GREAT ADVENTURES IN THE SOUTHERN APPALACHIANS

GREAT ADVENTURES IN THE SOUTHERN APPALACHIANS

by

g. forest

JOHN F. BLAIR, PUBLISHER
WINSTON-SALEM, NORTH CAROLINA

All photographs and maps by the author
unless otherwise noted

MANUFACTURED BY R. R. DONNELLEY & SONS
DESIGNED BY DEBRA LONG HAMPTON

The paper in this book meets the guidelines for permanence and durability of the Committee on Production Guidelines for Book Longevity of the Council on Library Resources.

Photographs on front cover:
Hot-air ballooning in the Moon Shadow, by Joy Sudderth;
Cross-country skiing in the southern Appalachians, by g. forest;
Whitewater rafting on the Chattooga River by Bruce Nelson, Photocrafts

Library of Congress Cataloging-in-Publication Data

Forest, G., 1949–
Great adventures in the southern appalachians / by G. Forest.
p. cm.
Includes index.
ISBN 0-89587-113-0
1. Outdoor recreation—Appalachian Region, Southern. 2. Appalachian Region, Southern—Description and travel. I. Title.
GV191.42.A66F67 1994
796.5'0974—dc20 94–18780

To My Parents,

the late Dr. Earl F. Hargett
and Dr. Martha Louise Freeman Hargett,
who taught me by example that life itself
is the essence of adventure
and every moment an opportunity for exploration

CONTENTS

Preface

I was ecstatic to learn that John F. Blair, Publisher, wanted to publish *Great Adventures in the Southern Appalachians.* With the air of an innocent, I readily signed the contract. It wasn't until I talked with an insurance agent a week later that my lights turned on and the elevator reached the top floor. No one would issue any kind of policy protecting my family against the possibility that I might be disabled while rock climbing, motorcycling, kayaking, rafting, fly-fishing, hiking, hot-air ballooning, caving, hang gliding, bungee jumping, cross-country skiing, horseback riding, ORVing, etc. Adventurers were not their idea of a good bet. I was on my own. As my wife confided after I informed her of the insurance situation, "Don't worry, Gil. If you get disabled, I'll kill you. You're not going to be lying around my house, moaning and groaning for eternity."

Southern women have always been great motivators, and my wife is no exception. Her observation, "Do you want to be a writer or not?" was the throwing down of the gauntlet. Now, I had to go out and actually do things I'd always said I wanted to do. And I would have to take risks—risks I was unfamiliar with—in performing a variety of physical exertions that I'd avoided the previous four decades.

Numerous factors influenced my decisions to select the adventures I've included in this book. I was familiar with some of the areas like Joyce Kilmer and Fires Creek. Other activities, like paddling the Chattooga, the Nantahala, and the Ocoee rivers, I felt comfortable performing. And still others, like hang gliding, rock climbing, and caving, offered me a challenge that I felt I needed to face.

Outdoor activities have always played a big part in my life. Every summer, when I hear the rivers and mountains of the Appalachians calling my name, I grab my gear and go to the river seeking adventure. Hopefully, I'll enjoy many more years of exploring the rivers, mountains, and valleys of the southern Appalachians, the chunk of the eastern United States that extends the length of West Virginia all the way south into north Georgia.

Adventure, by definition, entails risk. Sometimes, the risk is so slight that we readily accept it in our day-to-day lives. It is real nonetheless. While writing this book, I came to appreciate all the unsung athletes—the outdoor adventure guides and instructors—who led this novice step by step as I learned new sports. The key word here is *novice.* I took some licks in some of my adventures and found out that I'm not the natural athlete I once thought. I made mistakes and sometimes failed to achieve my goals. Hopefully, you can avoid the pitfalls I encountered, or at least be prepared to encounter and deal with them on your own outings.

I guess what I'm trying to say is be careful out there. Reading this book will not make you an expert at anything, but the information within it can help lead you to the right people, who can then provide good instruction. Every time I ventured into an unfamiliar sport, like hang gliding, rock climbing, or caving, I tried to find the best possible instructors with proven safety records to guide me. I advise you to do the same.

If you're planning back-country travel in Joyce Kilmer–Slickrock Wilderness, Fires Creek Bear Sanctuary, Shining Rock Wilderness, Great Smoky Mountains National Park, or Linville Gorge, I highly recommend that you secure detailed maps such as the ones available from the Forest Service. There are excellent trail guides that cover individual trails and trail systems in great detail, such as Allen de Hart's *North Carolina Hiking Trails* and Tim Homan's hiking guides. Lori Finley's series, *Mountain Biking the Appalachians*, provides a good deal of information about mountain biking. Countless other publications can aid you as you plan your own great adventures. Take advantage of them. And be sure to look at the maps before you go.

Great adventures await you in the vast playground called the southern Appalachians. Enjoy your exploration of these ancient mountains and their people, always remembering that without the life force of nature binding our footsteps together, our trails would all differ.

Acknowledgments

I am deeply indebted to my family—Joy, Dylan, Callie, and Cory—for tolerating my absences, participating in my adventures whenever possible, and yielding to my demands for prime computer time. Their constant willingness to venture into the wilderness inspires me. May we always explore new horizons and share adventures.

To all the folks who have helped me survive my adventures, thanks. If I have failed to mention you here or in the stories, know it was done intentionally to protect the innocent. Key individuals deserving my thanks include Tim Meaders, a.k.a. Gator, who has come to my rescue time and time again; John Gibney and his wife, Sherry, for being cross-country ski bums and getting me out there; Theo and Hayden Copeland, for showing me first-class fly-fishing; Tarp Head, the best—and only—hot-air balloonist I've ever flown with; Jerry and Sherry Collins, for introducing me to rock climbing; Robbie Robinson and Tom Wilkes, two longtime friends, for their bear tales and fish stories; Billy Crisp, for trusting me with his Gold Wing; Martin Sachs and Doug Drew, for riding the Blue Ridge Parkway with me during the hardest part of my journey, the beginning; Russ Miller, for taking me spelunking and showing me a whole new world underground; Buzz Chalmers, Daniel Jones, and the rest of the gang at Lookout Mountain Flight Park, for introducing me to hang gliding; Doyle Smith, for washing his dirt bike after I used it in the Tellico; and Greg and Linda Kerr, who made this whitewater river guide think he was an honest-to-god cowboy, at least for a couple of days.

Photographers who submitted work for possible inclusion in this book include Americo "Rick" Ardolino, Visions Photographic; Hugh Morton, Grandfather Mountain; Sherry Collins, Backcountry Photo Gallery; Bruce Chynoweth, Southern Exposure Studios; Tom Stults and Bruce Nelson, Photocrafts; Tim Dockery; Susan Scott; Danny Heatherly; Dylan Hargett, my son; and my longtime adventure companion, Joy Sudderth.

Special thanks go to Alfred W. Brown, publisher of *Brown's Guide to Georgia*, and Frank Bradley, publisher of *Mountain Home Companion*, for granting me permission to adapt articles and use photos that originally appeared in their publications.

Mapmakers who assisted me are Shannon Cox, who sketched the horse-trek map, and Frank Drago, who drew the original maps of Joyce Kilmer Memorial Forest and Fires Creek Bear Sanctuary. My Mac and I take the blame for all the other maps. Thanks also to George and Mike Kelischek of Mouse Pad Studios for their assistance whenever I had computer problems.

Several people who were experts in their fields read over the final drafts just to make sure there weren't any glaring errors. Thanks go to Jay Jorden of the National Speleological Society; Joe Nicholson, Thurmond Parrish, Larry Fleming, Pat Lancaster, and Bill Champion of the U.S. Forest Service; Dave Van Kleeck of the Nantahala Outdoor Center; Theo Copeland of Appalachian Angler; Buzz Chalmers of the Lookout Mountain Flight Park; Lawrence Robinson of Great Smoky Mountains National Park, and Phil Noblitt of the Blue Ridge Parkway.

The folks at John F. Blair, Publisher, have been real good to me whenever I've talked with them or camped behind their office in Winston-Salem—that's another adventure, yet unwritten, titled "Urban Camping." Thanks to Steve Kirk for his editing, Debbie Hampton for her design, and Anne Schultz for her sales efforts. I deeply appreciate the faith in this project and this writer shown by Carolyn Sakowski, the president at Blair. Without her direction, I would have been lost in the wilderness.

Last but not least, I want to thank Dotsy Carringer for encouraging me all these years to write. Thanks all. It's been a great adventure.

GREAT ADVENTURES IN THE SOUTHERN APPALACHIANS

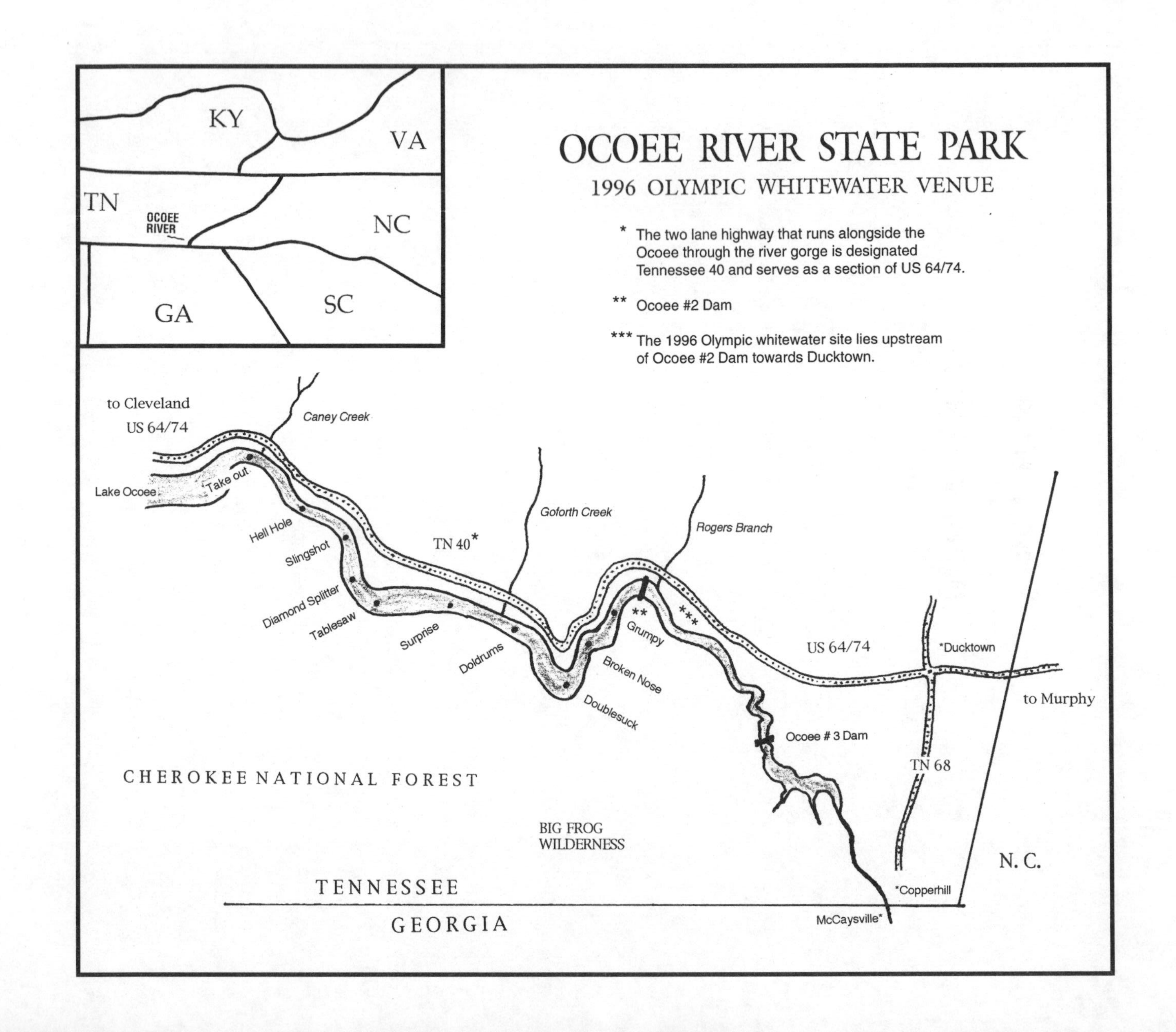
OCOEE RIVER STATE PARK
1996 OLYMPIC WHITEWATER VENUE
* The two lane highway that runs alongside the Ocoee through the river gorge is designated Tennessee 40 and serves as a section of US 64/74.
** Ocoee #2 Dam
*** The 1996 Olympic whitewater site lies upstream of Ocoee #2 Dam towards Ducktown.
KY
VA
TN
OCOEE RIVER
NC
GA
SC
to Cleveland
US 64/74
Caney Creek
Lake Ocoee
Take out
Hell Hole
Slingshot
Diamond Splitter
Tablesaw
Surprise
Doldrums
TN 40*
Goforth Creek
Rogers Branch
Grumpy
Broken Nose
Doublesuck
US 64/74
*Ducktown
to Murphy
Ocoee # 3 Dam
TN 68
CHEROKEE NATIONAL FOREST
BIG FROG WILDERNESS
N. C.
TENNESSEE
GEORGIA
*Copperhill
McCaysville*

THE OCOEE

A River for the World

My first encounter with the Ocoee was in the summer of 1974, when I accompanied a group of adventurous spirits I worked with at Nantahala Outdoor Center to the river. These guys had heard that the Ocoee was running all week due to problems with the TVA's generating facility, and they flat didn't care about the information coming out of Tennessee that the river was all but unrunnable. Rumors circulated that the rapids were too treacherous, too numerous, too continuous to be run safely. That just got this gang pumped up.

Since I was a first-year guide with only a handful of trips down the Chattooga under my belt, I kept my mouth shut. I told myself that these guys knew what they were doing. It never crossed my mind to question their sanity.

At the put-in, being the junior member of the expedition, I was the natural selection to stay with the raft and our paddling gear as they ran shuttle and scouted the section of river visible from the road. For what seemed an eternity, I sat by the river as it roared past and studied the imposing, half-the-river's-width hydraulic that would in later years be known as "Grumpy." The way it was shaped reminded me of Woodall Shoals on the Chattooga, a powerful hydraulic that has claimed numerous lives. Fortunately, we were putting in below this ledge and its pour-over rock. I couldn't help wondering what lay downstream.

Two hours later, the trio of Donnie, Bob, and Tom appeared, riding in the back of an old pickup truck complete with a 12-gauge shotgun hanging in the rack. As Donnie rolled his 300-pound bulk out of the tailgate, he hollered, "You know what the Indians used to say?"

"No," I said.

"'It's a great day to die!'" he boomed.

The old farmer who had given them the ride stood there with tobacco juice dripping down his chin. "You boys gonna try to go down this here river?" he finally asked.

Bob looked him straight in the eye and responded, "That's our intention."

"Well, I reckon I'll be reading about y'all in the paper."

With those encouraging words, we prepared to cast our raft on the waters. I was the grim one in the crowd. The others were downright exuberant.

Our trip down the Ocoee demanded teamwork and quick responses. Outside of one incident where I was tossed out of the raft and ingloriously pulled back in by my life jacket, it was uneventful. Like many folks who tackle a whitewater river for the first time, I found that the Ocoee was one continuous blur of rapids, crashing waves, and powerful eddies. It was difficult to separate the individual rapids from each other. Our experience was heightened by the knowledge that not many had gone before us. The Ocoee opened new insights for each of us that day, teaching us that the unknown is an obstacle to be confronted and challenged.

Since that day in 1974, the number of times that I have canoed, kayaked, or guided a raft down the Ocoee numbers in the four digits. Like other old-timers on the river, I have come to love the Ocoee, the beauty of its gorge, and the playfulness of its white water.

The headwaters of the Ocoee originate in the north Georgia mountains and Chattahoochee National Forest, where the river is known as the Toccoa. Flowing in a northwesterly direction, the river feeds Lake Blue Ridge in Georgia and Parksville Lake in Tennessee, also called Lake Ocoee. Once the river crosses the state line between the twin cities of McCaysville, Georgia, and Copperhill, Tennessee, it's called the Ocoee. John Harmon, a staff writer for the *Atlanta Constitution* who covers the tristate region, thinks that the difference in the names—Toccoa and Ocoee—was the result of two separate groups of early settlers attempting to pronounce the Cherokee name for the river—Tagwa-hi, "Place of the Catawba." Others say that Ocoee translates as "Land of the Maypop."

It is believed that an ancient people settled the Ocoee region 3,000 years before Christ, long before the arrival of the Creek and Cherokee Indian nations. Archaeologists know that Cherokees lived along the Ocoee and had an elaborate system of trails that facilitated trade of agricultural products between villages.

De Soto was the first documented explorer of European descent to visit these parts, arriving in 1540. Life for the Indians would never be the same again. By the early 1700s, the Cherokees felt pressure from the white man for possession of their lands. In 1715, Major General George Chicken led the first English military expedition against the Cherokees. By 1838, the Cherokee nation in this part of Tennessee was gone, a victim of the Trail of Tears, the forced march to Oklahoma that decimated the nation's numbers. A small group of Cherokees led by a man named Tsali managed to hide in the Great Smoky Mountains and avoid the Trail of Tears. Tsali was later executed by soldiers under the leadership of General Winfield Scott. The Eastern Band of the Cherokees was able to maintain some claim to its ancestral lands, which ultimately resulted in the

Running through Hell Hole
Photo by Susan Scott

establishment of the Qualla Indian Reservation, centered around Cherokee, North Carolina.

In 1840, a prospector found a copper vein by the Ocoee that literally changed the face of the earth in this region and led to a new name: the Copper Basin. Mining operations boomed. Thousands of acres of timber were harvested, to be used as lumber for building and as fuel to run the smelters that separated the copper from the sulfides. Open-pit smelting released sulfuric acid into the atmosphere, and the toxic fumes settled onto land devoid of trees, with catastrophic results. All the remaining vegetation died. With nothing left to hold it in place, the topsoil and its witches' brew of contaminants washed downstream, partially filling in lakes and killing all aquatic life in the Ocoee.

It wasn't until the early 1900s that it was discovered that the sulfuric acid being burned off during smelting was worth more than the copper itself. Sulfuric acid is a corrosive liquid used in making dyes, paints, fertilizers, and explosives.

In recent decades, mining supported 4,500 workers and their families in the Copper Basin. Economics finally caught up with the basin when foreign copper grew cheaper than domestic copper. The mines were closed in the mid-1980s. Currently, a foreign-owned corporation employees 450 people in the basin in the manufacturing of sulfuric acid.

The effects of over 100 years of environmental abuse are still visible in the basin. Kudzu, the bane of Southern forests, has gotten a grip on most of the barren gullies and hills, lending them a green aura during summer. Reforestation efforts by the Forest Service, corporations, and private individuals are paying off. But though the basin is greener and the river running clearer, there are serious environmental problems still confronting the region.

Commercial whitewater rafting came to the Ocoee during the summer of 1977. The TVA gave up its effort to maintain the flume line that diverted water from the river to a power station, and for the first time in seven decades, water flowed in the riverbed regularly. There's some debate over who actually ran the first commercial trip down the Ocoee that summer, but five guys got businesses going. J. T. Lemons and James Torrence founded Ocoee Outdoors. Marc Hunt and Bill Chipley named their operation Sunburst Adventures. Roger Lozier started Ocoee Rafting.

Since 1977, commercial rafting on "the Big O" has grown from those three companies and a few hundred rafting guests to 24 outfitters and over 180,000 rafting guests each season.

It almost didn't happen. In the early 1980s, the TVA decided to rebuild the flume. There would be no more water in the riverbed after construction was completed. The river was fixing to be "dewatered."

Commercial outfitters and private paddlers organized letter-writing campaigns to senators and congressmen. Petition drives yielded several hundred thousand signatures. Members of the media were courted. Soon, it was understood what the Ocoee means to the people of this region—whitewater recreation is the number-one industry in Polk County, Tennessee, today, for example.

Congress mandated that the TVA provide 116 days of recreational release each season. Naturally, the TVA was able to get its bureaucratic finger in the whitewater pie. For each person a company takes rafting on the Ocoee, a portion of the proceeds goes to the TVA to help recoup the revenue lost by providing recreational releases.

A normal release of water on the Ocoee these days is 1,200 cubic feet per second. If my math serves me correctly, that means approximately 9,000 gallons of water pour over the dam every second. It staggers the mind. Often, guests question why we don't run the dam. It looks like fun. And yes, it has been run, by a wide assortment of river guides and boaters in kayaks and canoes. I once photographed a group of Sunburst guides successfully running "the chute," the mega-turbulence created when the TVA opens the steel floodgate right next to the flume. Big rapid. Absolutely crazy.

But it's been a long time since I've seen the dam run. Nowadays, it brings a $500 fine per person. If you're a river guide, you' re banned from the river for two years by the state of Tennessee. Inner-tubing the river isn't permitted anymore, either, at least not in the section between Ocoee Power Unit #3 and Unit #2.

Over the years, what were once class V rapids on the Ocoee have been downgraded to class IV rapids. This is due to a combination of factors. Whitewater sports have progressed rapidly in terms of equipment and the overall skill level of paddlers. Innovative designs in decked and open boats and the advent of self-bailing rafts have led to a leap in popularity, as has new gear that protects paddlers from hypothermia and other river dangers. River rescue techniques are constantly being refined.

Although the Ocoee is a very forgiving river, it still has the potential to render paddlers bodily harm. The most common accident on the Ocoee is the T-Grip Sandwich, in which folks let go of the paddle's handle—the t-grip—and it tries to rearrange their face, teeth, and nasal passages, often with success.

A powerful hydraulic can hold an entire raft and its occupants for an indefinite period. Being caught in a hydraulic—also called hole, sousehole, vertical eddy, reversal, keeper, or soup—is a turbulent, exciting experience that leaves you thankful to have escaped the power of the river. River hydraulics are formed when water crashes over an obstacle, such as a ledge, then takes a dramatic drop into a pool. The water boils to the surface and is caught in a circular motion. As new water falls over the ledge, it forces the water it's replacing out the back of the hydraulic.

One school of thought on escaping a hydraulic says you should ball up into a tight configuration and let the hydraulic take you down to the river bottom, where the flow escapes the grip of the hydraulic. In theory, once you start bouncing along the river bottom, your life jacket will float you to the surface downstream of the hydraulic, and you can continue your river trip duly aware that you have just escaped the jaws of death.

And believe me, the river is powerful. In 1992, I had the experience of body-surfing the hydraulic called Grumpy in my personal flotation device when I got bounced out the back of a raft. I knew precisely where I was as I landed in the backwash just below the ledge. I started swimming furiously downstream. Later, my buddies said I looked like I was trying to moonwalk in the water. Regardless of my efforts, Grumpy pulled me steadily backwards. I was caught. No way out.

Luckily, I recollected Jeff Parker's Richard Nixon act in a powerful hydraulic on the Gauley River in West Virginia in 1985. With the instincts of an FBI SWAT team member—which he was—Jeff turned and went eye to eye with that wall of water with his arms spread wide, body-surfing the hole for a solid five minutes. Downstream, Gary Rady and I watched helplessly with our crews as Jeff tired from his efforts to survive. John Miller, running sweep, dropped his raft right in on top of Jeff to rescue him. However, Jeff's simple act of grabbing hold of Miller's raft caused enough loss of momentum for the hydraulic to grab the entire raft and its occupants. They surfed seemingly forever, but by now we were all laughing at their predicament. The danger Jeff Parker had faced was past. Let the river roll on.

I turned and faced Grumpy, my arms spread. The tongue that normally allows you to skirt the hydraulic ran close to my right side. I surfed in its direction and felt tremendous relief when I reached it and it began pulling my body downstream. Then, to my dismay, I found myself helicoptered right back into the heart of Grumpy. I could have sworn I heard a man on the bank hollering to his wife, "Honey! Get the video camera quick! This guy's gonna drown!"

Three times I reached the tongue, only to be helicoptered back into Grumpy's raging waters. At that point, I was seriously considering testing the theory about balling up and letting the hydraulic take me to the bottom and spit me out downstream, but I gave the tongue one more try. For some reason, it didn't spin me back into Grumpy, but let me float free, feet up, downstream. I had found religion. During my extended time in Grumpy, I saw Elvis at the bottom of the suck hole with a Bible in his right hand. His other hand was reaching toward me.

The river gave me a reprieve that day. Others have not been so lucky. Grumpy has claimed one life and has several near-drownings to its credit.

A fair number of rafters and private paddlers owe their continued existence to the quick reactions of Ocoee River guides. Such was the case in October 1982 when High Country guides rescued John Norton. After successfully running a portion of the river called Hell Hole, John got blown river left and, as he tried to ferry river right, wrapped his open canoe around the pylon supporting the old bridge leading to Ocoee Power Unit #2. Nine High Country guides had stopped to prepare their guests for the run through Hell Hole. They immediately ran to the bridge and lowered Karen Berry of Valdese, North Carolina, to the accident site. Karen was able to get John's head above water by running a rope around a web belt he was wearing. Using a knife, Karen then freed the semiconscious John Norton from his canoe, thus saving his life.

The Ocoee will continue to lure people to its white water. In fact, they will come from all over the world in 1996 to watch the Olympic competition on the Blue Holes section of the river.

And, as always, people will come to raft, kayak, and canoe the lower portion of the Ocoee. They will experience the excitement of racing downstream toward Grumpy, a true class IV rapid, right out of the put-in eddy. They'll punch through the double ledges at Broken Nose and work their way through the gate rocks at Heroes Go Right/Turkeys Go Left before bouncing over Double Suck, a small but powerful hydraulic. Double Trouble will make a "Kodak moment," the guide catching air in the rear and water trashing the entire crew. They'll paddle through Flipper before heading upstream and surfing Hollywood Hole.

After a brief lull called the Doldrums, they'll skirt Razor Rock and line up for Surprise. They can only hope their guide is paying attention to the river and not the boulder bunnies at Table Saw, where the river narrows dramatically and drops quickly, a series of holes and curling waves waiting for action. There is scant time for jubilation below Table Saw. Diamond Splitter looms downstream with its favorite play spot, Witches Hole. The brave will abandon ship at Swimmer's Rapid and try their luck assuming the whitewater swim position—feet downstream and elevated to avoid being trapped. Next, rafters will suddenly find themselves airborne and having an "out-of-raft" experience when their guide takes them sideways over the Nose—also affectionately called the Juicer—at Cat's Pajamas.

Their wild whitewater trip will culminate at Hell Hole, a large standing wave just below the new bridge at the powerhouse, a favorite spot for boaters to do pop-ups, pirouettes, and enders, to the delight of bystanders oohing and aahing on the rocky banks. Next, they'll punch through the middle wave called Bullseye before blasting into Powerhouse, the last hydraulic on the Ocoee. They'll float down to the take-out, board old school buses painted a variety of colors, and ride back to the outpost, a class VI outing in itself. Adventure fulfilled, they'll go home. The TVA will put the Ocoee to bed and get about the business of making electric power.

But when the river is running again, the visitors will come back. Just like me. They always do. They like the challenge of the world's first Olympic river, the magic feel of its waters splashing across the bow, engulfing their entire being. Ecstatic.

Let the river flow and the games begin.

Kayaking the Ocoee is a challenge even for the skilled paddler.

Whitewater Rafting on the Ocoee River

WHO

Regulations governing commercial rafting operations require that guests be at least 12 years old. All participants are required to sign a waiver recognizing the extreme risks associated with rafting and assuming those risks. All guests must wear a helmet and a type V life jacket their entire time on the river. They are subject to a citation and fine if caught on the water without them. Guides trained in CPR and first aid and having a minimum of 10 training trips down the Ocoee captain all commercial rafts, which normally carry four to seven passengers. Rafting guests are expected to paddle—in fact, the Ocoee demands it to safely run its numerous rapids.

Commercial outfitters pay the TVA a set fee for each guest they take down the Ocoee, but private paddlers still paddle free on the river. Equipment used by private parties must meet acceptable standards. Park rules no longer allow inner-tubing on the Ocoee.

All participants, private and commercial, should be in good physical condition. If you're an adventurous being with physical handicaps, do not be discouraged. People missing limbs have successfully paddled the Ocoee in rafts, kayaks, and canoes. One year, I carried an entire crew of six adults down the river. Every one of them was legally blind. I have often attempted to run a rapid "blind," but I just can't do it. I open my eyes every time. Trust me. It just looks like they're closed in the photos.

WHEN

TVA starts making scheduled whitewater releases on Saturdays and Sundays in late March of each year. During June, July, and August, water releases for recreational purposes are scheduled five days a week, with no water released on Tuesdays and Wednesdays. Scheduled water releases then revert to weekends only through September and October, with some releases in early November.

WHERE

The whitewater portion of the Ocoee River lies in Polk County, Tennessee, which shares state lines with Georgia to the south and North Carolina to the east. Copperhill and nearby Ducktown, Tennessee, are located within 15 miles of the put-in. Cleveland, Tennessee, approximately 20 miles west of the Ocoee, offers numerous dining and lodging facilities.

The two-lane U.S. 64/74 runs alongside the Ocoee. During summer, it is a bottleneck, jammed with outfitters' buses shuttling people to and from the river, rubberneckers stopping to watch the whitewater junkies do their thing, and tractor-trailers taking up both lanes as they try to negotiate the curves in the gorge. Be prepared for sudden stops, and don't be surprised if you see vehicles run off this snaky two-lane into the river. It's even happened to a ranger. Rock slides are common. Note that where the guardrails look new, they have been replaced. Drive defensively and slowly along the Ocoee. Your kayak may depend on it. Special provisions for limiting traffic in the gorge will be in effect during certain periods of the 1996 Olympic season.

HOW

If your whitewater paddling skills are not up to the rugged class III-IV rapids of the Ocoee, take my advice and go rafting with one of the following licensed outfitters:

Adventures Unlimited	615-338-4325
Cherokee Rafting, Inc.	800-451-7238 or 615-338-5124
Cripple Creek Expeditions	615-338-8441 or 800-338-RAFT
Eagle Adventure Company	800-288-3245 or 706-492-2277
High Country, Inc.	800-233-8594 or 615-338-8634
Infinity Rafting	800-442-0386
Nantahala Outdoor Center	800-232-7238
Ocoee Inn Rafting, Inc.	800-272-7238
Ocoee Outdoors	800-533-PROS or 615-338-2438
Ocoee Rafting, Inc.	800-251-4800 or 615-496-3388
Ocoee River Rats	615-338-4222
Outdoor Adventures of TN, Inc.	800-627-7636 or 615-338-8914
Outland Expeditions	800-827-1442 615-478-1442
Quest Expeditions	615-338-2979
Rafting, Inc.	800-338-RAFT or 615-338-8441
Rolling Thunder River Company	800-344-5838 or 704-488-2030
Smoky Mountain Expeditions	800-338-RAFT or 615-338-8441
Southeastern Expeditions	800-868-7238 or 615-338-8073
Sunburst Adventures, Inc.	800-247-8388 or 615-338-8388
USA RAFT	800-USA-RAFT
Wahoo's Adventures	800-444-RAFT or 704-262-5774
Whitewater Express, Inc.	404-325-5295 or 800-676-7238
Whitewater Tennessee	800-533-7767 or 615-338-2438
Wildwater, Ltd.	800-451-9972 or 615-496-4904

RESOURCES

Taking the Ocoee Challenge is a 64-page booklet that contains information about the river, the history of the region, and the formation of the whitewater industry in the area. It's available from Clayton News Service, #186 County Road 255, Athens, Tenn. 37303.

Each year, Polk County Publishing Company distributes thousands of copies of *Polk County, Tennessee: An Undiscovered Treasure*. This tabloid lists a multitude of activities in the area, including those in Hiwassee Scenic River Area and Cohuta Wilderness Area. It's available from the *Polk County News* Office, Main Street, Benton, Tenn. 37307.

Although commercial outfitters operate under a licensing agreement with the TVA, management and operation of Ocoee River State Park falls to the Tennessee Department of Environment and Conservation, Hiwassee/Ocoee River Ranger District, P.O. Box 255, Delano, Tenn. 37325 (615-338-4133). For hiking and campground information, contact Ocoee Ranger District, United States Forest Service, Route 1 Parksville, U.S. 64, Benton, Tenn. 37307 (615-338-5201).

OLYMPIC INFORMATION

The Ocoee River will be the site of the 1996 Olympic whitewater slalom venue, with competition scheduled to take place July 26–28. The Ocoee is the first natural river in the world to be so chosen. Previous Olympic whitewater venues have been man-made courses with water diverted into them.

The slalom venue is on the upper part of the river between Ocoee Power Unit #3 and Dam #3. This section of the Ocoee is commonly referred to as the Blue Holes, due to the numerous large pools of water, ideal for swimming. The Blue Holes section lies just upstream of the portion used by commercial rafting operations and is normally void of significant water flow, due to the fact that the water is diverted from the riverbed into a tunnel and used to power generators farther downstream.

Tickets to the whitewater slalom venue will be issued by the Atlanta Committee for Olympic Games. For information about ticket sales, contact Games Services, 250 Williams Street, Suite 6000, P.O. Box 1996, Atlanta, Ga. 30301-1996. For information about the actual site of the venue, contact Olympics Project Coordinator, Cherokee National Forest, Cleveland, Tenn. 37312 (615-339-8687).

EMERGENCY INFORMATION

Both Polk County and Bradley County, Tennessee, have the 911 system. Use it first in a true emergency.

Near the end of the 1993 rafting season, a pay phone was located at the put-in at Roger's Branch.

Copper Basin Medical Center (615-496-5511) is located approximately 12 minutes upriver (east), at the junction of U.S. 64 and Tenn. 68 at Ducktown, Tennessee. To reach it, turn right (south) onto Tenn. 68 before the underpass on U.S. 64 and travel approximately 0.25 mile to the entrance.

Rangers and park attendants have radio equipment and can save time in an emergency. Park attendants can generally be found at the put-in and the take-out during scheduled water releases. Rangers also patrol U.S. 64. These rangers and park attendants deserve medals for consistently coming to the aid of motorists, spectators, kayakers, canoeists, and rafters.

Bradley Memorial Hospital Cleveland, Tenn.	615-559-6000
Polk County Sheriff's Department Benton, Tenn.	615-338-8215
Hiwassee/Ocoee River Ranger Station Delano, Tenn.	615-338-4133
Ocoee Ranger District USFS Benton, Tenn.	615-338-5201
Hiwassee Ranger District USFS Etowah, Tenn.	615-263-5486

FREEDOM ALOFT

A Story of Hot-Air Balloons

"I normally don't launch above six knots surface wind," Tarp said matter-of-factly.

We were standing under a large circus tent attending the pilots' briefing. The balloon *meister* reported surface winds of five to seven knots. A hundred pilots and several hundred members of launch crews and chase teams stood attentive. Wind speed and direction at specific altitudes were duly recorded by pilots and copilots. Maps were spread open, and restricted areas where balloon flight was prohibited were marked in red.

The safety of all participants—pilots, ground crews, and chase teams—was stressed by race officials: "If you don t feel safe launching in these conditions, don't."

The sky was crystal blue. A few wisps of clouds snaked through the azure atmosphere, dispersing into the void of the sky. Although all signs pointed toward a beautiful day for ballooning, high surface winds threatened to cancel the launch, scheduled for six o'clock.

Tarp looked at me and said, "Conditions change rapidly. We can always wait and watch to see how the other balloons handle the wind if they fly. If it looks good, we'll fly with them. I like a little adventure, don't you?"

Two hare balloons were chosen. One was to leave from the western section, one from the eastern end. These hare balloons would inflate, launch, travel a predetermined length of time, land, and place a big *X* on the ground. The chase balloons—ours and 97 others—could not start inflating their envelopes until the hare balloons were airborne. It was our task to come as close as possible to the large *X* placed by one of the hare balloons and drop our beanbag as close to the center of the *X* as we could.

It sounds easy. But after being in a hare-and-hound hot-air balloon race, I can tell you that it is anything but.

Welcome to Freedom Weekend Aloft.

Man's love affair with flight is ancient.

Greek mythology tells of Icarus, the son of Daedalus, who flew so close to the sun that the heat melted the wax holding his feathery wings together. He fell to his death in the sea.

Man's first recorded successful attempt at defying gravity took place on November 21, 1783, when Frenchmen Jean François Pilatre de Rozier and the Marquis François d'Arlandes flew their smoke-filled balloon from Versailles over Paris at 3,000 feet. Their flight lasted about 20 minutes and was witnessed by King Louis XVI and Marie Antoinette. Unfortunately, two years later, de Rozier became the first recorded aviation fatality when his balloon exploded in flight.

Ballooning came to the United States in 1793, when Jean-Pierre Blanchard flew from Philadelphia to Depford, New Jersey. During the Civil War, gas-filled balloons were used for observing enemy troop movements during battle.

When the hydrogen-filled dirigible *Hindenburg* exploded in 1937, killing 35 of its 97 passengers, interest in lighter-than-air flight evaporated for nearly 25 years.

In 1960, Captain Joseph W. Kittenger, Jr., of the United States Air Force jumped out of a helium balloon at 102,800 feet and free-fell more than 16 miles. In 1961, Commander Malcolm Ross of the United States Naval Reserves ascended to 113,739 feet to establish the altitude record for class A balloons. On August 17, 1978, Ben Abruzzo, Larry Newman, and Maxie Anderson became the first team to cross the Atlantic Ocean by balloon; their flight lasted 137 hours. Three years later, Abruzzo and Newman teamed up with Ron Clark and Rocky Aoki to become the first balloonists to cross the Pacific Ocean; their helium balloon, the *Double Eagle V*, covered 5,208 miles from Japan to California.

Moon Rise **is airborne.**
Photo by Joy Sudderth

One of ballooning's more unusual events occurred on July 2, 1982, when a commercial airliner spotted Larry Walters, a 33-year-old truckdriver, flying 16,000 feet above Los Angeles. Tied to his lawn chair were 42 weather balloons and cradled in his arms was a BB gun, which he used to pop some of the balloons when he wanted to descend. Despite hitting power lines when he landed 10 miles from his launch site, Walters was able to fold up his lawn chair and head home. The Federal Aviation Administration was not amused. It fined him $4,000 for violating the airways.

On September 7, 1983, the Hutyra family flew a hot-air balloon to freedom, escaping communist Czechoslovakia. Numerous times, members of the family had almost been caught as they built and tested their balloon in secrecy. Their 11-mile flight in their 66-foot-high balloon made of raincoat material took 55 minutes and landed them in Austria, free to pursue a new life in a new land.

In my original flight of fantasy for this book, I envisioned traveling to Helen, Georgia, to be a participant in the Helen-to-Atlantic Balloon Race, sponsored each year by Head Balloons and the Helendorf Inn. How exciting it would be to lift off in the north Georgia mountains and float on invisible currents to the coast! Who could predict which way the wind would blow? Would we balloon toward the East Coast, or head south to the Gulf of Mexico?

Tarp Head, owner of Head Balloons, burst my bubble. First, balloonists are licensed pilots and must pass FAA tests that include actual flight. Second, participants have to provide their own balloons, which cost anywhere from $12,000 to $20,000.

Preparations for extended hot-air flights such as the Helen-to-Atlantic Balloon Race are extensive. Loads are calculated. Chase-team members prepare checklists, study road maps, keep a constant ear to wind reports, and test mobile communication systems that will allow them to stay in contact with their balloonists. Pilots and copilots train year-round. Months are spent planning and making sure all the equipment—the basket, the tanks, the burners, the envelope, the skirt—are in perfect working order.

Race day is electric. Crowds mingle with balloonists and support staff, getting first-hand insight into the sport of ballooning and why folks do it.

Those entering the Helen-to-Atlantic Balloon Race are the hardy and the few. Kit Weathers, a dentist from Griffin, Georgia, won the 20th annual race in record time. After lifting off on the morning of June 3, 1993, Dr. Weathers landed 10 hours and eight minutes later near Dillon, South Carolina, after crossing I-95, which served as the finish line. *Supertooth*, his lightweight balloon, broke the old mark in the 225-mile race by eight minutes.

Eighteen balloons lifted off that day in 1993. Only five were competing in the Helen-to-Atlantic Balloon Race. Some of the balloons were on tethers that stretched several hundred feet, and crews were busy hauling the lines in and out. Visitors could pay a small fee and take an actual balloon flight that let them rise above the tree line to see the surrounding mountains unobstructed. I didn't get a ride that day. The idea of going up on a tether just didn't appeal to me.

The following week, I visited Tarp Head at his balloon-manufacturing facility outside Helen and watched multicolored panels being stitched together in a "gore." Fourteen panels aligned vertically comprise one gore in a 77,000-cubic-foot envelope; it takes 24 gores to make the entire envelope. Talking with Tarp, I realized how little I knew about ballooning. It's easy to get caught up in the sport with this energetic Georgia Tech engineer. Since he started flying in 1973, Tarp has logged over 1,000 hours aloft in a hot-air balloon. Since I was going to talk my way into a flight with him, I liked the facts that he had a perfect safety record and appeared to have all his body parts.

The element of risk, the potential for bodily harm or death, is very real in ballooning. At least five people died trying to be the first to cross the Atlantic. Others have perished when their balloons struck power lines or trees. Others have fallen into the sea, like Icarus.

Tarp is methodical in his quest to eliminate potential equipment failure. He and his crew make the entire balloon envelope. They inspect and double-check seams and the nylon webbing that runs vertically the length of each gore. Nomex, a rugged, flame-resistant fabric, is used to make the number-one envelope panel. It is also used to make the skirt, or scoop, that channels air into the envelope. Tarp personally weaves the basket, using a mixture of strong, resilient natural rattan and round-reed rattan around a framework of nylon rods and aluminum tubing.

One of the innovative features of Tarp's balloons is the DB II burner system, which is actually two complete redundant systems. The burner system heats the air inside the envelope. Two separate fuel systems feed two separate blast valves mounted in a polished stainless-steel housing. Normally, only one blast valve is used during flight. Using both can increase the output by 45 to 70 percent. At 80 degrees, one blast valve can deliver 15.5 million BTUs at 140 pounds per square inch. Four 10-gallon aluminum tanks—one in each corner of the basket—filled with liquid propane provide fuel for the burner.

I left Tarp that afternoon in good spirits. He had invited me to fly with him during Greenville, South Carolina's, Fourth of July celebration, called Freedom Weekend Aloft. The ride home caught me daydreaming scenes out of *Around the World in Eighty Days.*

Flight day finally arrived. My family, minus Dylan, departed early for Greenville. Somehow, we missed getting a pass into the balloonists' gate, but we managed to catch a ride with Earl Miller and his *Wild Thang* crew to the Donaldson Center, just south of Greenville. It was at the pilots' briefing under the big tent that we finally caught up with Tarp and the rest of the crew. They welcomed my wife, Joy, and our two girls, Callie and Cory, and invited them to ride in the chase vehicle.

It was the first day of the three-day festival. A crowd numbering in the thousands wandered up and down the concourse viewing the exhibits, enjoying carnival rides, buying T-shirts, and eating chili dogs. Sound technicians tested 50,000 watts of speakers and microphones by pounding on a drumhead and yelling, "Testing, testing, one, two, three!"

Excitement built as launch crews spread out balloon envelopes on the grassy field and started rigging baskets. Launching nearly 100 balloons simultaneously requires a large amount of space. From our end of the field, we couldn't see the balloons at the other end. Just prior to launch, the wind calmed and the hare balloons began inflating. We scrambled to get everything ready. Within minutes, the two hare balloons were soaring steadily upward and flying in a northeasterly direction. They intentionally played with the wind currents at different altitudes to make it harder for us to follow their flight path. It would be a real test to get close enough to toss a beanbag at the *X*.

Activity around us intensified, as engines were cranked up to run the fans used to blow cold air into the envelopes and give them shape. Tarp quickly informed us, "We do not blow up a balloon. We inflate it."

We waited until the majority of the balloons were inflated and clear of the area before we cranked our engine. Halfway into inflating our envelope, the engine died. Out of gas. We suspected sabotage. Balloonists are characters who love to pull practical jokes on each other. Actually, chances are that it was an oversight on our team's part. The tank looked fuller than it was. Nobody ever claimed credit if it was a practical joke. If a balloonist gets one on you, don't worry, he'll let you and everybody else know about it.

Our launch, the maiden flight of *Moon Rise*, an 88,000-cubic-foot balloon decorated with the moon surrounded by stars, found me hanging on the outside of the basket as we were pulled along the field on our side. Tarp and Dave, another first-timer, hoisted me over the side and into the relative security of the basket just as the envelope righted itself and we were airborne. I'm not sure how much more exciting a launch can be. My first balloon ride. And I almost missed it.

Thanks to the large envelope and the efficient burners, we ascended rapidly. Soon, we were floating among the other 90 or so balloons of various colors, sizes, and configurations. With the burners shut off, we could converse with other balloonists at great distances using moderately projected voices. The background noise from the busy metro area below faded into nothingness as we rose to 4,000 feet. Cars resembled ants scurrying about, and people afoot were but specks on the ground.

The roar of the burner was another matter entirely. It was similar to standing on a runway as a 747 cranks its engines. The DB II roared with serious intentions, jetting a flame 25 feet into the depths of the envelope. During inflation, Tarp had been extremely careful not to let the flame melt the 1.9-ounce ripstop nylon that comprises the bulk of the panels.

Although we stayed aloft nearly an hour, the flight passed all too quickly. I had the strangest sensation that I could step over the edge of the basket and float softly to the earth. Such is the illusion of balloon flight. You are one with the sky, riding invisible winds, free of all earthly constraints. The only limitations are your imagination and the four tanks of propane.

I wish I could report that we nailed the *X* with our beanbag, but that would be lying. The crew of the hare we chased had done a great job of juggling altitudes, and we weren't even close. Now, we needed a landing area.

Early in the flight, we had lost radio contact with Moon Shadow, the name bestowed upon our chase team. We knew the team was down there somewhere tracking the general flight of the balloons. We just didn't know where. Tarp scanned the horizon for a suitable spot.

"Gil, I don't want you guys to get excited, but we're going for that field dead ahead," he said.

All I could see was a narrow strip just beyond a stand of trees, bordered on the opposite edge by power lines. Great.

"I'm going to drop the basket into that stand of trees and let it drag. That'll help slow us down. These winds must be gusting up to 15 knots. It'll be tricky, but we can do it. As soon as we clear the trees, I'll pull the parachute top, and we'll settle in way before we hit the power lines."

I didn't figure Tarp was serious about dragging the bottom of the basket along the tops of the trees. My mistake. Before I knew it, branches were slapping me upside the head. Needless to say, adrenaline levels were running high in the basket. But Tarp pulled it off with an excellent demonstration of his flying skills. We landed well clear of the power lines, and before we knew it, people were coming out of their houses and parking their cars to stare at *Moon Rise*, a beautiful flying machine, as she sat inflated at the completion of her maiden voyage.

Later, after the Moon Shadow team tracked us down and we deflated *Moon Rise* and loaded it in the trailer, Tarp had Dave and me kneel as he christened us with champagne and recited the Balloonist's Prayer:

> The winds have welcomed you with softness.
> The sun has blessed you with his warm hands.
> You have flown so high and so well that God has joined you in your laughter.
> And he has set you gently back again into the loving arms of Mother Earth.

Life is not the same after having flown with the wind. Like Tarp said, "It's the second-greatest sensation."

Being ignorant, I had to ask, "What's the first?"

"A good golf shot."

Hot-Air Ballooning

WHO

Flying a balloon is an expensive proposition. While it is possible to enjoy a 15-minute tethered flight at a reasonable price, an actual hour or hour-and-a-half ride can cost between $150 and $250 per person.

If you're serious about purchasing a balloon for yourself or your company, you can probably talk a manufacturer into a demonstration flight.

Many corporations sponsor flights at the major balloon outings.

If you're afraid of heights or confined areas like a balloon basket, ride in the chase vehicle. According to my wife, it's a wild experience, trying to keep one eye on the highway while scanning the skies for the particular balloon you're tracking. The roads don't always go where you think they're going, and there's no telling where the pilot will set down. Your task is to be there ready to help deflate, disassemble, and load.

WHEN

Most ballooning activities are held in the warm months, although individuals have been known to fly in the winter when they can catch a warm spell. Major considerations on whether to launch on a particular day include weather conditions, forecasts, and wind speed. There are "only" three times you are actually at risk when ballooning: at launch, in the air, and at landing.

WHERE

Balloon events are held all over the Southeast. Greenville's Freedom Weekend Aloft is held annually around the Fourth of July. The Helen-to-Atlantic Balloon Race is conducted the first full weekend in June. Macon, Georgia, holds its Cherry Blossom Festival the last weekend in March; the event attracts numerous balloonists. Nashville has a balloon event the third weekend in June. Atlanta's Dogwood Festival in May features balloons. The National Balloon Rally is held in Statesville, North Carolina, the third weekend in September.

HOW

Free and tethered rides are available for a fee at all the major ballooning events. It is an experience you will never forget.

Sometimes, corporate sponsors have open spaces on their flights.

It is also possible to serve on a chase team in exchange for a ride. Being on a chase team requires training in how to help assemble and disassemble the balloon, basket, and propulsion system. You may have to be a chase-team member for several launches and recoveries before your number comes up.

RESOURCES

Ballooning: The Journal of the Balloon Federation of America, P.O. Box 180, Post Mills, Vt. 05058. This excellent quarterly magazine contains informative articles and full-color photos. The Balloon Federation of America also publishes a monthly newsletter, *Skylines*, for federation members. The yearly federation dues of $40 include a subscription to both publications.

Balloon Life, 2145 Dale Avenue, Sacramento, Calif. 95815. This monthly full-color publication covers the technical side of ballooning and offers educational and safety information. The subscription price is $30 annually.

Up, up and away!

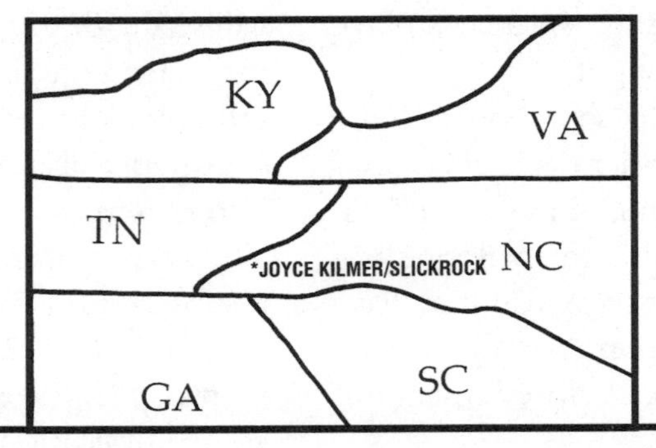
KY
VA
TN
NC
*JOYCE KILMER/SLICKROCK
GA
SC

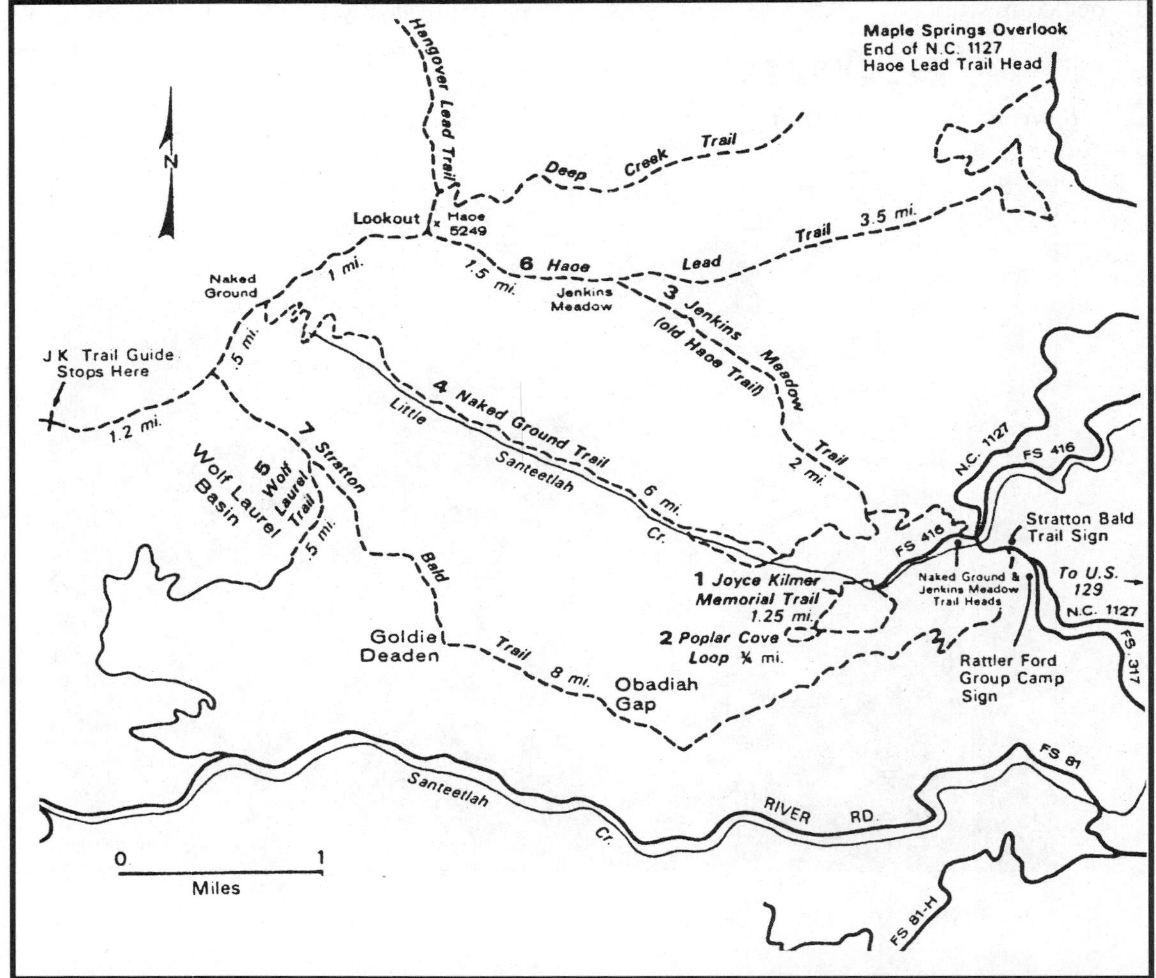
Maple Springs Overlook
End of N.C. 1127
Haoe Lead Trail Head
Hangover Lead Trail
Deep Creek Trail
Lookout
Haoe 5249
Trail 3.5 mi.
6 Haoe Lead
1.5 mi.
1 mi.
Naked Ground
Jenkins Meadow
3 Jenkins Meadow Trail
(old Haoe Trail)
2 mi.
.5 mi.
J K Trail Guide Stops Here
1.2 mi.
4 Naked Ground Trail
6 mi.
Little Santeetlah Cr.
7 Stratton Bald Trail
8 mi.
5 Wolf Laurel Trail
.5 mi.
Wolf Laurel Basin
Goldie Deaden
Obadiah Gap
1 Joyce Kilmer Memorial Trail
1.25 mi.
2 Poplar Cove Loop ¾ mi.
N.C. 1127
FS 416
FS 416
Stratton Bald Trail Sign
Naked Ground & Jenkins Meadow Trail Heads
To U.S. 129
N.C. 1127
FS 317
Rattler Ford Group Camp Sign
FS 81
Santeetlah Cr.
RIVER RD.
FS 81-H
0
1
Miles
N

A POET, A POEM, A PRIMEVAL FOREST

An Adventure in Joyce Kilmer Memorial Forest and Slickrock Wilderness

Dawn had not yet broken, although a faint glow above us hinted at its arrival. A massive storm front passing over us promised rain or, if we were lucky, a November snowfall. For an instant, the front yielded and the sun appeared, rising sleepily over the faraway mountains to the east. Briefly, our tents were filled with its warming rays before the sun was once again obliterated.

From our vantage point on Jenkins Meadow, 4,600 feet above sea level, we watched as the front moved in and dropped large, fluffy flakes of frozen moisture on our camp. Our view of the Little Santeetlah Creek watershed, the whole of Joyce Kilmer Memorial Forest, disappeared. As we worked to bring a fire to life despite the falling snow, our visibility now measured in feet, I thought of a fifth-grade class that long ago stood and recited in unison:

I think that I shall never see
A poem lovely as a tree.

A tree whose hungry mouth is prest
Against the earth's sweet flowing breast;

A tree that looks at God all day,
And lifts her leafy arms to pray;

A tree that may in summer wear
A nest of robins in her hair;

Upon whose bosom snow has lain;
Who intimately lives with rain.

Poems are made by fools like me,
But only God can make a tree.

Fourteen years after my introduction to poetry, in the fall of 1974, several friends introduced me to Joyce Kilmer Memorial Forest. It was a clear, cool day when we hiked the short Joyce Kilmer Memorial Trail to the large boulder and its bronze marker eulogizing Joyce Kilmer. As we stood surrounded by virgin poplars and hemlocks, I read about the man who'd written the poem "Trees" and later given his life in World War I. My notions of a poem learned long ago tumbled and fell. For the first time in my life, I stood in a virgin forest and truly appreciated "Trees."

The man who wrote "Trees," Joyce Kilmer, was born December 6, 1886, in New Brunswick, New Jersey. His parents, Frederick B. and Annie E. Kilmer, both had an interest in literary pursuits. Frederick, a doctor, helped edit *Johnson's First Aid Manual*; after her son's death,

The virgin forest of Joyce Kilmer Memorial Forest is lush with greenery, massive hemlocks, and poplars.
Photo by Americo Ardolino

Annie wrote *Memories of My Son* and other pieces. But when Joyce Kilmer's first volume of poetry—*Summer of Love*—was published in 1911, he could hardly have imagined that two years later he would compose one of the most widely known poems of the 20th century. After "Trees" appeared in 1913, Kilmer tried writing other poems using the same kind of simple philosophy and sentiment. But he was never again able to capture the public's attention quite so strongly.

When World War I threatened Europe and tensions at home mounted, Kilmer enlisted in the Seventh Regiment of the New York National Guard. When America joined the war in 1917, he was transferred to the 165th Regiment of the Rainbow

Division. On July 30, 1918, his 32 years on earth came to an end as he scouted an enemy machine-gun nest, as one source remembered, taking a bullet in the brain. Buried beside the Ourcq, a French stream not far from the village of Seringes-et-Nesles, Kilmer was posthumously awarded the Croix de Guerre by the French government.

Years later, Joyce Kilmer Memorial Forest was created at the request of the Bozeman Bulger Post of the Veterans of Foreign Wars, a New York post which apparently was interested in Kilmer because he had served in a New York unit. After a thorough search of all national forest lands in the United States, the Little Santeetlah's watershed was selected by the Forest Service. The area, acquired by the government in 1935, was dedicated as Kilmer's memorial on July 30, 1936, 18 years to the day after his death.

Prior to its acquisition by the government, the Little Santeetlah watershed had been threatened by logging more than once. Before proposed logging in the area actually began, the construction of a dam and a reservoir downstream forced the closing of the only railroad into the area. Since the railroad provided the only means of hauling logs to market, extensive logging operations were abandoned, and the virgin forest was allowed to stand virtually unmolested. Remnants of the abandoned narrow-gauge railroad can still be seen in parts of the memorial forest today. Later, when another logging company thought it could harvest the area's massive trees profitably, it went bankrupt before reaching the Little Santeetlah.

Although Joyce Kilmer Memorial Forest's small size (3,840 acres) would normally have prohibited it from being classified a wilderness area, Congress passed a law in 1975 creating a number of instant wilderness areas, and the Kilmer forest was included. Combined with the 11,060 acres in the neighboring Slickrock watershed, the area is now known as the Joyce Kilmer–Slickrock Wilderness. Adjoining the Joyce Kilmer–Slickrock Wilderness is the Citico Creek Wilderness. Combined, these areas total 32,904 acres, making them the second-largest wilderness area in the South.

It took a great effort for Joy and me to get our fire going that frozen, snow-encrusted morning on Jenkins Meadow. As the day brightened, our spirits strengthened as we broke camp and shook two inches of feathery snow off our tent and packs. We climbed westward towards Haoe, a 5,249-foot knob, losing our footing numerous times in the blanket of powder. We stashed our packs on Haoe and carefully made our way along the trail through Saddle Tree Gap to Hangover, which offers a grand vista of the Great Smoky Mountains. We then retraced our steps to Haoe and made for Naked Ground, a pronounced saddle in the ridge line between Haoe and Stratton Bald, which at 5,341 feet is the highest mountain in the Kilmer-Slickrock and Citico Creek wilderness areas.

Joy and I made our way through Naked Ground and descended northward into the Slickrock portion of the wilderness. The trail drops more than 2,000 feet as it meanders down the steep northern slope on a ridge between Hangover Creek and Naked Ground Branch, and hiking it is an arduous affair. For miles, our headlong plunge into Slickrock exceeded 500 vertical feet per mile and found us butt-scooting, tree-hugging, and scrambling over significant rock outcroppings.

Hiking down extreme terrain covered by snow and ice is hazardous. Each step must be firmly planted, particularly when you are burdened by a 40-pound backpack. Such demanding hiking puts unusual stress on your muscles, bones, and joints, makes you burn energy rapidly, and can leave you vulnerable to hypothermia. When we finally reached Slickrock Creek, we congratulated ourselves for not getting hurt during the descent. Cups of hot coffee and a bowl of steaming chicken noodle soup restored our lagging spirits and exhausted bodies.

At that point in our trek, a warming trend set in and rains hit. Within minutes, the rain washed away all traces of the earlier snowfall, and as we hiked along Slickrock Creek, we saw it transformed from a beautiful, snow-encrusted branch into a torrent rushing downstream.

We camped in a steady rain alongside the creek and vainly attempted to wring all the moisture from our boots and socks. We had a great night secure under our nylon enclosure, the ever-faithful VE-24, as rains pounded Slickrock and lightning danced across the darkened sky. At times, the flashes were so brilliant that we could peer through the tent fabric as the bolts crashed and see trees silhouetted in an eerie forest. Virtually exposed to the elements, we faded into well-deserved sleep, arms and legs intertwined in our sleeping bags for added security against the howling night. There is nothing like the comfort of a lover on a night like that, alone in a fragile world, surrounded by wilderness.

Morning broke to a steady drizzle. Joy expected me to crawl out of the tent and fix breakfast. Not wanting to abandon the warmth and dryness of our shelter, I managed to fire the cookstove outside the tent from under the fly. We had oatmeal with raisins, steaming coffee, and fruit for breakfast in bed. We lingered, postponing breaking camp until the day brightened.

Slickrock Creek was racing downstream, and I wondered about the wisdom of continuing down the trail toward Calderwood Lake. I knew that numerous fords awaited in that direction and that Slickrock Creek

Slickrock Creek cascades through the middle of the Slickrock Wilderness.

would only get bigger as other branches fed into it. The fords would get tougher. But Joy said, "Let's go for it. My boots are already wet, and they won't get any wetter. Besides, it won't hurt to have a little adventure in our lives."

We hiked toward Wildcat Falls. The trail crossed Slickrock Creek just above the falls, but there was no way for us to ford the strong current encumbered by heavy packs. We found a well-worn path through the rhododendron thickets along the rock formations and made our way around the four levels of Wildcat Falls. I couldn't imagine attempting to paddle such a creek, but I have heard tales of "hair boaters" carrying their boats in from Big Fat Gap and running the drops of Wildcat Falls. Not me. The 20-foot drops, pronounced ledges, and pulsating chutes are just too much.

Pushing our way through rough terrain, we stumbled onto the carcass of a well-preserved eight-point buck. Close inspection revealed that he had broken a foreleg—perhaps while fleeing a wildcat or a bear through the forest—and frozen to death earlier in the week. We left the carcass untouched. Scavengers of the forest would soon gather and feed upon the remains. Bones would be picked clean. The antlers would decompose with time. With the next falling of the leaves, little sign of this young buck's life and death would be left in the wilderness.

Our attention turned again to creek crossings. Below Wildcat Falls, we found a twisted tree trunk fallen across the creek and used it to avoid another ford. As I made my way out onto the log, I found myself in a position where I could neither advance nor retreat. Above the roar of the creek, I heard Joy yelling for me to reposition my feet. Slowly, I managed to scoot sideways across the raging water.

Then it was Joy's turn. Halfway out on the log, she halted. "I want to think about it." She looked down and started swaying, her balance abandoning her.

Quickly, I shed my pack and climbed back onto the log. Instead of trying to walk to her, I straddled the log and scooted; there was no way I could have rendered her any aid standing up. From my semi-secure position, I was able to help her get down onto the log like me. We sat silent and still just like that for a matter of minutes. Repeatedly, I asked myself how long we could survive in 35-degree water with backpacks on. Finally, we worked our way off the log and continued our hike on Slickrock Creek Trail.

Confronted by another ford, Joy suggested we skirt it by attacking the steep cliff to the side and dropping over the ridge to the next bend in the creek. Hanging by our fingernails, we managed to gain the top of the 60-foot cliff with great difficulty. Once committed, there was no turning back. We finally made our way back to the trail, only to be challenged by another ford, which we waded. We passed Nichols Cove Trail and rapidly covered the short distance to Stiffknee Trail, which joins from the west.

Half a mile downstream, we momentarily considered hiking the trail that connects Slickrock Creek Trail and Ike Branch Trail, which would lead us to our shuttle vehicle, parked off U.S. 129 near Tapoco, North Carolina. I voted for leaving the creek and avoiding any more fords, but Joy wanted to see Lower Falls. "It's only three or four more creek crossings, Gil. Come on."

Reluctantly, I followed her lead. Earlier, I had photographed Joy trying to tiptoe rock to rock across Slickrock Creek. I couldn't help laughing when she stepped waist-deep into a hole during the next crossing. Cold and wet, she never complained, her desire to see another waterfall overriding her physical discomfort. I got thoroughly soaked, too, when my feet shot out from under me and I sat down smack in the middle of the creek. It was Joy's turn to laugh then.

Lower Falls is spectacular, with two main chutes spilling over a small upper ledge before plunging 15 to 20 feet into a deep, picturesque pool.

We waded through the last ford between Lower Falls and Calderwood Lake gritting our teeth, then hiked the remaining 2.5 miles to our vehicle at a pace dictated by wet clothes, wet boots, and numb toes. At the car, we stripped naked and briskly rubbed circulation back into our limbs. Warm, dry clothes! What a wonder!

When we warmed up, we felt invigorated by our weekend in the woods and proud of our perseverance in the face of adverse weather and unexpected challenges during our 20-mile traverse of Joyce Kilmer–Slickrock Wilderness.

One aspect of the Slickrock portion of the wilderness that I like is the absence of blazes every 50 feet and the minimal signs. A good map, a compass, and common sense are necessities for any person venturing into this remote area on the North Carolina–Tennessee border. Ranger Jim Burchfield of the Forest Service stated to me in a recent conversation, "Wilderness skills are essential and often make the difference between a great experience in Joyce Kilmer-Slickrock and a bad one. If you're planning an extended stay in the wilderness, go prepared. If you get into trouble, it's best to stay on trail and not attempt cross-country travel. It's big country out there."

Over the years, Joyce Kilmer Memorial Forest and Slickrock Wilderness have afforded me numerous adventures. After one such visit in January 1976, during which I listened as a giant poplar crashed to earth, I was moved to write the following poem as my tribute to the forest:

Virgin Timber Still Grows
Among America

Winds of Unity prevail amid Storms of
 Discontent
and white dove Breezes caress Our Faces,
 as we please . . .
 (a life grows, self seeds sprout
 and Humanity's Tree is strengthened . . .
 Our Dawn Cracks oblivious Night
 brightly . . .
 We have come of age)
As We please,
The White Dove flies
She silhouettes The Sky with Silent
 Mountains
and Reigns The Oceans with High Tides . . .
 A gibbous Moon
 A star Cluster called Pleiades
Yes, Our White Dove soars above
 These inlets to Golden Shores
 Where Virgin Timber still grows

If you are searching for a wilderness experience amid high places offering panoramic views, or if you're simply longing for a leisurely stroll beneath a virgin canopy of hemlock, poplar, beech, and birch trees, Joyce Kilmer–Slickrock Wilderness will inspire you and call you back time and time again.

A Life-and-Death Experience in Joyce Kilmer

In the fall of 1982, I accompanied Murphy, North Carolina, Scout Troop 402 on a weekend hiking expedition into Joyce Kilmer-Slickrock. We had hiked up the tough Naked Ground Trail roughly two miles when Paul Taaffe, one of the Senior Scouts, was stung repeatedly by a horde of yellow jackets. Immediately, the youth's face began to swell.

We prepared to evacuate Paul. The Scouts quickly made a litter and loaded him as I raced two miles down the trail to alert Oleta Nelms—the Forest Service assistant patrolling the Joyce Kilmer picnic area—who I hoped could radio for an ambulance.

After explaining the situation, I ran back up the trail, only to discover that Paul's condition was deteriorating rapidly and that the Scouts had not made much progress moving him down toward the trailhead. Realizing that Paul's breathing was becoming more labored and that we were faced with a life-threatening emergency, Senior Scout John Ammerman and I took turns carrying Paul down the trail.

I was stunned when we burst into a totally deserted parking area. Oleta Nelms was nowhere to be found. There was no one to assist us. Doing the only thing I could, I left Paul with the rest of the Scout troop and ran the mile down to where my old Volvo was parked. Luckily, the PV544 cranked with little fuss, and I raced back to the picnic area. After we loaded Paul into the back of the car, I screamed toward Robbinsville.

Murphy Troop 402

Recognizing Oleta in her vehicle as I zoomed up the road, I honked the horn and continued on my way, trying to figure out what to do.

On a straight stretch of road near Snowbird Creek, I saw an ambulance approaching, siren blaring. I blocked the road, forcing the ambulance to a stop. The irate attendants spilled out of the emergency vehicle, yelling for me to clear the road. When informed that I had a victim suffering from anaphylactic shock in the back of my Volvo, they quickly went to work transferring Paul into the ambulance. Once again, we sped toward Robbinsville.

Later, I discovered that Oleta had not been able to raise anybody on the radio down in the Joyce Kilmer basin and had driven to the top of the ridge so the signal would alert the EMTs. Her actions that day were critical in saving Paul's life, since I had no idea where to go in Robbinsville for such an emergency. The nearest hospital was in Andrews, 25 minutes away. I'd determined that Paul's best bet was for me to quickly locate the police or a doctor's office in Robbinsville. By requesting that ambulance, Oleta saved precious minutes that may have made a difference in Paul's survival.

When the ambulance pulled into Tallulah Health Center, smoke was billowing from its engine, and open flames soon appeared from under the hood. As one EMT grabbed a fire extinguisher, the other EMT and I pulled Paul from the ambulance. Ignoring the danger posed by the burning vehicle, the doctor and his staff, alerted to Paul's condition, immediately administered epinephrine and fluids.

I finally calmed down long enough to contact Paul's parents and let them know what was happening. Within minutes of that conversation, I found myself sitting in a chair in the waiting room shaking uncontrollably.

Hiking in Joyce Kilmer always reminds me of that day on Naked Ground Trail. Realizing that I needed to be better prepared to deal with wilderness emergencies, I took EMT training and maintained my certification for nine years.

Governor Jim Hunt recognized Troop 402 and myself for the quick actions that saved Paul's life. Within a year, the North Carolina legislature passed a law permitting EMTs to administer epinephrine shots. Before that time, only physicians and registered nurses had been allowed to do so.

As a result of what happened that day on Naked Ground Trail, other lives may have been saved across the state of North Carolina. Every time I see Paul Taaffe or any of the other Scouts of Troop 402 these days, a feeling of relief overwhelms me.

Backpacking in Joyce Kilmer Memorial Forest and Slickrock Wilderness

WHO

Both the memorial forest and the wilderness are for the enjoyment of the public. A wide range of trails—some with easy grades and benches, others quite difficult—permit adventurers of all ages and physical abilities to share their secrets. Maple Springs Overlook and the memorial forest's picnic area are wheelchair accessible.

At present, permits are not required for primitive camping in the combined wilderness. Areas where fees are charged include Horse Cove Campground and Rattler Ford Group Camp.

WHAT

The Trails of Joyce Kilmer Memorial Forest

Within recent years, the trails of the memorial forest have undergone some important changes: new trailheads have been established, sections of old trails have been reclaimed, and new trails have been blazed.

Visitors are strongly encouraged to stay on all trails, and to be especially careful to do so on Joyce Kilmer Memorial Trail and Poplar Cove Loop Trail, where traffic is expected to increase substantially in the coming years.

Joyce Kilmer Memorial Trail (1)

Enchanting, mystical, and *enthralling* are words often used to describe this 1.25-mile loop trail leading to the bronze plaque commemorating Joyce Kilmer. The plaque is roughly in the middle of the loop.

Accessible from the picnic area, the trail contains some of the forest's virgin timber. Easy grades, footbridges, steps built into switchbacks, and log benches aid foot travel through the forest. Walking in the lower section of the Little Santeetlah watershed is a worthwhile experience any time of year. The elevation gain from the picnic area (2,200 feet) to the plaque is 560 feet. During peak use, as many as 600 people hike this trail in a day. Combined with Poplar Cove Loop Trail, this trail is now referred to as Joyce Kilmer National Recreation Trail. Backpacking and camping along the trail are prohibited due to sensitive plant life.

Poplar Cove Loop Trail (2)

Most of the giant timber in the forest is located along this 0.75-mile spur trail, which breaks off from Joyce Kilmer Memorial Trail at the plaque. There is very little change in elevation over the trail.

Poplars 15 to 20 feet in circumference

and over 100 feet tall remind viewers of Kilmer's parting line: "But only God can make a tree." Hiking this spur trail requires only 30 minutes of walking, but be sure to allow time for hugging these giants and straining to see their uppermost branches. The virgin poplars are estimated to be over 200 years old, with the oldest pushing 300. Some of them probably sprouted about the time La Salle crossed the Great Lakes and navigated the Mississippi River back in the 1600s. In 1990, ranger Jim Burchfield counted 430 rings on a fallen white oak in Joyce Kilmer.

Jenkins Meadow Trail (3)

Years ago, this trail, formerly called Haoe Trail, began at the Joyce Kilmer picnic area. The new trailhead serves both Jenkins Meadow and Naked Ground trails and is located where you turn from S.R. 1116 onto F.R. 416. The trail climbs 600 feet within the first half-mile. At the ridge line, Jenkins Meadow Trail heads north and Naked Ground Trail south. Jenkins Meadow Trail is two miles in length and very steep, following the ascent of the ridge. It ends at Haoe Lead Trail just below Jenkins Meadow.

Naked Ground Trail (4)

Naked Ground Trail leaves Jenkins Meadow Trail, heads in a southerly direction, and descends sharply 400 feet in elevation. Eventually, the trail begins an ascent along Little Santeetlah Creek. In this section, I have seen the night forest's display of foxfire, the luminescence caused by the action of various fungi upon decaying wood and plants. The last two miles of this six-mile trail are extremely difficult and contain numerous sharp switchbacks.

If the parking area at the trailhead is crowded, use Rattler Ford Group Camp. Overnight parking in the picnic (day-use) area is prohibited.

Ranger Jim Burchfield, who has found several Indian relics in the Naked Ground area, believes that this flat area on the main ridge once served Cherokee braves as a hunting camp.

Wolf Laurel Trail (5)

Two miles before reaching F.R. 416 on S.R. 1127, turn left at Santeetlah Gap onto River Road; you will see a sign for Tellico Plains and Stratton Meadows. Follow River Road for seven miles to Wolf Laurel Road. Turn right and wind along this rutted road for three miles to the trailhead. Wolf Laurel Trail leads 0.6 mile to Stratton Bald Trail.

Haoe Lead Trail (6)

This trail starts outside Joyce Kilmer Memorial Forest. It departs from Maple Springs Overlook, located at the end of S.R. 1127, and proceeds to Jenkins Meadow, where it joins Jenkins Meadow Trail. Approximately a mile into the hike, a giant boulder affords an excellent view of the mountains to the east. After entering Jenkins Meadow, follow the trail 1.5 miles upward to Haoe Lookout. Note the short trail that skirts the lookout to the left and rejoins the main trail. Haoe Lookout no longer offers good views, since scrub brush has grown up around it. Descend a mile to Naked Ground Camp, where Naked Ground Trail and Slick Rock Trail intersect. The ascent to Stratton Bald Trail is a steady half-mile climb; the trail junction is marked by a sign directing you uphill to Stratton Bald. This intersection marks the end of the 6.5-mile Haoe Lead Trail.

Stratton Bald Trail (7)

Though I personally prefer going uphill, I recommend hiking this trail down from Stratton Bald (5,341 feet) rather than up from Rattler Ford Group Camp (2,200 feet) because the climb is difficult.

From the junction of Haoe Lead Trail and Stratton Bald Trail, hike a mile west on Stratton Bald Trail to Bob Bald—old-timers call this whole section Bob Stratton Bald—to enjoy a mountain meadow with excellent views. Retrace your steps to the trail intersection and descend Stratton Bald Trail. Approximately half a mile down, Wolf Laurel Trail intersects Stratton Bald Trail; as you descend, you'll pass several portions of the old Wolf Laurel Trail. Continue your descent through Goldie Deaden, named after the first white settler in the area, and skirt the 4,060-foot unnamed peak rising to the north of the trail. Along this section, open areas yield views of Little Huckleberry Knob (5,360 feet) to the south. At Obadiah Gap, just down the trail from Goldie Deaden, there is a small camping area. Beyond this point, an impressive rock formation looms over the trail. Several tent sites are available where the trail leaves the south side of the ridge and crosses the ridge line just below Obadiah Gap. Steadily descend the northern slope of the ridge for 2.5 miles to the trailhead near Rattler Ford Group Camp.

WHEN

During the summer months, Joyce Kilmer-Slickrock is flooded with people. I prefer hiking in this area during the winter months, when everyone is gone except those who want to test new equipment and old skills. Early-spring hikes yield abundant viewing of blooming Appalachian flora like trailing arbutus, spring beauty, and birdfoot violet. In May and June, mountain laurel will dazzle you with its magnificent flowers; underneath this canopy, a host of trilliums show three leaves, three sepals, and three petals. Whatever time of year you visit, Joyce Kilmer-Slickrock offers an unparalleled experience.

WHERE

Joyce Kilmer–Slickrock Wilderness lies immediately south of the far western portion of Great Smoky Mountains National Park. While all of the memorial forest and the bulk of Slickrock are located in North

Carolina, a significant part of the wilderness lies in Tennessee and abuts Citico Creek Wilderness.

To reach Joyce Kilmer Memorial Forest, travel north approximately one mile from Robbinsville, North Carolina, on U.S. 129 and turn left onto S.R. 1116, which is clearly marked with signs for the Cheoah Ranger District headquarters and the memorial forest. Continue past the ranger station on S.R. 1116 for 3.3 miles to an intersection with S.R. 1127. Turn right onto S.R. 1127 and travel north approximately 8.5 miles to F.R. 416, the half-mile paved entrance to the picnic area and Joyce Kilmer National Recreation Trail. At one point, S.R. 1127 runs alongside Snowbird Creek. At the end of a long straight, the road forks, with the left fork crossing Snowbird Creek. Bear right at this fork; do not cross Snowbird Creek. You will pass the entrances to Snowbird Mountain Lodge and Blue Boar Lodge as you gain altitude and crest the ridge at Santeetlah Gap. As you descend into the massive basin that harbors the memorial forest, note the immensity of Stratton Bald to the northwest and the sharply defined pitch of Hangover to the north.

HOW

For those who want a wilderness experience in Joyce Kilmer–Slickrock Wilderness but are hesitant to venture into such rugged terrain on their own, Gary Galloway operates Trail Blazers Hiking and Backpacking, a guide service that offers expert guides, shuttles, and backpacking equipment for group outings in the wilderness. His company holds a Forest Service permit for commercial operations in the wilderness and meets all insurance regulations. For information, contact Trail Blazers Hiking and Backpacking, 41 Connahetta Avenue, Andrews, N.C. 28901 (704-321-2346).

Group reservations for Rattler Ford Group Camp can be made through Cheoah Ranger Headquarters, Nantahala National Forest, Robbinsville, N.C. 28771 (704-479-6431).

Hunting and fishing are permitted in Joyce Kilmer Memorial Forest, but permits and licenses are required. Violators are prosecuted by a vigilant enforcement division. For current hunting and fishing regulations and maps, contact North Carolina Wildlife Resources Commission, Division of Game, 512 N. Salisbury Street, Raleigh, N.C. 27611 (919-733-7291). License information number is 919-662-4370. General information is 919-662-4381.

Although permits are not required for hiking in the memorial forest, they are being considered. It's a good idea to file an outline of your planned stay in the back country with the Cheoah Ranger Station, located north of Robbinsville on S.R. 1116 a mile west of U.S. 129. Information should include when and where you plan to hike and camp and the number of days you plan to stay. Also include the name and phone number of someone to be contacted in case of an emergency, the make and license number of your car, and where you plan to park it. If no one is at the ranger station, just slide this information under the door.

Should winter weather conditions prevail, be prepared for sub-zero temperatures, particularly during January and February.

There are numerous lodging facilities in the area. Three that I recommend are Fontana Village Resort (704-498-2211 or 800-849-2258), a year-round resort with a multitude of activities; Snowbird Mountain Lodge (704-479-3433), with its rustic cabins of stone and wood and its majestic view of the entire Little Santeetlah watershed; and Blue Boar Lodge (704-479-8126), known for good cooking and gracious hospitality.

Balance is tricky and footing slippery when fording Slickrock Creek.

RESOURCES

Allen de Hart's second edition of *North Carolina Hiking Trails* offers abbreviated trail descriptions of routes in Joyce Kilmer Memorial Forest. It is available from Appalachian Mountain Club, 5 Joy Street, Boston, Mass. 02108.

Tim Homan's *Hiking Trails of Joyce Kilmer-Slickrock and Citico Creek Wilderness Areas* makes interesting reading. His precise trail descriptions are complemented by his accounts of spring wildflowers and his insight into the total wilderness experience. This guide is available from Peachtree Publishers, 494 Armour Circle NE, Atlanta, Ga. 30324.

U.S. Geological Survey maps of Santeetlah Creek, North Carolina; Tapoco, North Carolina; and Whiteoak Flats, Tennessee, all contain parts of Joyce Kilmer Memorial Forest. They are available from U.S. Geological Survey, 120 South Eads Street, Arlington, Va. 22202; Tennessee Valley Authority, Chattanooga, Tenn. 37401; and the Cheoah Ranger Station.

EMERGENCY INFORMATION

Joyce Kilmer–Slickrock Wilderness is

devoid of phones. Your best bet for getting assistance quickly is via two-way radio or CB. Tallulah Health Center (704-479-6434)—a short distance south of Robbinsville on U.S. 129, approximately 20 minutes from the Joyce Kilmer picnic area—is the nearest medical facility. District Memorial Hospital (704-321-1200) in Andrews, another 25 minutes away, is the closest hospital. To reach it, travel on U.S. 129 past Robbinsville and Topton to Andrews. Continue on the four-lane bypass for four miles to the stoplight at the western end of town; a shopping center is on your left. Turn left, pass the shopping center, and take the first right. District Memorial Hospital is on your right.

Graham County has an enhanced 911 system; call that number first in a true emergency.

The number for the Graham County Sheriff's Department in Robbinsville is 704-479-3352. The number for the Graham County Rescue Squad is 704-479-3333. The number for the Cheoah Ranger District office is 704-479-6431.

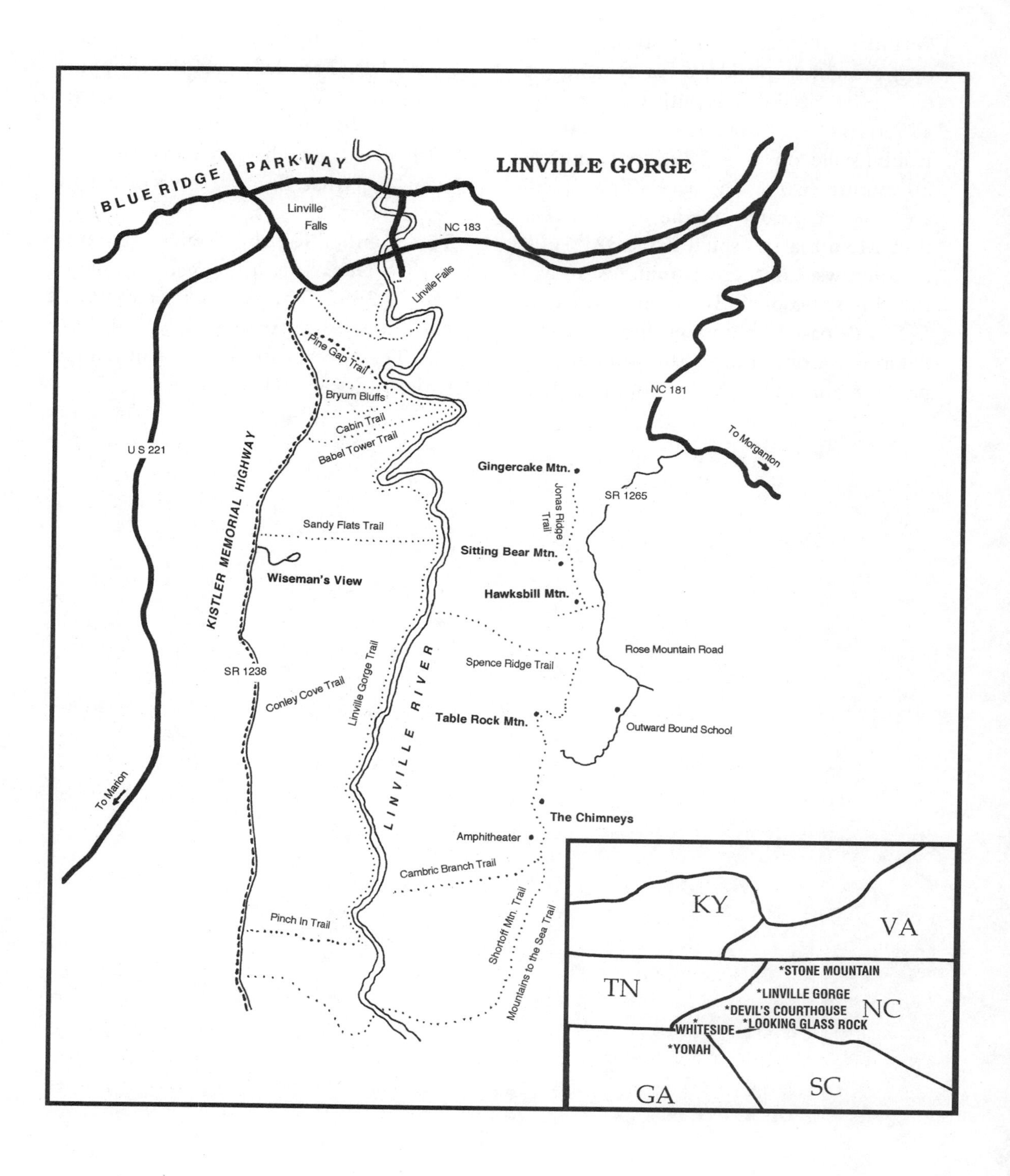
LINVILLE GORGE
BLUE RIDGE PARKWAY
Linville Falls
NC 183
Linville Falls
Pine Gap Trail
Bryum Bluffs
Cabin Trail
Babel Tower Trail
NC 181
To Morganton
US 221
KISTLER MEMORIAL HIGHWAY
Gingercake Mtn.
Jonas Ridge Trail
SR 1265
Sandy Flats Trail
Sitting Bear Mtn.
Wiseman's View
Hawksbill Mtn.
Rose Mountain Road
Spence Ridge Trail
SR 1238
Conley Cove Trail
Linville Gorge Trail
LINVILLE RIVER
Table Rock Mtn.
Outward Bound School
To Marion
The Chimneys
Amphitheater
Cambric Branch Trail
Pinch In Trail
Shortoff Mtn. Trail
Mountains to the Sea Trail
KY
VA
TN
NC
*STONE MOUNTAIN
*LINVILLE GORGE
*DEVIL'S COURTHOUSE
*LOOKING GLASS ROCK
WHITESIDE
*YONAH
GA
SC

YONAH AND LINVILLE

Hard Rock Cafes

I should probably abort this adventure. Rock is hard, and you only get one free bounce at this cafe. I crane my neck, scanning the chunk of granite that rises skyward. We're going to climb that? I ask as I lean against the monolith, seeking comfort. Surprisingly, the rock is warm compared to the air temperature. I turn and give it a great big hug, arms stretched wide. I suspect that's the way I'll be spending most of the day: hugging rock.

Yonah juts out of the earth just northeast of Cleveland, Georgia, where the Appalachians meet the plateau that eventually falls away into the coastal plain. A favorite haunt of the Atlanta climbing community due to its proximity, Yonah is known as an excellent rock for beginners developing their technique. The United States Army Rangers stationed at Dahlonega are often found climbing and rappelling on Yonah.

My instructors are Jerry and Sherry Collins of Murphy, North Carolina. Jerry practices law like he attacks the leisure sports of ice climbing, rock climbing, paddling, and mountain biking. *Tenacious* and *unyielding* are words that come to mind in describing him. His basic approach to anything embraces thorough planning and attention to detail—overwhelming attention. Sherry, on the other hand, is a motivator who keeps her partner focused. She also knows how to focus a camera to catch the essence of adventure. Walking through Sherry's Backcountry Photo Gallery and looking at her collection of adventure photos lets you know immediately that these two take their outdoor activities seriously. They also make a great climbing team, Jerry leading, Sherry on belay. Or vice versa. They're both good, experienced, and adventurous.

Rock climbing is new to me, and many questions float through my mind as we ride toward Yonah. Jerry assures me we'll take it slow, step by step. Sherry informs me that the hardest thing to do will be to push away from the wall, the rockface, with my upper body.

"What?" I ask.

"Gil, you've got to. Think about it. You're not going to pull yourself up with your arms. You could, but basically you're going to be using your feet. Put your weight on your feet. Push your upper body away from the face. Your hands are free to grab new rock. You can see up the rock and pick your route easier, allowing you to make a series of moves. Don't try to make big steps up the rock. Use small, well-placed steps, and maintain your balance. Remember, this is basic rock climbing. Think of it like a dance lesson."

No hugging the rock.

After turning off Ga. 17 onto F.R. 324 between Helen and Cleveland, we encounter a steep, rutted road that leads past a few cabins as it winds its way up Yonah. We park in a large, wooded lot shy of the summit. After organizing our gear, we hike up the hill 200 yards. We branch off right and start traversing the mountain's western flank.

Almost immediately, we enter a rock garden, with chunks of granite fractured, tossed, rolled, and positioned every which way. Jerry leads the way through the boulder field to a section of rock called the Concave Wall, a 20-plus-foot, smooth, concave piece that looks impossible to climb. Close inspection reveals chalk marks left by someone who ascended recently. So much for my knowledge of climbing. Serious free climbers carry bags of gymnastic chalk to improve their grip on the rock. There is some debate in the climbing community about the use of chalk, due to the fact that it leaves a residue that some consider unsightly. Personally, I would have been proud to make those chalk marks up the Concave Wall. Chalk marks are very temporary, usually disappearing with changing weather conditions.

My first test comes almost immediately after leaving the boulder field, on a wide stretch of smooth, sloping granite. The Vibram soles of my boots slip on the damp rock as I vainly try to follow the sure-footed Collinses. "Why aren't we roping up?" I ask. Their answer, that it's just a small slide down the rockface to the edge of the woods, isn't what I want to hear. It looks like 40 feet of bruise city, if you ask me. Later, Sherry confides in me that on one occasion, several members of their party stopped their Yonah experience right there and refused to cross the open rock slide.

After passing my first hard rock exam, I arrive with the Collinses at the base of the 350-foot granite face of Yonah, where we proceed to examine a number of climbs. Dihedral, rated 5.5, is a bit much for a beginner, they decide. We continue around the rock to the area designated by the United States Army Rangers as climbs 1, 2, and 3, as noted by the large numbers painted on the rockface. It is now time for a serious introduction to climbing equipment, tools, aids, and techniques.

First, I cast my hiking boots aside for a pair of Merrill rock-climbing shoes, featuring sticky rubber coating on the soles, across the front and top of the toes, and up the back of the heel. An inch-wide rand of this super-traction material runs around the entire outside lower edge of the shoe. The rigidity of the shoe and the sharply defined edges permit a climber to gain secure purchase on the rockface with surpris-

Jerry leading Yonah checks his equipment before attacking second pitch.
Photo by Sherry Collins

ingly little of the shoe in contact with the rock.

Now, I'm ready for some bouldering—the art of executing climbing moves only a few feet off the ground. Sherry patiently shows me how to gain holds where I can perceive none. A small bump, a slight depression in the rock, an eyebrow, a crack, a crevice, a ledge—all provide means for negotiating a rockface. "It's simply a matter of picking your route and executing the moves. Remember, climb with your feet," she keeps telling me.

I'm impressed with the climbing shoes. You feel like your toes are hot-glued to the rock. Pushing your chest away from the rock actually aids your balance as you work the face of a cliff. The dance has begun. Slowly and with great care, I learn my partner's nuances. She is steady. Like a rock.

While I fill in my dance card, Jerry is

occupied setting up a top rope. Using cables placed by the Rangers, he scrambles 50 feet up the rock, secures webbing, biners, and rope, and drops back to the base. I struggle into a seat harness, which Jerry pulls tight and double-checks. The climbing rope is then looped into the seat harness and tied off with a figure-eight knot backed with a half-hitch. This rope, my safety line, runs the 50 feet up the vertical rock wall, hooks into the locking carabiner secured by at least three points of protection, and then returns to the base. Jerry, on belay, instructs me in the proper form of climbing communication.

"On *belay?*" I query.

"*Belay is on!*" Jerry responds.

"Climbing!" I yell.

"Climb on."

The use of standard climbing signals can help eliminate accidents. It's one thing, though, to be standing near your instructor in ideal conditions and quite another to be on a rockface separated from the lead climber by 150 feet of rope and rock with a howling wind in your face. Yelling gets lost in the turbulence. Sometimes, echoes confuse matters. Safe climbing requires undivided attention. You cannot daydream while belaying a climber. Climbing partners often develop communication links based on tugs of the rope, with a certain number of tugs meaning that the climber needs more rope to maneuver, for example. When a climber knocks a rock loose, it is paramount that he yell "Rock!" as loud as possible to alert those below.

My instructors keep filling my head with these informative tidbits as I slowly work my way up the wall. I feel secure, though. Even if I slip and fall, I can't go far. Jerry keeps the slack out of the rope as he works the belay. I'm beginning to like rock climbing.

In the 1930s, the Sierra Club developed a classification system for climbing. It features six distinct classes. Class 1 climbing, requiring no special equipment or moves, is basically walking up a mountain. Class 2 climbing involves scrambling uphill and using your hands for balance. A rope is recommended for class 3 climbs, particularly for the inexperienced. Class 4 routes have the potential for fatal falls, and ropes and belays are encouraged. Class 5 denotes difficult climbing on which the lead climber should use protection anchors to limit falls should they occur. Class 6 climbs are the most dangerous, requiring the use of ropes, anchors, and other means of assistance; these climbs are generally referred to as "aid climbing" and are denoted by the letter *A*.

By the early 1950s, a decimal system denoting the degree of difficulty of class 5 routes was developed at Tahquitz Rock in southern California. Under that system, 5.9 described the most difficult class 5 routes, while 5.0 described the easiest routes. Today, the decimal system has been expanded beyond 5.9 to 5.14, with only a handful of climbers capable of making the most demanding climbs. Additionally, each designation beginning with 5.10 is now followed with a letter *a, b, c,* or *d* to further aid in judging the climb's difficulty.

Jerry is dying to get me to try a 5.8 climb on Yonah called Stairway To Heaven, but Sherry's good sense prevails, and we work on climbs rated 5.4 and 5.5. Harder climbs can follow later, when I develop the feel and confidence I so sorely need.

I watch Jerry gear up to lead the first pitch on Yonah. He clips biners of various shapes and sizes to hooks on his seat harness. Quick draws—small loops of webbing—are placed within reach. Standard runners are looped around his neck and under his arm for easy access. A rack of numerous chocks, all different sizes and configurations, dangles around the side of his chest. A host of active cams like "Black Diamond Camalots" and "Wildcountry flexible friends" completes his armor. He jingles like Santa when he moves.

After making sure that the bottoms of his climbing shoes are free of dirt and grit and that his helmet is secure, Jerry starts working his way up the rockface. A foot positioned here lets a hand grab a new hold there. Every 10 to 12 feet, Jerry halts his upward progress and selects the proper piece of equipment to wedge in a crack to provide some protection in case he falls.

Leading is the most demanding activity in climbing. The leader often climbs the rockface with a ton of equipment draped around his body and hanging on his seat harness. He must select the proper anchors—otherwise known as "pieces of protection"—and make sure that each fulfills its intended purpose. Chocks—pieces of metal that come in a great variety of shapes and sizes—are slid into cracks in the rock until they wedge themselves in tight. A rope sling or wire attaches to the chock and then to a quick draw or runner. Finally, a carabiner is clipped on, and the rope is passed through it. As the lead climber progresses up the rockface, another climber positioned below belays. Should the leader fall, the belayer checks the fall by applying friction on the belay device. Hopefully, the last piece of protection installed by the leader will hold and limit the distance of the fall.

In the early years of rock climbing, climbers used pitons and bolts for points of protection. The lead climber would climb up the face and use a hammer to drive a piton or bolt into the rock. Occasionally, the climber would have to use a star-pointed chisel to create a hole for the piton. Since they were actually driven into the rockface, pitons were commonly left in place.

With the development of chocks and cams, clean climbing came into vogue. Instead of routes being marred by the placement of pitons and bolts, each point of protection is removed by the last climber. Even though a route has been conquered, the rockface remains clean. Today, pitons and bolts are frowned upon by many in the climbing community, although their use is still acceptable in big-wall climbing and on many sport climbs.

Another mechanical device used in clean climbing is called a cam. With its trigger depressed, a cam aligns itself into its smallest possible configuration and is wedged into a crack or natural depression in the rock. Releasing the trigger allows the cam to spread out in the crack and provide a secure point of protection. Sometimes, cams and chocks get wedged so tightly that it is impossible to free them using only your hands. Jerry hooks a metal pick onto my harness and tells me how to use it to free the cams and chocks he has installed as I follow him up the wall.

Another style of climbing that has gained popularity is solo climbing. Soloing involves using only the holds that the rockface provides. No ropes or mechanical devices are involved. Basically, this means that the climber has no protection in case of a fall; only his skill prevents disaster. While we climb Yonah, we watch another climber as he solos the face. With my limited experience, I am awed. On the other hand, I do not want to witness his sudden demise should he fall. Rock climbing is a high-risk sport. Soloing takes it to another level entirely and is the ultimate challenge for advanced climbers.

I am exhilarated by my ability to climb Yonah, even though the route we're ascending is pretty basic. Knowing that I can't fall far with all the protection Jerry has placed gives me a sense of freedom. Looking down doesn't send butterflies through my stomach like I had envisioned. Occasionally, I stop and enjoy the unobstructed view from the rockface. A hawk soars effortlessly above me. Numerous turkey vultures cruise past the face with wary eyes as they search for a tasty morsel. Sherry tells of watching a hang glider launch from the top of Yonah one day as they climbed, and how the pilot caught an uplifting thermal and soared for an hour around the mountaintop.

At the completion of this first pitch, Jerry has me rappel down the rockface. My previous experience rappelling involved the use of a figure eight and a rack. Both of these devices are used to apply friction to the rope, thus slowing or halting the rate of descent. Jerry introduces me to the Black Diamond ATC, yet another rappelling device. With Jerry on belay, I smoothly descend to the base of the cliff. My ego is inflated, and the Collinses' words of encouragement only serve to boost my confidence. Naturally, I then proceed to commit my first cardinal sin: I step on the rope.

A climber should never step on the rope.

Dirt, grit, and grime from the bottom of his climbing shoes work their way into the strands of the rope and can seriously detract from its integrity. Chastised, I resolve not to commit such a felony again. The rope is a climber's lifeline and must be treated with respect. Climbers are constantly inspecting their ropes for signs of stress. If a rope is subjected to the harsh tension of a bad fall or is frayed or cut, climbers will discard it. When your life is hanging in the balance, $150 is an insignificant sum.

Our next task is to climb Yonah via a more difficult route. Jerry will lead both pitches while Sherry photos our ascent and climbs last. One of the things I notice about Sherry is that as she climbs, she ignores easy handholds and foot placements, thus making her ascent harder than necessary. Jerry explains that a lot of climbers do that to increase the challenge and expand their skills when climbing relatively easy routes. Naturally, I don't feel the need to do that. I take advantage of every crack and ledge.

On the first pitch, I commit two more cardinal sins of rock climbing.

First, as I am removing a cam Jerry has placed, I drop it. I do have the presence of mind to yell "Rock!" to alert Sherry that an object is falling, and we are later able to recover the device. In this particular situation, it's no big deal. However, if we'd been scaling a big wall and I'd dropped one of the mechanical devices, it could have been disaster for the team. Every piece of equipment is critical, not to mention expensive. A climber simply does not drop cams, chocks, or biners.

The author studies a particular problem. How am I going to do this?
Photo by Sherry Collins

Needless to say, I'm a bit embarrassed as I reach Jerry's position, which marks the end of the first pitch. As I slide past him, I place my knee in a depression in the rockface and am promptly informed that the use of knees is a no-no. Your knees don't have the traction that climbing shoes provide and are easily injured. Can you imagine getting halfway up a difficult route and hurting your knee? It could put undue pressure on your teammates and force them to expend their energies evacuating you. Again, I bow my head in shame and resolve to do better on the second and final pitch to the summit.

Yonah provides relatively easy routes that let beginners get the confidence they need. That fact, however, does nothing to diminish the feelings that rush over me when I reach the top. I have climbed my first rockface and am proud of the fact. We celebrate at a little restaurant in Helen called Cannibals. The beer is cold and the hot wings spicy. What a way to end the day! And I still have my free bounce tucked away safely in my pack.

One of the finest wilderness areas in the continental United States, Linville Gorge is 10,975 acres of prime, rugged terrain that offers everything from rock climbing to fly-fishing, from hiking to hunting. Named for the explorer William Linville, who, along with his son, is believed to have been scalped by Cherokee Indians in the gorge in 1766, Linville Gorge was carved by the river of the same name on its 2,000-foot descent to the Catawba Valley. The Cherokees called the river Eeseeoh, which means river of many cliffs. Linville Mountain forms the western flank of the gorge, while Jonas Ridge is its counterpart to the east. Numerous cliffs and rockfaces are on Jonas Ridge, including Sitting Bear, Hawksbill, Table Rock, the Chimneys, the Amphitheater, and the North Carolina Wall.

Although we have come to the gorge to do some serious rock climbing, we first hike the short distance from the National Park Service visitor center—located off a spur of the Blue Ridge Parkway not far from the community of Linville Falls—to an overlook affording an excellent view of Linville Falls. There's something about water dropping over a sharp precipice that captures the imagination.

After returning to our vehicle, we decide that a journey out Kistler Memorial Highway, which runs the length of the western edge of the gorge to Wiseman's View, is in order. Don't let the term *highway* fool you. Kistler Memorial Highway is a narrow track of road along a rugged piece of real estate. Getting out to Wiseman's View is no problem, though, as most of the highway is paved and in fairly decent condition. Beyond Wiseman's View, it's a different tale. The highway, now primarily gravel, is paved only in sections that are extremely steep. Where the pavement ends and the gravel begins, the road is marked by deep swells where tires have spun desperately for traction.

Wiseman's View is named after LaFayette

"Uncle Fete" Wiseman, who often camped at this incredible overlook as he wandered the mountains tending his cattle. In the old days, farmers didn't have fences to restrain their cattle and just let them meander. They located their cattle by means of the "bell cow"—the one with a bell around its neck—and left salt licks in accessible locations like Wiseman's View.

Standing there looking down into the depths of the gorge can leave you disorientated. Wiseman's View is 3,400 feet above sea level, and it's 1,200 feet down to the river. You get the feeling that with a good throw, you could hit the water's surface with a rock. Believe me when I say it's steep. Several deaths have occurred here when folks didn't respect the signs warning them of danger.

We abandon all pretense of climbing that day and drive a short distance to a campsite outside the wilderness boundary. Later that evening, after dark, we make our way back to Wiseman's View in hopes of catching a glimpse of the famous Brown Mountain Lights. We strike out on the lights but enjoy sitting exposed under the stars at the edge of the world, feeling the wind against our faces as it rushes out of the void below us.

Across the gorge, a scant half-mile as the crow flies, Table Rock stands silhouetted like a mighty fortress. Called Attacoa by the Cherokees, Table Rock was once a favorite spot for sacred ceremonies. Today, it is prime rock-climbing territory, with numerous routes leading up its face, including My Route (5.6), Skip to My Lou (5.6), Helmet Buttress (5.6), Cave Route (5.5), Crackerjack (5.8), Rip Van Winkle (5.7), Blood, Sweat & Tears (5.7), Second Stanza (5.8), and North Ridge (5.5). Incidentally, the 1992 movie *Last of the Mohicans* contained a lot of footage shot in and around Linville Gorge and Table Rock.

We break camp early the following morning and drive Kistler Memorial Highway north toward the community of Linville Falls, where we pick up N.C. 183 and follow it to N.C. 181. After turning onto the gravel road that runs along the eastern edge of Linville Gorge, it takes us almost an hour to reach the parking area in the saddle just south of Table Rock Mountain, even though it's less than a mile across the gorge from where we camped.

After organizing our gear, we head south on Shortoff Mountain Trail and hike past the Chimneys, on our left, for approximately 15 minutes until we come to a small, blazed yellow pine on our right. This small pine, approximately eight inches in diameter, with a white blaze at eye level, marks the main approach to the Amphitheater. The approach leads downhill, terminating at a buttress overlooking the climbing area. Looking south from the buttress, I can see the Mummy (5.5) and the Daddy (5.6), sheer vertical climbing routes compared to the friction climbing we had done on Yonah.

While backtracking from the buttress to the faint trail that leads steeply downhill to the bottom of the couloir, I fall and suffer a severely twisted ankle. I can barely walk, much less climb. Resigning myself to being a spectator, I wonder whether I can sit safely on the buttress without endangering myself further as my partners tackle the Daddy. I endure a steady stream of condolences and urge them to push on without me. I'll be all right, and my bruised ego will heal with time.

I watch as Jerry, Sherry, and her two sons—Josh, age 14, and Cory, age 10—work their way down the gully to the base of the Daddy. Jerry leads, placing protection for Josh, climbing second. Cory exhibits no fear climbing third, with Sherry following sweep. A finger crack leads to a large ledge that marks the completion of

Table Rock, a massive outcropping of granite, is a popular climbing spot in North Carolina.
Photo by Sherry Collins

the first pitch. The next pitch begins with an extremely dangerous move up a crack on fresh rock. The group face-climbs up to another ledge and the end of the second pitch. They zigzag across the face of the rock to a large boulder just below an overhang. I watch through binoculars as Jerry slings his left leg up and over the overhang and proceeds upward, using anything he can find for handholds.

Just watching this family climb has me nervous. They climb exposed on a vertical wall that appears to be 500 feet or more. The Linville River snakes along far below in the depths of the gorge. Several times, I close my eyes and try not to think bad thoughts. Hours pass as they work their way slowly up the rockface. Near the end of the route, they disappear under and over huge granite blocks to an alcove below an open book—a configuration of rock where two walls come together at right angles. Jerry free-climbs the vertical wall without stopping. As he tells me later, he has to do this quickly, due to the fact that there are good handholds in the crack but no good footholds, and he fears that if he takes too long, his arms will flame out and he'll fall. It definitely isn't a good place for that, since he hasn't placed a lot of protection, and the granite blocks below have numerous sharp, ragged edges.

I watch as Jerry attacks the final head wall—30 feet of vertical rock with a slight negative incline—and tops out with a graceful exit over the final piece of rock. Soon, the entire family is standing and waving on top of the freestanding pinnacle of rock. We exchange hoots and hollers. They are ecstatic. I watch them work their way around the lip of the Amphitheater, dangerously close to the edge, to the narrow piece of land that leads from the pinnacle to the main ridge. They then negotiate their way through the boulders on their way toward the trail.

Linville Gorge is a rock climber's heaven. The many exposed faces offer technical routes ranging from 5.5 to 5.11 in difficulty. The scenic beauty of one of the East's deepest gorges, complete with impressive stands of poplar and hemlock and the powerful Linville River, adds to the adventure.

Table Rock is one of the most popular cliffs in the state. This jutting chunk of granite dominates the countryside for miles. The view from its summit leaves a lasting impression of the southern Appalachians. On any given day, students and instructors from the North Carolina Outward Bound School—located on the eastern flank of Table Rock—can be found crawling up its cracks and crevices, bonding with their climbing mates, and finding strength in meeting new challenges.

As we work our way back to the trailhead and begin our journey home, I know that what I have seen and been a part of is incredible hard rock, a cafe with an expansive menu.

In Search of the Brown Mountain Lights

The year's last snow had barely melted when we set off in search of the lights.

I had talked with folks who had witnessed North Carolina's famed, and as yet unexplained, Brown Mountain Lights. They had spoken of globular lights meandering up and down distant mountains. Some had said the lights moved with calculated intent. Others had seen irregular bursts, rapid accelerations, and sudden stops—rolling balls of light aflame on the mountain.

Raised in the Asheville area, Elaine Dumas of Murphy, North Carolina, recollected trips to Wiseman's View, just off Kistler Memorial Highway, to see the lights. She, her father—C. M. Owenby—and other family members and friends would not depart Asheville until after dark. By the time they arrived at Wiseman's View, it was usually after midnight.

In the mid-1980s, Elaine's brother, Frank, returned to Asheville from his home in Savannah and accompanied his father to Wiseman's View to witness the lights. Frank had always been a skeptic. He figured the lights were some kind of put-on, an excuse for his father to escape to the mountains. That night, a brilliant fireball rolled up the mountain close to where they were standing and nearly engulfed Frank. After his "close encounter of the third kind," Frank became a believer.

Numerous explanations have been offered for the Brown Mountain Lights. Several murder tales circulate in the region, and some people think the lights are associated with those murders. There are also legends of lovers looking for their lost companions. And there is a dubious theory involving big lightning bugs. The most logical explanation, though, involves an illuminating gas that escapes from the earth's depths through fissures and collects in small pockets under rocks and ledges. Random gusts of wind set them free to wander on the mountain.

Our search for the Brown Mountain Lights began with finding Kistler Memorial Highway, located off N.C. 126 outside Nebo, near Lake James. We stopped at a country store and asked directions to the highway. The old man behind the counter peered out the store window at our Toyota van and laughed. "Son, I'd not try that road in that thing. It's four-wheel-drive country. It's rough. Oh, you'll get some nine miles up the road. But that's about it. No. You'd best drive up to Linville Falls. Come in that way."

After finally getting directions as originally requested, I thanked the old coot and relayed his concerns to Joy, my wife. She just smiled and said, "Let's go for it. We can always turn back."

The farther we traveled north on Kistler Memorial Highway, the rougher it got. Several times, we had to back up and get a running start to make it over the tremendous ruts. But we made it. As Joy said, "Me and my Toyota. What a feeling!"

Kistler Memorial Highway runs along the western boundary of Linville Gorge

Wilderness Area and offers exceptional views of the gorge and its massive rock outcroppings. At Wiseman's View, you can stand on a sheer precipice 1,200 feet above the Linville River. Across the gulf rises Table Rock, an ancient granite upheaval resembling an impregnable fortress. North of Table Rock rises Hawksbill Mountain. To the south is the North Carolina Wall, a jumble of spires, boulders, and overhanging cliffs.

We camped that night at a primitive site near Wiseman's View. As soon as the sun set, we anxiously began scanning the opposite ridge for the Brown Mountain Lights. The day's activities finally caught up with our children; Dylan, Callie, and Cory drifted into slumber disappointed. I watched the fire's embers fade and die and finally crawled into the tent with Joy and the kids.

Around three in the morning, something woke me from a deep sleep. I peered into the night. Lights bounced and flickered on the mountainside, weaving a magic spell in total silence. I watched amazed, not even thinking to wake the gang, as the lights disappeared as rapidly as they had come. I could offer no logical explanation and, worse yet, had no witnesses to collaborate the brilliance of the lights as they danced along the ridge. I was alone and the lights were gone.

Rock Climbing

WHO

Hard rock knows no age, as evidenced by young Cory's climbing skills. It is important that climbers know their limitations, have the proper equipment, and prepare mentally and physically before tackling technical routes. Regardless of the precautions, it remains a high-risk activity.

WHEN

Most climbers prefer spring, summer, and fall weather, though there are times when the summer sun shows no mercy and climbers must be concerned about dehydration. In the cool, wet months, hypothermia is an obstacle climbers must guard against. Climbing during the winter months is possible, provided the weather cooperates.

Linville Gorge is so steep that little sun reaches into its depths; the majority of climbing in the area is done during warm conditions. Yonah, on the other hand, offers plenty of sunshine; climbers can be found on it year-round.

WHERE

Yonah Mountain in Georgia is an excellent rock for beginners, as is Devil's Courthouse (5,462 feet), located on the Blue Ridge Parkway approximately 18 miles north of Balsam Gap, near Waynesville, North Carolina.

Whiteside Mountain lies between Highlands and Cashiers, North Carolina, and is the closest thing to big-wall climbing in the East. The routes are long, technical, and scary. Since the cliff faces south and west, good weather permits winter attempts. Many of the routes up Whiteside—such as Boulder Problem in the Sky, Hard up for Cracks, New Perversions, and Volunteer Wall—are rated 5.10 or better and have numerous pitches.

There are at least 45 different routes laid out on Looking Glass Rock, which rises out of Pisgah National Forest north of Brevard, North Carolina. Four different areas on the rock—the South Face, the Sun Wall, the Nose Area, and the North Face—offer routes of varying difficulty, from Good Intentions (5.6) to a host of 5.11 climbs, like Off the Wall, Chieftains of Creep, and Cornflake Crack. Cretins of Swing is rated 5.12.

Linville Gorge offers hundreds of climbs on Table Rock, the North Carolina Wall, Sitting Bear, Hawksbill, the Amphitheater, Shortoff Mountain, and Wiseman's View. Note that all the trails in Linville Gorge are rated "More Difficult" or "Most Difficult." And that's just hiking. Climbing routes in the area are vertical or nearly vertical and are extremely dangerous. Do not attempt climbing them without advance training, proper equipment, and the expertise to execute the ascent safely.

Another popular area for rock climbing is Stone Mountain State Park, near Roaring Gap, North Carolina. This 13,378-acre park, established in 1969, features Stone Mountain, a dome-shaped granite mass that rises 600 feet from the land surrounding it. At least 13 routes—with descriptive names like Grand Funk Railroad, Taken for Granite, Electric Boobs, and Fantastic—lead up Stone Mountain's face. Many rock climbers feel this rock offers some of the best friction climbing in the South. Stone Mountain State Park is located in Wilkes and Alleghany counties approximately halfway between Elkin and Sparta and should not be confused with Georgia's Stone Mountain, just east of Atlanta. The state park is open year-round, with family, group, and back-country camping facilities available. The rock is closed to climbing when wet. All climbers must self-register and follow established routes. No fees are charged for climbing. For more information, contact Stone Mountain State Park, Star Route 1, Box 17, Roaring Gap, N.C. 28668 (910-957-8185).

At the time of this writing, the policy of allowing rock climbing at selected North Carolina state parks was coming under review, due to the death of a young climber.

HOW

Most people end up trying rock climbing because friends talk them into it. I was fortunate to have two excellent instructors who, after being introduced to the sport by friends, took the time to enroll in rock-climbing clinics conducted by Nantahala Outdoor Center (704-488-2175), headquartered in Bryson City, North Carolina. Atlanta-based High Country Outfitters (404-391-9657) sponsors rock-climbing classes that are frequently conducted at Looking Glass Rock in North Carolina. Eagle Adventure Company (800-288-3245) offers an introduction to rappelling at Gee Creek, along the Hiwassee River in Tennessee. Southeastern Expeditions (800-868-7238) has a very popular ropes course at its Chattooga River outpost.

The North Carolina Outward Bound School (704-437-6112 or 800-841-0186) is headquartered in Morganton, North Carolina, with its main base camp 1.5 miles from Table Rock at Linville Gorge. This program prides itself on excellent rock-climbing instruction and a heart-stopping ropes course that gives individuals confidence in newly found skills and friends. The Outward Bound School is highly recommended.

Numerous colleges sponsor outdoor programs that introduce participants to rock climbing.

Whatever route you take in learning to climb, keep in mind that it is a high-risk sport that involves heights. It is not for the faint of heart. You only get one free bounce. As I was constantly reminded, "It's not the fall that kills you. It's the sudden stop."

RESOURCES

Published by the Sierra Club in 1981, Michael Loughman's *Learning to Rock Climb* makes use of excellent black-and-white photos and a step-by-step approach to rock climbing. This book really helped me prepare for my introduction to rock climbing.

The Climber's Guide to North Carolina, by Thomas Kelley, published by Earthbound Books, utilizes full-page black-and-white photos of the actual rock formations to depict charted routes. Good photos of climbers solving technical problems are accompanied by line drawings denoting specific obstacles. All known routes are rated. This book is a must for the serious climber exploring North Carolina rock. Jerry Collins's copy, reluctantly loaned out to me, was dog-eared, stained with assorted liquids, and chock-full of notations about specific climbs he has made over the years.

Basic Mountaineering, edited by Henry I. Mandolf and published by the San Diego chapter of the Sierra Club, provides a general overview of climbing and mountaineering.

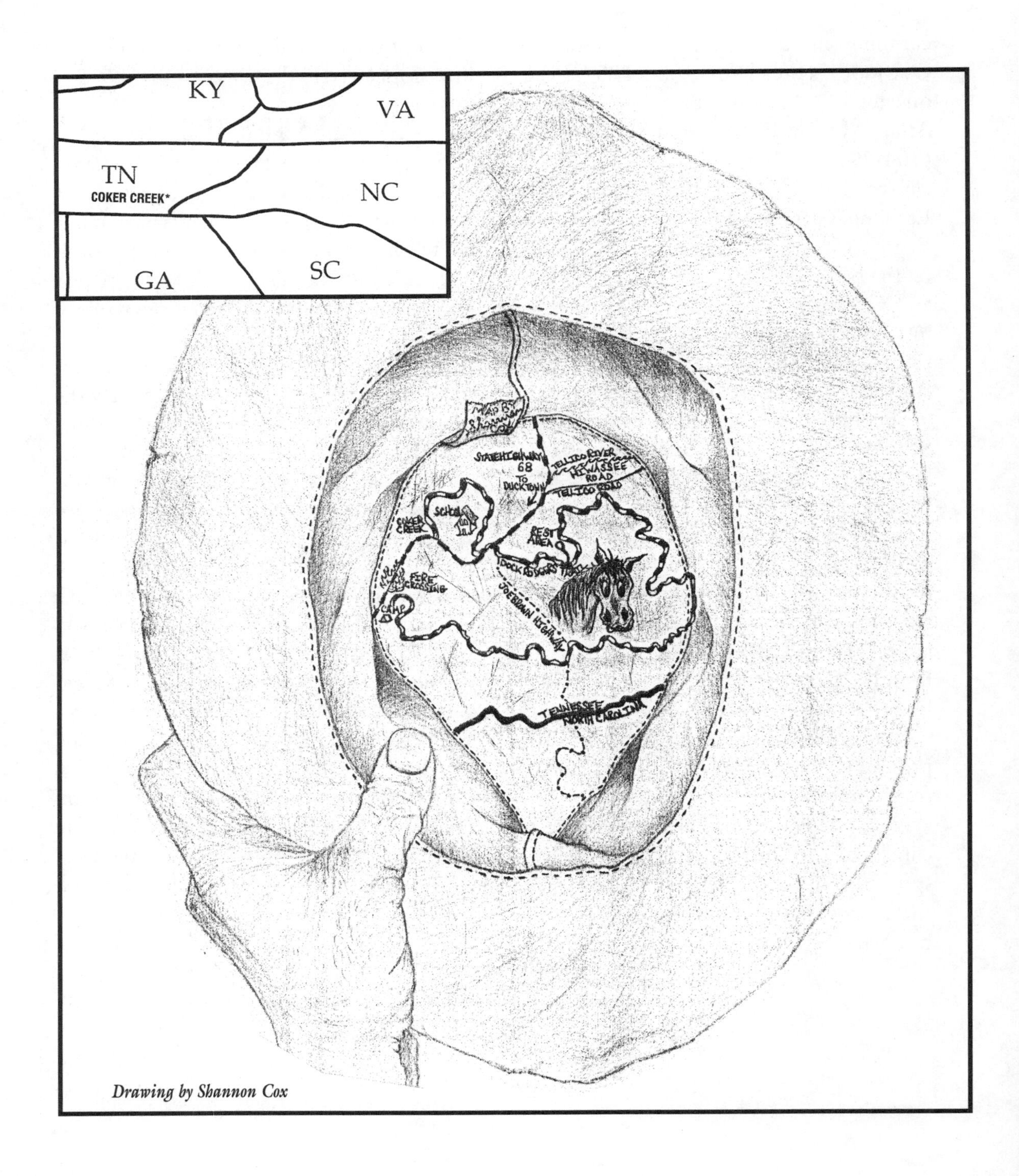

Drawing by Shannon Cox

MAD MAX, BLACK ATTACK, AND THE COKER CREEK HORSE TREK

"Yee-ha! Let's ride!"

With a spin of his steed and a quick slap of the reins across its neck, Greg was gone, a blur of horse and cowboy riding toward the top of the ridge. They flew upward, Greg balanced in the stirrups, weight forward, giving Black Attack free rein, urging the horse on with swats of his cowboy hat, held securely in his left hand. The noise of hooves meeting earth excited our waiting mounts. We were trail riding with Eagle Adventure Company. Yee-ha!

Mad Max snorted and stomped the ground, impatient at having to wait. Fortunately for me, his days as lead horse had passed several years ago, and our gallop up the steep climb was not nearly as dramatic as Greg's on Black Attack. Believe me, though, it was a handful. Nine hundred and fifty pounds of horse knew where he wanted to go, and I was determined to keep my 200 or so pounds on his back. Already, I could tell that riding this horse was going to teach me about some muscles I had always taken for granted.

When I think of horses and the role they have played in man's conquest of North America, I envision a Plains Indian riding a painted pony hard alongside a stampeding herd of buffalo, armed only with a spear. Killing a buffalo meant life for the tribe, and although the buffalo was fast, the horse was faster.

Interestingly, horses were indigenous to North America, only to disappear from the continent around 6000 B.C. when they migrated over land bridges to Asia and Europe. Early Native Americans led quite a different life prior to horses' reappearance. Their travel was limited, as camps had to be moved on foot, with only dogs to drag baggage secured to long wooden poles. The vast majority of Indians depended on the fertile forests—not the open plains—for food. But the coming of Spanish explorers with horses in tow in the early 1500s changed all that.

As early as 1540, Native Americans discovered horses, descendants of those that escaped from the Spaniards or were stolen and traded from tribe to tribe. By the mid-1700s, horses transformed the life of virtually all Native Americans. It was now possible to journey great distances and move easily from camp to camp. Native Americans claimed the vast plains on horseback. Unfortunately for them, in the decades to come, horses also served to hasten the influx of European settlers, who

Unless Greg and Black Attack were stopped, they were going too fast for me to get a shot.

were followed by the United States Cavalry.

On this overnight horse trip with Eagle Adventure Company of McCaysville, Georgia, I would not be galloping alongside buffalo or saddling up after reveille to ride with General Custer. My main concern was my lack of riding experience. I'd watched Roy and Dale, "The Lone Ranger," and "Wild, Wild West." I was a card-carrying member of the Howdy Doody Club. While I was in college, a friend took me riding one afternoon, and I ended up plastered to the side of the barn as my horse ducked at a full gallop to enter the sanctity of its stall. Years later, someone stuck a burr under the saddle blanket of the horse I was riding to test my skills. Since then, I'd stayed clear of horses.

Eagle's ranch operation is located at Coker Creek, Tennessee, 24 miles north of McCaysville. I traveled Tenn. 68, a scenic mountain road that winds along a section of the Hiwassee River and crosses portions of Cherokee National Forest. I passed through Ducktown, Dogtown, and Turtletown, whose names came from the various clans of Cherokees who originally settled these lands. Rich in Native American history and Cherokee lore, Coker Creek is the burial site of Coqua Bell, for whom the area was named. Legend has it that if you place a rock on her grave, good fortune rides as your companion. If you steal a rock, bad luck haunts your days on earth. A spur of the Trail of Tears runs alongside Coker Creek near Coqua Bell's burial mound and is a sad reminder of the thousands of Cherokees forced to leave their ancestral homes, many of whom died during their march to Oklahoma.

Greg and Linda Kerr, part-owners of Eagle's equestrian center, were busy with last-minute details when I drove up. Linda and a partner had just completed saddling the horses and were brushing manes and securing saddlebags. Across the field, Greg and a couple of friends were gathered around the chuck wagon grilling burgers. I made my way over to see if they needed any assistance and to taste the cuisine.

"Glad you made it. Hope you're ready for some riding," Greg said. "Meet Alan and Candie Canon. These folks are going to be our heroes tonight. They'll have camp pitched and dinner cooking when we ride in. They'll also help with the horses. Couldn't do without them. With them packing everything to camp, we can ride fast and hard. Still, it'll take four to five hours for us to get there. Some steep trail we've got to tackle, creeks to ford. Eat hearty."

It wasn't long before the other riders started showing up. Dr. Preston, a pediatrician from Oak Ridge whose excellent health belied his 77 years of age, was joined by Nancy Schultz and Arlene Lulavage from Asheville, North Carolina. Ellen LaFond and Cindy Beets, both from Knoxville, soon followed.

After lunch, Linda Kerr led us across the

field to where the horses were tethered. She explained that even though three riders were missing, we couldn't afford to wait on them if we were to make camp before dark, which comes early in late November. "The sun sets at 5:40 tonight. We really don't have a lot of leeway."

With practiced ease, Linda talked with each of us to give her an idea of our riding skills, in order to better match rider and horse. After taking over 2,000 cowboys and cowgirls riding that summer, Linda was very familiar with each of the 17 horses in her stable and knew their capabilities and temperaments well. Dr. Preston was assigned Iraq, a powerful, smooth gelding. Nancy Schultz drew Sinbad, and her friend Arlene Lulavage was placed on Chester, Jr. Mad Max was mine. "He's solid. You won't have any problems, Gil. If you do, whisper 'Mel Gibson' in his ear over and over," Linda chuckled. Cinnamon was given to Cindy Beets, due to the fact that she'd been paired with that horse on an earlier ride. Ellen LaFond, with her extensive credentials, which included riding equestrian in college, was seated on Diablo, a spirited creature that knew only one speed: flat out.

Stirrups were adjusted and girths double-checked and snugged tight. I loaded my camera, notebook, rain gear, and water bottle into my saddlebag and studied Mad Max intently as Linda went over the do's and don'ts of trail riding. Mad Max looked pretty much like a horse. Four legs. Long tail. Mane. Saddle in the middle. I could only hope that he didn't object to my inexperience.

At the precise instant we were all saddled up and headed out, the missing riders pulled up. They were three sisters from the Clinton, Tennessee, area—Shirley Inabinet, Barbara Hagan, and Pat Byrd. Each appeared to be in her 50s. After listening to them explain that they thought they were an hour early, I wondered what this ride had in store for us. They were also a bit dismayed to discover that the ride was four hours in length, not one hour, as Pat had led her sisters to believe. With a flurry, they signed the waiver forms and gathered their gear from their vehicle while their mounts—Ginger, Boy Gorge, and Halloween—were prepared for the ride.

I wheeled Mad Max back to the hitching post and dismounted. I actually contemplated snapping a few shots with the trusty Nikon, getting in my car, and heading home. Mad Max didn't seem thrilled that I sat so heavily. Besides, he was wide. I'd only been sitting in the saddle 10 minutes and already the insides of my thighs were tight as a drum. Could I take four hours of this?

Once again, we all mounted up, and with Greg leading, we strung out the line, each of us careful to maintain distance, as a few of the steeds were prone to kicking. As we rode by Coker Creek General Store, I could hear the sisters questioning their sanity and Ellen LaFond asking if Diablo meant "devil" in Spanish. We crossed Tenn. 68 and headed up an old road leading into the woods. A short trot later, we reined in. Greg and Black Attack waited in the middle of the road.

"Ladies and gents, this is the first piece of trail riding," Greg said. "It's tight. Watch your knees. Sometimes, these horses will get real close to the trees. Remember, keep your distance. This is your first test, and it's easy. It'll prepare you for what's later. Let's do it."

Greg and Black Attack left the road and plunged up the hill on a narrow mountain trail, both horse and rider working to avoid low-flying branches and trees close to switchbacks in the trail. We followed gamely, each of us learning our steeds. A quick half-mile found us exiting the woods near Coker Creek Elementary School. We then proceeded to walk the horses through downtown Coker Creek. Not all 51 residents were home, but a bunch of them waved or stopped their cars as we paraded past. The slight grade of the paved road caused several horses to lose their footing momentarily, giving their riders a brief thrill. All the horses were fully shod, and the metal horseshoes failed to yield the same traction on blacktop as a Goodyear radial.

We regrouped at the trailhead for Doc Rogers Trail. Greg and Linda did a quick check of all the saddle girths and cinched a couple tighter. We were then ready for our first run with the horses.

After passing through the off-road-vehicle restraints single file, the horses burst into pursuit of Black Attack, galloping with abandon down Doc Rogers. Immediately, we were confronted with a stretch that descended before curving left onto the flats. Mad Max barely slowed, and I was proud of the fact that I was still not holding onto the horn; my weight was balanced in the stirrups as I bounced in the saddle. Cavalry to the rescue! I flew on my magic steed confident that the Indians couldn't catch me. Mad Max was magnificent.

A scream interrupted my reverie. I turned in the saddle as much as I dared and was astonished to see Pat and Halloween crashing to the earth. Quickly, I reined Mad Max in, hollering, "Whoa, boy! Whoa!" and pulling hard on the bit. Max protested as I turned him back up the trail and yelled for Greg: "Rider down!"

I dismounted and grabbed Halloween, who had scrambled up and was skittish, frightened by the fall. By the time I got the horses hitched to trees and started making my way to Pat, who was lying by the side of the trail, other riders arrived. Linda took control, checking Pat for injuries. She was okay. Pat had a little hitch in her getalong, and her pride hurt as much as her hip, but she got back on that horse. I was impressed. This lady wanted to ride, and her resolve strengthened ours.

Subdued, we remounted. Much to my surprise, Greg and Black Attack bolted. It was no holds barred down Doc Rogers.

Instantly, we were at full gallop, Mad Max's hooves churning the earth as he hurtled down the lane. It was then that I noticed: though I held the reins expertly with one hand, my free hand had found a secure notch beneath the horn. I was holding onto the saddle. What a shame. Then again, nobody could see. The main task, as I saw it, was survival. For both me and the horse.

At Doc Rogers Fields, we forded Coker Creek and, at Greg and Linda's urging, let our mounts drink as much as they wanted. Mad Max didn't linger at the watering hole. He wanted trail, or so he acted.

We made our way deeper into Cherokee National Forest, working our way up the western flank of Peels Hightop, headed for Peels Gap. At one point, I could see the gap. It was a long way off and mostly uphill. With mixed emotions, I overheard that it marked only the halfway point in our trek toward camp. I hadn't been beaten up this badly in years.

We rode through a tight canopy of mountain laurel and rhododendron amid a mixed hardwood forest. Damage from the blizzard of 1993 was evident in many places. Whole stands of young pines had been bowed by the massive weight of three feet of snow. We saw large oaks and white pines uprooted by the snow and wind. Now and then, we had to skirt fallen trees by getting off the trail. The horses snorted and pranced when we passed a standing dead pine trunk that had been mostly debarked by black bears in search of grubs and beetles.

A short ways after skirting a burned area, we reached our first major ascent. Greg cut loose with Black Attack. Scenes from *The Man from Snowy River* flashed through my consciousness. I couldn't help admiring Greg's showmanship and skill. He was a natural, and his horse was well trained. Ellen's years of riding were evident as she followed quickly up the trail. Diablo was determined to catch Black Attack, and Ellen urged him to do so.

Three-quarters of the way up this first steep slope, Mad Max ran out of juice and was instantly transformed into an old plug, laboriously placing one paw in front of the other. Cindy had to pull up on Cinnamon to keep from running over us. At the next major pull, Mad Max made a halfhearted attempt to run with the big dogs, but he just didn't have it. The steep climbs—combined with a heavy rider—winded him. Holding on for dear life had gotten a little old, and I was glad for the respite.

It didn't last long. When we reached the vicinity of Peels Gap, Mad Max knew the uphill climbs were history. He was energized by the fact that we were headed toward camp and he knew the way. It was along this section of trail that I complimented Barbara, one of the three sisters, on how well she was riding.

Shortly afterwards, we hit a long gallop on slightly descending terrain with numerous low-flying branches, one of which knocked my hat off. I reined in Mad Max, dismounted, and grabbed the hat quickly due to the fact that I could hear a horse pounding down the trail behind us. It was Boy Gorge, going flat-out and riderless. A rider was down up the trail—Barbara. Somehow, I managed to grab her horse by the halter as it raced by and hold onto Mad Max at the same time.

Both horses were spooked. They just plain didn't like me leading them back up the trail. I finally had to mount Mad Max. To my astonishment, Boy Gorge began trotting calmly alongside us.

Linda was already with Barbara by the time I arrived. Barbara was gamely trying to walk off the injury to her right leg and hip. She looked at me with distinct displeasure. "Gil, don't you jinx me again," she said as she mounted her horse with a grunt of pain. After a meek "Yes, ma'am," I turned Mad Max back down the trail and slunk out of sight.

It was a wild ride back toward Coker Creek. We passed a crew operating a dredge in a feeder stream. They were searching the streambed for gold nuggets, grains, and flakes. Coker Creek was the second area in North America where gold was found by the white man; the first discovery was in North Carolina in 1799. Legend has it that in the mid-1820s, a soldier courting an Indian maiden noticed a gold nugget in her neck ornament and asked where it came from. Yielding to his persistent questioning, she revealed Coker Creek as the source. For decades, the Cherokees had kept the source of their gold secret from white settlers and soldiers. No more. The sudden influx of fortune seekers drove the Cherokees off their ancestral lands. The Trail of Tears in 1838 was merely the *coup de grâce*. The discovery of gold had sealed their fate years earlier.

Day was fading when we hit the ridge line leading down to camp. I was bushed. My legs ached. I looked across the valley and saw a fire I thought marked our camp. All the riders hustled to beat the darkness. Soon, the campfire was in clear view.

As it turned out, the fire I had seen earlier was another one across the road. By the time we galloped into camp, the other blaze was a full-scale forest fire sweeping up the opposite ridge, threatening homes and livestock.

We left the horses on the hitching rack. I watched as my fellow riders stiffly "bow-legged" their way the 100 yards to the refreshment tent. Greg, Alan Canon, and I grabbed a few essentials before jumping into Greg's father's vehicle to help fight the fire.

Firefighting is not my idea of a good time. My adrenaline was pumping as I followed Greg and Alan up the hill, putting out small patches of fire as we went. Pulling a wet handkerchief around my nose and mouth, I now sported the complete cowboy bandit look. But instead of a gun, I carried a shovel.

As we worked our way uphill, we met other folks helping manage the blaze. I was encouraged. Local people had turned out instantly to help preserve their neighbors' way of life.

Greg, Alan, and I manned a hot spot that threatened to get into the tops of the trees. Within half an hour of our arrival, the volunteer fire department took control of the blaze and mop-up operations. The fire was beaten. It was with great relief that we descended and made our way back to camp. This adventure was turning out to be more than I had bargained for.

The mood in camp was festive. The horses, brushed down and settled into a small field for the night, were no longer snorting and pawing at the smell of smoke and the sight of a mountain afire. Chili and cornbread hit the spot as Cindy entertained the group around the campfire with her insights into the art of riding, the mental makeup of horses, and what the horn on the saddle could be used for. It was a great way to end the day. Even Pat and Barbara, the fallen sisters, joined in the laughter, ignoring their aches and pains. Dr. Preston had long since hit the hay, and I couldn't blame him. Underneath a brilliant canopy of stars, I headed for my tent one tired cowboy.

Day two on the range started early. Cowboy coffee and a hearty plate of meat, potatoes, eggs, and fresh-made biscuits got us hustling. I helped saddle the horses under Linda's watchful eye. It was obvious that Barbara wouldn't be riding that day, as she limped around camp using a walking stick. In fact, all three sisters decided they'd had enough. I talked Greg into giving me more horse and got Halloween, the horse that had stumbled and fallen the previous day. Helen, Greg's mom, ended up on Mad Max, a much happier horse with 100 fewer pounds on his back.

"Gil, make that horse pay attention and pick her feet up," Greg said. "She's four years old and wants to run if you let her. She might be a little smaller than Mad Max, but your weight won't bother her. Keep her tight. Yee-ha!"

Greg burst out of camp and up the trail. Another day in the saddle, flying with the Eagle. Our newfound confidence led us to attack the hills more aggressively and give the horses free rein on all-out gallops down the mountain tracks. As I galloped down the trail, I could hear a familiar song from my youth ringing in my ears:

Happy trails to you, until we meet again.
Happy trails to you, keep smiling on till then.
Happy trails to you.

This young prospector thinks he sees gold as he tries his hand panning.

Glitters of Gleaming Gold

The first twitches of yellow fever hit me in 1982 while I was preparing for a trip to Alaska. I bought a gold pan and secured a book that promised to lead me to rich finds of the precious metal. Tales of gold veins in rocky hillsides and nuggets as big as bird eggs lying exposed along creek banks whetted my appetite.

Gold, one of 92 naturally occurring elements found on earth, is an amazing metal. No known natural substance can destroy it. It possesses tremendous malleability. Gold can be pounded so thin that you can look through it. It is so ductile that a single ounce can be stretched into a strand of wire 35 miles long. Although gold is not magnetic, it is an excellent conductor of electricity. It cannot be corroded or oxidized. With a specific gravity of 19.3, a single cubic foot of gold weighs approximately 1,200 pounds. Gold's many uses range from jewelry to dental fillings to coins to thousands of electronic and technological applications.

To the novice prospector, the whole process of locating and extracting gold from the earth appears simple. You grab some dirt from the bottom of a creek, slosh some water around in a pan, and pick out the gold. Nothing to it. Then you take your gold grains, flakes, and nuggets down to the man who can assay them. Then you grab the money and run.

Over the course of that Alaska trip, I panned a lot of worthless grit. Although I witnessed prospectors exchanging gold for drafts of beer in several bars, the nuggets I so ardently searched for remained hidden. My gold pan ended up in the trunk of the Volvo, where it remained for several years.

It wasn't until 1987 that I got up with Hank Fonda of Andrews, North Carolina, who rekindled in me the virus called gold fever. Hank instructed me in the fine art of panning. There is a certain way to swirl the grit around in your pan so the water sloshes over the side and the heavy valuables are caught in the ridges on the pan's side. It is a task that requires patience and a subtle expertise.

The next step in my learning came when Hank dragged out a 2.5-inch dredge complete with hoses and nozzles, a powerful pump, and a sluice box. The dredge is a wonderful device for gold seekers. It can suck up the bed of a creek and process tons of material in a short span of time. Material is sucked through the nozzle and into the hose, which leads to the sluice box. As the watery portion runs over the top of the sluice, the heavy portion sinks and is trapped in the riffles at the bottom of the sluice. Among the concentrates gathered on the backside of the riffles are black sands rich in microscopic gold and other heavy metals. That is, if you happen to be prospecting in the right area. Hank and I dredged for days in numerous creeks and rivers. Our finds were scant. Finally, the dredge ended up serving Hank as a means to draw water from his pond and irrigate his garden. The fever died.

My horse trek through Coker Creek, an area rich in gold dating back to the time of the Cherokees, carried me past several groups using pans and dredging equipment in their effort to find gold.

Unfortunately, a dredge, whether a small recreational rig or a large commercial operation, has a tremendous impact on the environment. Sucking the bottom out of a creek harms a wide variety of aquatic life and adversely affects water quality, potentially disrupting an entire watershed. Currently, recreational dredging is prohibited in North Carolina's national forests, and all commercial mining operations are heavily regulated and monitored. A recent influx of requests for recreational dredging permits in national forests has caused the Forest Service to review its policy banning such activities. Conservation groups, however, anticipate no change in the ban on recreational dredging in the foreseeable future.

Panning, on the other hand, impacts lightly and offers those struck with gold fever a chance to try their luck in tracking down a vein.

It is theorized that gold found on the surface or in the earth's outer crust was formed deep inside the earth's core and was brought to the surface by volcanic activity. With erosion and changes in streambeds and rivers, new veins are always being brought closer to discovery.

It is of prime interest to prospectors that gold has been found in some measurable quantity in every county of the continental United States. In Georgia, the famed Dahlonega gold belt runs from the Alabama line, near Bremen, northeast to the North Carolina border, near Dillard, varying in width from half a mile to nearly 13 miles. Gold has been discovered in many sections of North Carolina, from the Koneheeta Valley, near Andrews, to McDowell and Rutherford Counties, near Morganton, to the rich deposits surrounding Charlotte in Mecklenburg County and nearby Union County. And there is always Coker Creek, north of Ducktown, Tennessee, on Tenn. 68.

The hard work of panning for gold, of spending hours up to your knees in a cold mountain stream, pales beside the thrill of discovery. A fleck of yellow can make a prospector's day. The odds of striking a vein are about as likely as those of winning the lottery—slim to none—but then that's the glitter of gleaming gold.

Horseback Riding

WHO

Before you start organizing a horse trip for yourself and 20 friends, I recommend checking out the outfitter and finding out the rules and the cost. Some outfitters can't take kids under 12 due to insurance regulations, while others take riders as young as six. Riding helmets are often available upon request, but in this day of lawsuits, don't be surprised if you're required to wear one. Getting to know the outfitter and the services offered will help you plan your trip and the composition of your group. Be sure to inquire about group rates.

WHEN

Riding horses is great any time of year. In winter, when the leaves are off the trees, the views are open and bugs virtually nonexistent. Unfortunately, most commercial riding stables close during the off-season, but some operate all year. Check with the stables for a complete schedule of trips.

WHERE

In recent years, the Forest Service has included riding activities and trail use in its management plans. The vast majority of districts have areas open to horse travel. Some old logging roads on national forest lands have been closed to vehicles; these make excellent horse trails.

Recently, my daughter Callie and I went mountain biking in the Tsali Recreation Area, near Robbinsville, North Carolina, where trails are open to horses and mountain bikes on alternate days.

HOW

To locate a riding facility near you, try the yellow pages. Excellent facilities are located throughout the southern Appalachians. The following outfitters, all located in the tristate area of North Carolina, Tennessee, and Georgia, offer mountain trail riding:

Eagle Adventure Company
104 Toccoa Street
McCaysville, Ga. 30555
800-288-3245

Track Rock Riding Academy
Route 2, Box 2310
Blairsville, Ga. 30512
706-745-5252

Cataloochee Ranch
Route 1, Box 500
Maggie Valley, N.C. 28751
704-926-1401

Nantahala Village Riding Stables
30 Watkins Cemetery Road
Bryson City, N.C. 28713
704-488-9649

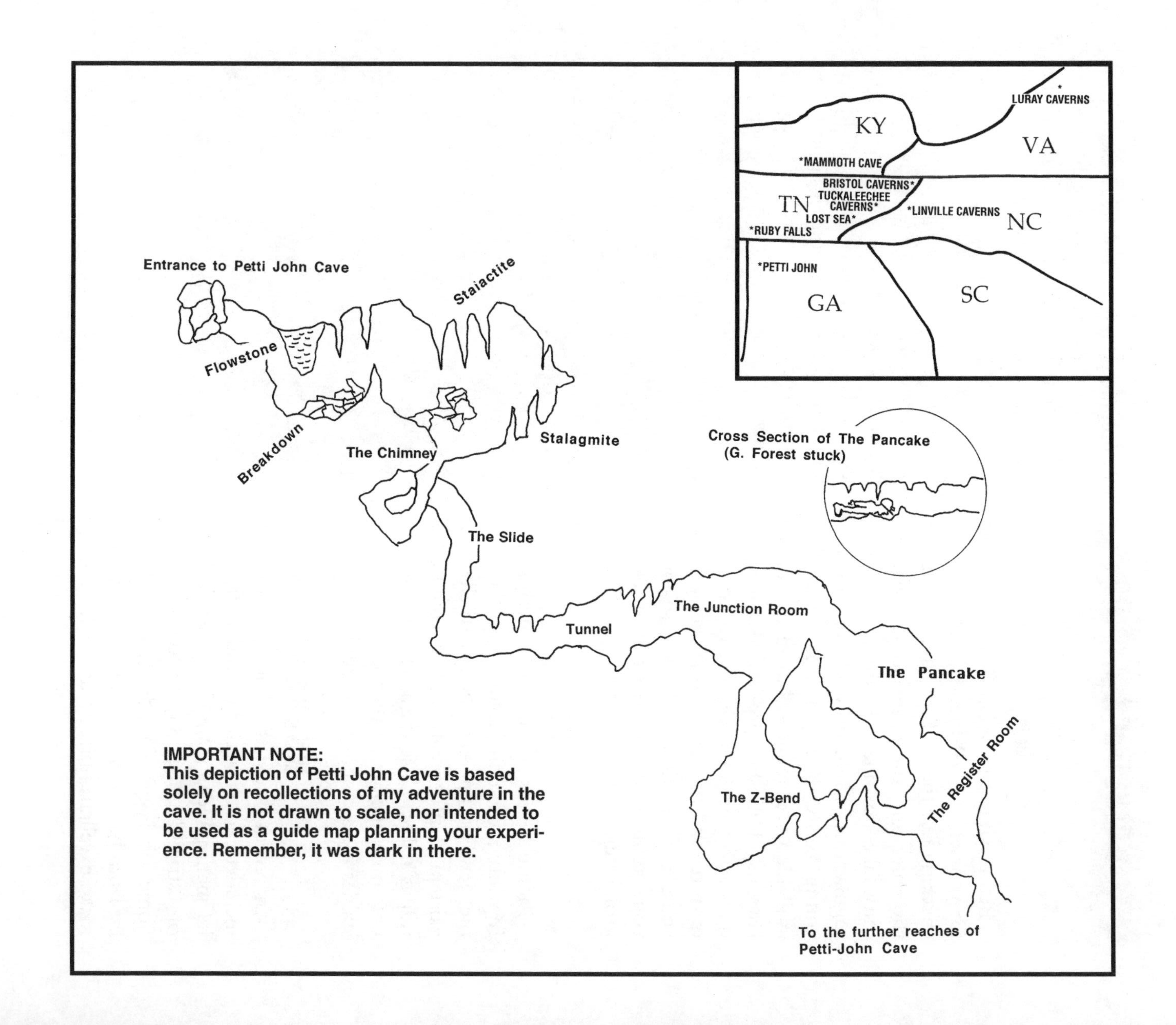
LURAY CAVERNS
KY
VA
*MAMMOTH CAVE
BRISTOL CAVERNS*
TUCKALEECHEE CAVERNS*
TN
LOST SEA*
*LINVILLE CAVERNS
NC
*RUBY FALLS
*PETTI JOHN
GA
SC
Entrance to Petti John Cave
Staiactite
Flowstone
Breakdown
The Chimney
Stalagmite
Cross Section of The Pancake
(G. Forest stuck)
The Slide
Tunnel
The Junction Room
The Pancake
The Register Room
The Z-Bend
To the further reaches of
Petti-John Cave
IMPORTANT NOTE:
This depiction of Petti John Cave is based solely on recollections of my adventure in the cave. It is not drawn to scale, nor intended to be used as a guide map planning your experience. Remember, it was dark in there.

DOWN UNDER, HORIZONTAL AND VERTICAL

Two Stories About Spelunking

Reservations flooded my thoughts as I pondered my upcoming caving expedition. Outside of a few family outings where we strolled down steps carved and poured that led to caverns popularized and commercialized, I had never been spelunking. This weekend was showtime. Would I be able to handle the confined spaces, the darkness, the knowledge that thousands of tons of earth lay above me? Would I suffer from claustrophobia? How would my fellow adventurers react?

Caves have shielded man and beast from the elements and each other for many centuries. The cave man is no joke. He's our ancestor. Imagine huddling around a fire a few feet inside the entrance to a cave while a blizzard raged through the countryside. It had to be a tough life. Little to eat. The big stick kept close to ward off all threats to survival, whether on four legs or two. Living hand to mouth. Who would have guessed that 20th-century humans would sometimes feel the need to return to their cave-man roots in the name of adventure?

Being a novice, I didn't know where to go for a real caving experience. I needed a guide. A list of qualifications formed in my mind. Wanted: Someone I could trust, who had knowledge of modern cave-exploration techniques. Medical and evac training preferred. Search-and-rescue training would also be nice.

Russ Miller fit the bill nicely. A veteran spelunker, Russ was once a professional caver, earning a living exploring and mapping caves for Mammoth Uplands Research Lab. A paramedic who is often called in to help conduct underground rescues, Russ knows the value of good leadership, of performance under duress. Having participated numerous times in the river rescue clinics Russ conducts for Ocoee River guides, I knew he was an instructor well-versed in ropes, knots, and rescue operations. Russ also teaches classes in vertical climbing, basic rappelling, and rope management at Chattanooga State.

I figured I'd talk some of my fellow river guides into going with us. I'd even get my son, Dylan, to do it. Safety in numbers, right? My wife wouldn't even think of going. "Have fun. Let me know if you make it back," she said.

Joy figured out real quickly why I was recruiting strong, young people to accompany me on this adventure. Russ and I had planned to go spelunking in late June 1993. Unfortunately, I injured my back and had to be carried off a raft trip. Strong, young river guides had come to my aid. I felt there was a real possibility I would have to be dragged out of some cave in Tennessee or Georgia.

Opal Petty showed up that Saturday morning at Ocoee Outdoors, our rendezvous point. My friend Tim "Gator" Meaders figured this would be an excellent opportunity for an adventure—as well as an opportunity to test a pet theory about group behavior. Dylan, my junior in high school, wasn't letting the old man

Russ and I pause as we descend into Classic Sinkhole.
Photo by Tim Meaders

get anything up on him. It would be radical, right? Russ's friend Margaret Hodge completed our group.

Russ planned a two-part introduction to spelunking: horizontal and vertical. The first day, we'd explore the early reaches of Petti John Cave, south of Lookout Mountain, Tennessee, near Lafayette, Georgia. For the most part, we'd stay horizontal: crawling, sliding, belly-scooting, ducking under, over, and through "breakdown," contorting our bodies through cracks and crevices. For the vertical experience, we'd travel to a place in Tennessee called the Classic Sinkhole and break out the racks, Gibbs ascenders, and chicken loops. We'd try a 160-plus-foot free rappel to the bottom of the sinkhole. The big tests for us novices would be going over the lip, then making the tough ascent without succumbing to entrance fever.

It was close to 11 by the time we parked our vehicles three-quarters of a mile off the Chamberlin Road entrance to Crockford-Pigeon Wildlife Management Area. We began gearing up for Petti John, paying close attention to Russ's instructions. "There's some basic rules all cavers should follow," he stressed. "Three separate light sources minimum per person, helmet-mounted preferred; at least three people in a group; and outside knowledge of where you are going and your E.T.A. surface. Everybody in my spelunking outings is furnished with a helmet and required to wear it. Gloves are highly recommended. We stay together as a group. Any questions?"

We hiked the short distance to the cave in silence. Each of us had questions, I'm sure. Mine were self-centered. Was I ready for this?

At the mouth of the cave, we counted off. I was number five, which would be my designation the entire time we were underground. Russ took the last number—six. He would alternate between lead and sweep. When he was in the lead, I was assigned the sweep, or last, position. In no uncertain terms, Russ reminded us that he was the trip leader and that he called the shots. He explained that the length of our stay and to what depth we journeyed depended on us. If one member of our party felt he'd had enough, we'd all exit together. There would be no splitting up.

The exposed rocks that form the entrance to Petti John lie near the edge of a beautiful, elongated valley on the eastern slope of the escarpment known as the Tennessee Valley Divide, an ancient geological formation that created the mountain ridges running south from Chattanooga deep into Georgia. A person-sized opening slips between boulders and spirals gently downward before opening into the first of numerous caverns. In fact, Petti John consists of more than 20 miles of caves. "Push cavers" haven't found the end of it yet, if there is one. What makes the entrance to Petti John impressive is the fact that it is the only known entrance to the largest cave system in Georgia. Characteristic of large caves with only one small opening, Petti John "breathes," as air is forced out the entrance.

As Russ led us through the cavern, he identified "fluting," where limestone, rock, and clay were scalloped by high-velocity abrasion. He pointed out flowstone, where a surface coating of mineral was deposited in midflow. He also explained the difference between stalagmites and stalactites, and how they can form columns when stalactites drooping from the roof meet stalagmites building from the floor. Pillars, as distinguished from columns, are what's left of the original bedrock of the cave.

Interestingly, I learned that all caves are in the process of falling down. That's just one of the hazards of caving. Others include flooding, snakes near entrance zones, bad air, injuries, hypothermia, getting trapped, and just plain getting lost.

We worked our way deeper into Petti John. At times, we had the option of either scrambling over or crawling through breakdown. I opted for the higher moves every time. Stepping carefully to avoid slipping and busting a kneecap—I'd left my kneepads safe at home—I made my way through a breakdown to the first intriguing move, a chimney down a narrow chute. The chimney was followed by a 20-foot feet-first slide that ended in a four- or five-foot-high tunnel leading to the left toward the Junction Room.

It was here that Gator decided to apply his test to the group. "I've had enough," he stated as Russ finished describing our next move, which would take us through The Pancake, a wide, horizontal slit in solid rock not more than 15 inches high at any spot. With aplomb, Russ cautioned Gator to think about it. On the other side of The Pancake was the Register Room, where we could attain the goal of signing the first register in Petti John and leaving proof of our penetration into the cave. It wasn't far to the Register Room. Thirty feet or so. Thirty feet of tight squeeze.

Group dynamics came into play.

"You can do it, Gator."

"Just think. You can say you did it."

"We'll have lunch there."

"Come on, Gator. Go for it."

He did. Flat on his stomach, he squirmed into The Pancake behind Russ, Dylan, and Opal. Then Margaret disappeared into the crack in the rock, and I was left to follow. As I inched forward over the thin coating of slime, it was impossible to lift my head and see forward. I had to look off to the side and pick my route. Once, my headlamp went out. Panic city.

I could hear my companions safely in the Register Room.

"Gil, are you coming?"

"Suck it in."

"If you can move an inch, you're not stuck, okay?"

With concentration and controlled breathing, I managed to repair the electrical connection to my lamp. It was reassuring to be able to see again. There is no natural light in a cave. It's just plain black. Totally black. Cavers are careful never to look another caver in the eyes with their headlamp on, as doing so defeats night vision.

With great relief, I fell out of The Pancake into the Register Room, amid laughter at my predicament. Gator took one look at me and said, "I think he's had enough, too."

As we ate, Russ told of passages beyond. Of the Pine Forest, a maze of stalactites and stalagmites. Of an underground stream not far ahead. Of daring moves over sheer drops. Of tunnels yet unexplored. Gator talked of entrance fever. Of going through The Pancake again. Russ mentioned the option of returning to the Junction Room via the Z-Bend. Gator and I both nixed that idea, since we already knew what it would take to get out through The Pancake. We'd lost our explorer's edge, at least for the day.

After signing the register, stored in a section of PVC pipe dangling from a bolt sunk in the roof of the cave, I brought up the rear again as we began our return trip to the surface. I tried to pick my moves through The Pancake based on Margaret's light as she smoothly negotiated ahead of me, but that only got me stuck. Jammed fast and breathing hard, with my head caught sideways, I lay still, collecting my wits. My first attempt at backing out was halted by the position of my right boot. Once I was able to reposition it, I backed up half an inch at a time until I reached an area in The Pancake with several inches of clearance. A new route led me to the rest of the team, waiting patiently in the Junction Room.

For a few moments, we rested. The group seemed subdued. I think two factors were at work. First, with my difficulty getting through The Pancake, they were relieved that we weren't penetrating Petti John deeper. What a monumental task it would be to haul me out of there! On the other hand, some members of the party were disappointed. They wanted to push on and explore the cave deeper, to see the Pine Forest and cross the bridge high above running water.

The Junction Room is so named because two separate routes lead from it to the Register Room: the path we took through The Pancake and the Z-Bend, a contortionist's dream. After thoroughly discussing the matter, and fully aware of the potential consequences, we opted to commit two cardinal sins of caving. We split up the group, and the members of the advancing party left their packs and most of their spare equipment behind. Gator and I would stay in the Junction Room while Russ led the other three members of the team through the Z-Bend into the Register Room and back via The Pancake, a 20- or 30-minute excursion. Though I would not recommend proceeding as we did that day in Petti John, it is

Margaret starts into the Pancake as Gator studies the situation. Vandalism of caves such as spray painting names is common and unfortunate.

common in modern cave exploration to establish base camps as teams spread out and explore new routes. It is also a technique used in search and rescue underground.

Gator and I had a frank discussion about caving as we waited in the darkness, conserving our batteries. We agreed: spelunking is not for everybody. Like Gator says, "Been there. Done that!"

Upon the return of the advance party and their tales of bending this way and that through the Z-Bend, we began our exit of Petti John. Some of the moves were tricky, but the allure of the unknown had faded. We were spelunkers, veterans of a horizontal cave.

Warm, life-sustaining sun welcomed us as we surfaced through the corkscrew opening of Petti John. A short ride later, we were all splashing in the cold, clear water of a swimming area called the Blue Hole, ridding our bodies of the dirt and slime of our horizontal experience. The water refreshed our spirits and washed clean the fears we each may have had underground.

Russ brought us back to reality. "A steep hike up from here lies Ellison Cave, the second- and third-deepest known cave drops in North America," he explained. "It is for expert cavers only. One drop is over 500 feet. For our vertical experience, we are going to travel north of Chattanooga to South Pittsburgh, Tennessee, and do the Classic Sinkhole. Don't worry, though, it's over 160 feet vertical, and once over the lip, it's a free rappel."

We camped that night barely off the rough mountain road that runs past the unmarked trail leading to the Classic Sinkhole. Russ was determined to get a jump on our vertical descent the next day, worried that with the TAG convention being held that weekend just south of Chattanooga, the Classic Sinkhole would be overflowing with cavers. The TAG convention started in 1978 when a small group of Tennessee, Alabama, and Georgia cavers organized an informal get-together. The annual event now attracts over 1,000 spelunkers. To secure our site, Russ, Opal, and Margaret hiked to the sinkhole late that evening and rigged the ropes we would use descending.

Morning broke clear. Russ introduced us to the equipment we'd be using. After determining that we'd used figure-eight descending rings in all our previous rappelling, he introduced us to the rappel rack, a variable-friction device invented by John Cole in 1966. The rack allows a person to maintain a safe rate of descent by changing the number of bars in contact with the rope, or by changing the distance between the bars. It has been called one of the greatest contributions to rappelling. Since this would be our first experience with the rappel rack, Russ decided to accompany us individually, both descending and ascending. That meant he would make three trips up and down the Classic Sinkhole, almost 1,000 vertical feet.

Opal would go first with Russ. Then Dylan. Then me. Margaret and Gator were opting to remain above ground and keep the water boiling for coffee and tea. The arrangement looked good for me. First, Opal would test the ropes she'd helped rig the previous night. Second, Dylan would tire Russ out on the next ascent. If Russ felt up for the third jump, he might not complain about my slow ascent out of the sinkhole.

Russ and Opal triple-checked everything from the tensionless anchor to the chest and seat harnesses to the locking carabiners and Gibbs ascenders. Nothing was left to chance. From a vantage point across the open gulf of the sinkhole, we watched as they worked their way over the lip and slid smoothly down into the chasm. We lost sight of them as they passed a rock bridge, only to see them reappear quickly much farther down, caught in golden shafts of sunlight. I could tell that Opal, a lead rappelling instructor, was in her element. Though she was learning new rope techniques and using new types of equipment, she made it look easy.

Dylan's descent with Russ into the Classic Sinkhole found me peering nervously at their every move. It was one thing to watch Opal and another to watch my offspring venturing into the unknown, confronting his destiny. I witnessed their ascent and return to safety with mixed emotions. I was glad Dylan was safe. But Russ didn't look worn out at all. After a quick cup of tea, he looked at me and said, "Let's get hooked up."

Gator laughed, "Have fun, old man!"

I made Russ double-check the triple-check. Dylan hooted. Even a week later, I was nervous as I started writing this account.

I made my way to the jump site and carefully, under Russ's constant supervision, got my rope securely through the rack and all the safety ropes attached. We walked through how to operate the rack one more time. I made my way awkwardly over the lip and somehow managed to make sure the rope was protected by the pad, so it would not fray on the rocky edge.

Once away from the lip and hanging free, suspended like a spider on a single, long, silvery strand, I gained confidence in my situation and equipment. The rack was amazingly effective. I could easily stop and hold my position while I studied the geological features of the sinkhole. Sunlight danced on the stream cascading into the pit on its northern flank. I was in another world.

Upon gaining the bottom, we unhooked our harnesses and explored the sinkhole. After climbing up a muddy bank, we descended a short distance to a cave that led about a half-mile before rejoining the stream at the bottom of the sinkhole. I assured Russ that I'd enjoyed yesterday's horizontal very much but that I was concentrating on today's vertical, more particularly the 160-plus feet up and out.

Russ helped me rig my equipment for the ascent. He'd chosen a modified Texas prusik method. In place of prusik loops, we used Gibbs ascenders, which employ cams to apply friction to the rope. First, I attached a Gibbs ascender system, with stirrups for both feet, to my rope and seat harness. After sliding the stirrups through the chicken loops—small pieces of webbing tied around my ankles that would prevent the stirrups from sliding off—I stepped into the stirrups, lowered my chicken loops, and hooked another Gibbs ascending unit to my chest harness. A safety prusik followed.

Getting started was difficult. Two hundred-plus pounds resisted. First, I had to slide the chest-mounted Gibbs system as high as I could reach, with my weight on the foot loops. After transferring my weight to the chest harness, I drew my legs up frog-style as I slid the lower Gibbs up the rope. Standing up in the foot loops again allowed me to slide the upper Gibbs ascender higher on the rope. I repeated this process what seemed like several thousand times.

I looked down and was dismayed to see I was only six or seven feet off the ground. Looking up, I saw a tremendous expanse of rock and only a thin umbilical cord as my salvation. Russ cautioned me to pace myself. The entrance wasn't going anywhere, and we had plenty of time to get there.

As we gained height, I found the modified Texas system easier and easier to execute. According to Russ, that was because the weight of the rope below us made it increasingly easy to move the lower Gibbs upward. The system also allowed us to rest comfortably by distributing our weight at three points: the foot loops, the seat harness, and the chest harness.

As I worked my way out of the sinkhole, I was able to study the nylon rope on which my life depended. All cavers use nylon-fiber ropes because they have a high shock-load capacity. The particular rope I was using was a Blue Water II, developed in 1966 by a textile mill in Whitesburg, Georgia, for use in the marine industry. My rope had a tight, braided sheath to protect the core from abrasion by continued rubbing on rocks. Russ was on a rope made by PMI in Lafayette, Georgia, a few miles from Petti John Cave. One of the first things you learn working with ropes is that you never step on them. Dirt works into the fibers and can cause serious internal abrasion. Acids of any kind can quickly destroy the integrity of a rope. Climbers and cavers pay strict attention to the care and condition of their ropes. Their lives hang on them.

When we were about halfway up, I noticed all kinds of activity above us. Hooked by a safety line, Gator was leaning over the edge taking photos of my epic struggle. All of a sudden, ropes started dropping into the sinkhole. TAG members had hit the scene. There must have been 20 or 30 of them preparing to enter the Classic Sinkhole. More than once, a rock accidentally kicked into the pit whizzed by our heads, seemingly long before we heard the warning yell.

A piece of cake, I told myself as I finally struggled over the lip and onto earth's precious surface. Thank God. Still alive.

Caving, whether horizontal or vertical, is not for everybody. The risks are real. The feeling of confinement can make the strongest weak. But it is easy to see why cavers enjoy the challenge of being underground. Caving requires training, tremendous self-control, and total appreciation of the dangers faced in every Pancake, every Z-Bend, every Classic Sinkhole, every tunnel leading to new discoveries. During my time down under, I came to the conclusion that caves do not call to me as they do to Russ Miller. I can honestly say that I wouldn't have done it without his leadership. Thanks, Russ. I'm out of here.

Spelunking

WHO

If you think you want to go caving, I recommend researching the matter thoroughly. Your local library probably has numerous books on caving. Talk to people who have actually been down under and experienced it firsthand. Find a caving club (a National Speleological Society Grotto) in your area and determine if any of its planned outings offer you the opportunity to participate. Remember, never go caving with people you are not comfortable with, whether because of their personalities or skill levels. Never hesitate to ask questions, especially if they pertain to safety and procedures.

WHEN

Caves are always pitch black, so it doesn't really matter whether you explore at dawn or midnight. Underground air temperatures are pretty constant, although cool. Howling blizzards up top have little effect once you're past the entrance to a cave. All the same, most people prefer to go spelunking during the summer months.

WHERE

For your first outings, consider taking a tour of a commercial cavern like The Lost Sea, near Sweetwater, Tennessee, or Mammoth Cave National Park in Kentucky. Ruby Falls on Lookout Mountain in Tennessee; Virginia's Luray Cavern; Tuckaleechee Caverns in Townsend, Tennessee; Linville Caverns near Linville, North Carolina; and Bristol Caverns outside of Bristol, Tennessee, offer you the opportunity to experience the wilderness underground without considerable equipment or expertise.

HOW

If you're looking for an in-depth spelunking experience, Russ Miller can be contacted through Ocoee Outdoors (800-533-7767). Bill Wallace leads group spelunking trips that explore Blowing Rock Cave near Scottsboro, Alabama. He can be contacted through Outdoor Adventure Rafting (800-627-7636 or 615-338-8914).

RESOURCES

Two resources all cavers are aware of are the National Speleological Society, Cave Avenue, Huntsville, Ala. 35810 (205-852-1300) and the Cave Research Foundation, 206 W. 18th Avenue, Columbus, Ohio 43210. Both publish excellent literature pertaining to man's adventures under the earth. Grottos—chapters of the National Speleological Society—are located across the country. Grotto members are always searching for individuals interested in experiencing the wonders of the underworld and are happy to introduce them to spelunking.

On Rope: North American Vertical Rope Techniques for Caving, Search & Rescue, Mountaineering, by Allen Padgett and Bruce Smith, published in 1987 by the Vertical Section of the National Speleological Society, is a detailed account of all aspects of vertical work. Chapters on rope, knots, rigging, rappelling, prusiking, belaying, long drops, domes, and walls are complemented by excellent graphics and artwork.

W. R. Halliday's book, *American Caves and Caving*, provides a wealth of information about caves, the various formations found in them, and all aspects of modern cave exploration. This book was published in 1974, and although there have been advances in spelunking and medical techniques since then, Halliday's account of caving is timeless. His book helped me prepare for an experience I never envisioned.

Prior to caving, I also read *Trapped*, by Robert Murray and Roger Brucker. This book delves into the attempted rescue of solo push caver Floyd Collins from Sand Cave in Kentucky during late January and early February 1925. I could not put it down. In some ways, it was reassuring to know that rescuers will go to great lengths and exhibit superhuman courage to aid a caver. You just hope they do it in time. Unfortunately for Floyd Collins, they didn't.

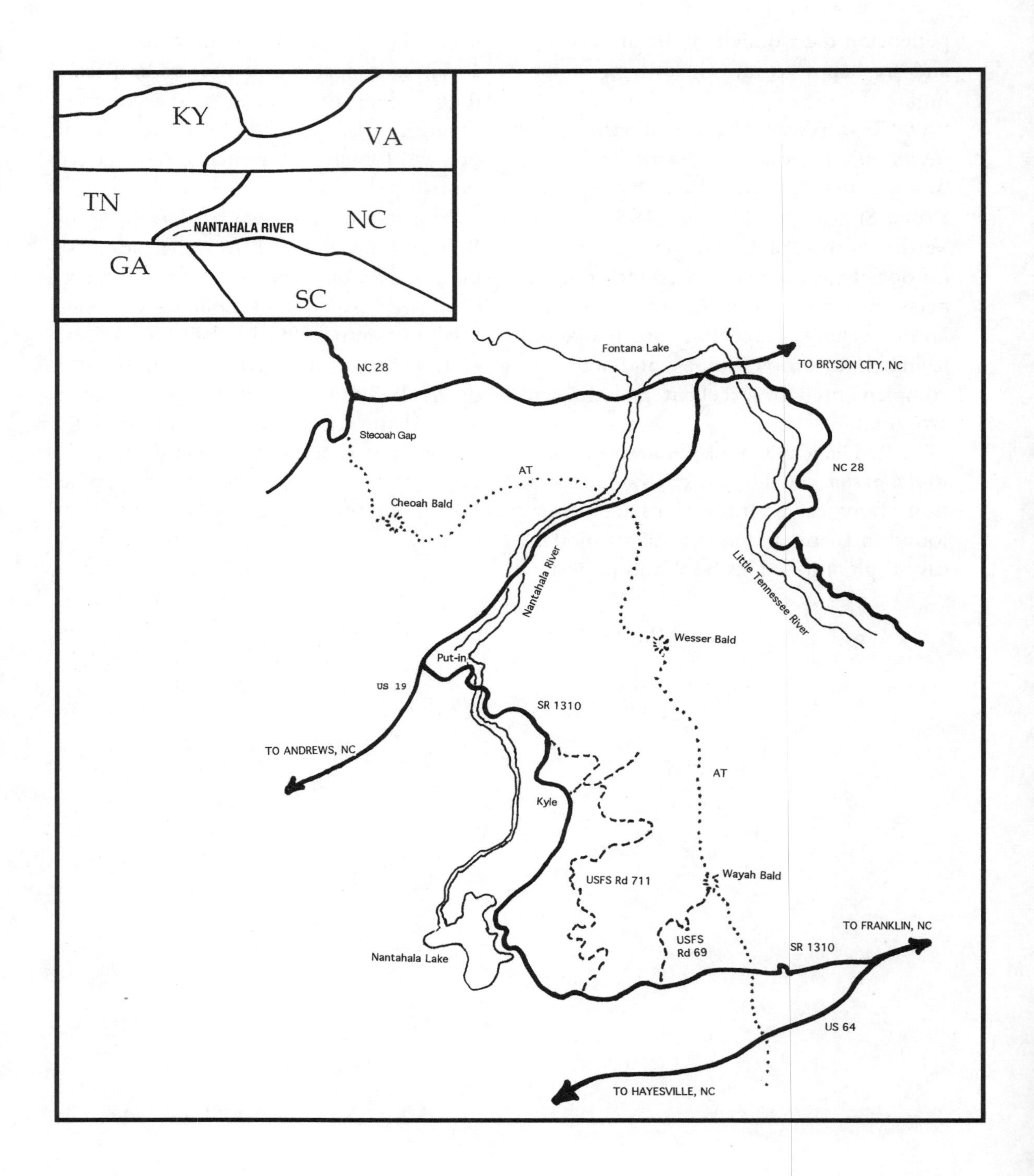
KY
VA
TN
NANTAHALA RIVER
NC
GA
SC
NC 28
Fontana Lake
TO BRYSON CITY, NC
Stecoah Gap
AT
NC 28
Cheoah Bald
Nantahala River
Little Tennessee River
Wesser Bald
Put-in
US 19
SR 1310
TO ANDREWS, NC
AT
Kyle
USFS Rd 711
Wayah Bald
TO FRANKLIN, NC
USFS
Rd 69
SR 1310
Nantahala Lake
US 64
TO HAYESVILLE, NC

THE MAD LUNAR ECLIPSE EXPEDITION

A full moon engulfed our camp below the tower rising from the summit of Wayah Bald. The clarity of the moonbeams bouncing toward our planet enthralled us earthlings. Craters on the moon's surface stood visible to the naked eye. Beneath stars glittering in the pale night sky, we were ready to be captivated by a startling display of the universe's power: a full lunar eclipse.

Amazingly, we had Wayah Bald to ourselves. Wayah, the Wolf, stands 5,342 feet above sea level and dominates the surrounding ridges with its majestic presence. With the brilliance of the moon's reflected sunlight, we could see Clingmans Dome and the Great Smoky Mountains to the north as the moon rose over Whiteside Mountain. Far below us in the eastern valleys, the waters of the Little Tennessee shimmered as they flowed through Franklin, North Carolina, on their way north toward Fontana Lake.

The power of the moon had drawn us to Wayah Bald, just as it influences the tides. There was no resisting it. The magic of witnessing the sun cast earth's shadow across the moon mystified early man. Copernicus was the first to explain the paths of the planets by the simple observation that the sun was the center of our solar system. He thus provided the basis for modern astronomy. Galileo and his telescope proved that the moon's surface was not smooth, like the Greek philosophers had speculated, and his observations of moons circling Jupiter brought Copernicus's postulation from theory to fact: Man was not the center of the universe. Not even of his own solar system. A mote in God's eye.

As we huddled around a small fire near the base of the tower, waiting for earth to align itself between the sun and the moon, we contemplated the insignificance of our so-called expedition. From various points in North Carolina and Georgia, we'd rendezvoused at Wayah for the eclipse. It was a chance to do something different. Our plans were simple. We'd camp and watch the eclipse that night on Wayah. The next day, we'd 10-speed-bike our way down F.R. 711 approximately 23 miles to the Nantahala River, where we'd climb into kayaks and paddle seven miles of class II and III waters to the Nantahala Outdoor Center. At the center, we'd jump on the Appalachian Trail for 11 miles of hard hiking north to Stecoah Gap. All in one day. Our own personal 40-mile triathlon, or as Joy aptly named it, The Mad Lunar Eclipse Expedition.

One of the members of our support team was Luke Bayless, from Murphy, North Carolina, who had agreed to be our main driver. He would shuttle the equipment we required for the different activities. We also solicited him to serve as the expedition's main photographer. Luke would join us in the last portion, hiking the Appalachian Trail to Stecoah Gap.

Joy wanted to ride her bike along F.R. 711 but had no desire to paddle the freezing waters of the Nantahala or tackle the Appalachian Trail. She offered to help Luke shuttle vehicles and look after our son, Dylan, who wasn't feeling too hot. Dylan's main goals were seeing the eclipse the first night and riding comfortably in Luke's shuttle the next day. He'd occupy his mind reading comic books.

The McKnight brothers, Robert and Linton, from Milledgeville, Georgia, would join us on the paddling portion of the trip and leave the rest alone.

Rich LaGrange and his two sons, from Hendersonville, North Carolina, had come to camp on Wayah and share the eclipse with us. They planned on heading home at first light.

Only my longtime friend and fellow adventurer, John Gibney, from Hayesville, North Carolina, and I would attempt all three phrases of the expedition. We both laughed as we pondered our chances of completing the course, knowing that our dreams of competing in the Iron Man were just that: dreams.

While Robert and Linton McKnight, the self-appointed chefs, prepared a meal of grilled sirloin, baked potatoes, and tossed salad, Rich LaGrange, an amateur astronomer, filled our heads with moon facts. The origin of the moon is much like that of the earth: mostly unknown. What is known about the moon is that it is lifeless, a sterile chunk of rock without water or air, and that it has always been that way. Since there is no atmosphere on the moon, there is no sound, no clouds, no weather to speak of. Although we call it a moon, many experts believe it is a dual planet captured by the gravitational force of the earth, and that it was never actually a physical part of the earth that ended up in space. Satellite or planet? You make the call. Keep in mind that the diameter of the moon is 2,160 miles, versus 7,927 for the earth. It has a mass 1/80 of the earth's. That's a pretty big chunk of real estate for a moon.

In 1966, Russia's unmanned *Luna 9* became the first spacecraft to cross the 240,000-mile gulf between the earth and the moon. Three years later, on July 20, 1969, Neil Armstrong became the first man to set foot on the surface of the moon, after he and Buzz Aldrin landed their lunar module, the *Eagle*, on the Sea of Tranquility. Armstrong's famous statement, "That's one small step for man, one giant leap for mankind," strengthened America's commitment to the exploration of space. At the time, many believed it would be a scant few decades before

America operated a permanent lunar base and the average citizen could purchase a ticket to the moon.

As a youth, I was caught up in the excitement of the Mercury and Apollo space programs. It was Buck Rogers come to life. On the night of the first moon landing, my dad and I made our way to a nearby golf course and watched the moon intently through binoculars. I thought I saw a blip flash across the surface of the moon and was convinced I had seen the orbiter, the *Columbia*, with Michael Collins aboard, on one of its numerous orbits as Armstrong and Aldrin prepared the *Eagle* for its historic flight. Although my dad cautioned that it was highly improbable for me to have seen *Columbia*, he encouraged me to see the universe with open eyes and appreciate man's efforts to challenge its great distances and discover its secrets.

Rich was a walking encyclopedia of lunar trivia. He said that most of the craters on the moon were created during the period of the "Great Bombardment" billions of years ago. It is believed that in 1178, a group of five monks in Canterbury, England, witnessed a comet or asteroid strike the moon. Their written account of the incident is vivid: "A flaming torch sprang up, spewing out fire, hot coals, and sparks." Rich also explained that lunar eclipses occur infrequently, due to the five-degree incline of the moon's orbit.

As the time of the eclipse drew near, we hustled up the tower to the observation deck and were rewarded with a 360-degree panorama of mountain peaks and valleys bathed in moonlight. The earth's shadow gradually turned the moon into a golden globe suspended in a darkened sky. To write of the event is not to capture it, but only to savor personal memories shared with friends and family high on a mountain in the Appalachians. When the eclipse peaked, we watched the moon hang silent in the sky. A nighthawk flew by and was briefly silhouetted by the faint, darkened moon before it dove off the mountain into night. It was with great expectations that we awaited the reappearance of moonbeams, the mere seven percent of reflected sunlight that reaches earth, thus illuminating the moon for us earthlings. Watching the trailing edge of the earth's shadow move across the lunar terrain got the crowd on its feet, and when the final shadow was gone, the eclipse finished, we broke into spontaneous applause. Cheers echoed down the far reaches of the mountain slopes. An omen had been witnessed, and it was good.

Camp came to life early the next morning. The LaGrange family headed out as we packed our tents and finished breakfast. The McKnight boys were a bit slow to get moving, but they had several hours before they were to meet us at the put-in. We transported our bikes down the four miles of F.R. 69 leading to Wayah Bald, knowing that the rough gravel road would destroy tires, tubes, and wheel rims. Luke

Full Moon

Photos by Bruce Chynoweth, Southern Exposures

Eclipse One

and Dylan let Joy, John, and me out at Wayah Gap, 4,180 feet in elevation, and disappeared down S.R. 1310 toward F.R. 711.

It was a good thing that everybody had brakes on their bikes because it was all downhill. We screamed alongside Jarrett Creek, dropping 400 feet in elevation in the two miles to the F.R. 711 junction. The shuttle bunnies were surprised to see us so quickly.

Government plans for F.R. 711 once called for it to be extended northward across Great Smoky Mountains National Park. The section we were riding was constructed in 1970 at a cost of $2 million. Thankfully, the rest was never built. To date, logging operations have been the primary beneficiary of this road, which is little used by the general public. Similar to the Blue Ridge Parkway in its scenic vistas, F.R. 711 winds 15.3 miles north from its beginning at S.R. 1310 to its terminus at S.R. 1397 near the small community of Kyle, North Carolina.

During its first 2.5 miles, F.R. 711 rises from 3,800 feet to 4,400 feet at Sawmill Gap, near Jarrett Bald. I was exhausted by the time I reached the gap, though I did manage to laugh at Joy's displeasure with her bike seat. John was on cruise control and showed no signs of distress at pulling that long climb. The descent from the gap went all too quickly, as we leaned into curves and let our hair fly. The Tusquitee Mountains, west of us, and the Snowbirds, to the northwest, kept us company. At the end of the second long climb, we were rewarded with a view of Nantahala Lake spread below us.

Eclipse Two

Eclipse Three

We had to negotiate a small piece of gravel road (S.R. 1397) at the end of F.R. 711 to reach S.R. 1310, which would lead us to the put-in. Riding along that smooth, descending blacktop alongside the upper Nantahala was a blur of curves and bridges. We caught up with Luke and Dylan at the put-in a scant two and a half hours after they had dropped us off at Wayah Gap. Even though we had covered a lot of miles, we still had a long way to go. There was no sign of the McKnight brothers.

The last seven miles of descending S.R. 1310 left me cool. Confronted with the 49-degree water of the Nantahala, I opted for polypro and a paddling jacket as I prepared for the second part of the journey. John zipped up his life jacket, secured his helmet, and grabbed his paddle, ready to go. Patton's Run lay just downstream around a bend in the river, the first of many rapids we would run that day. Patton's Run is exciting, with a rock ledge river left funneling the bulk of the water into a narrow, turbulent channel that hugs the right bank. I felt confident on this river, one I had paddled hundreds of times. My paddling strokes were strong as I eddy-hopped my way downstream toward Patton's Run.

John ran the rapid smoothly and was disappearing downstream just as I entered the top portion of Patton's Run. In what I can only describe as a freak natural act, a pair of boulders grabbed my right paddle blade and wedged it securely in their jaws. Immediately, my kayak swung crossways in the current as I gamely held on and tried to free my paddle from the boulder monsters. The turbulent river tugged and pulled on my kayak, popping my spray skirt loose. My boat rapidly filled with water, which applied more pressure on the lower half of my body. Hanging there upside down, it dawned on me that I was drowning in two feet of water. As soon as I let go of the paddle, it came free, but I was too busy banging my head on the river bottom to give it much thought. Lacking a paddle and the ability to roll my kayak upright without it, I ejected myself from the kayak in record time and brought into play one the strongest aspects of my paddling skills: the self-rescue.

Even though I was now blue and shaking from the frigid water, I grabbed my paddle as it floated by and managed to catch an eddy downstream, with boat in tow. It would have been so easy to drag the old Mirage up the bank to the road and forget continuing the river experience. But John was downstream, and the shuttle crew was laughing at my expense. With a stiff, shivering upper lip, I got back on the horse that had thrown me and paddled hurriedly downstream, out of sight of the shuttle crew.

The Nantahala was not supposed to do this to me. I had learned to paddle on this seven-mile stretch of white water in the early 1970s, and it had opened my world to other rivers and a career as a professional river guide. Later, I would be able to look back on the incident and laugh, but at the time it wasn't funny to me. Embarrassed after having been thoroughly trashed by a marginal class III rapid, I paid the Nantahala more courtesy as I pushed on. I'd done enough swimming for the day.

Since 1973, when Payson Kennedy and his wife, Aurelia, began full-season operation of the Nantahala Outdoor Center, whitewater rafting and paddling in the Southeast have shot off the chart. From its humble beginnings as the old Tote and Tarry, located in Wesser, North Carolina, the Nantahala Outdoor Center is now known as the world leader in whitewater instruction. It operates numerous outposts for whitewater rafting in the Appalachian region. In 1992, two NOC staff members, Joe Jacobi and Scott Strausbaugh, won the gold medal in C-2 at the Olympics in Spain. They did a lot of their training on the Nantahala.

Although an estimated 2 million recreational boaters have used the Nantahala since 1984, we were surprised to find the river virtually devoid of paddlers that day. There was nobody at Ferebee Park when we stopped for rest and food. Due to the coolness of the day, we did not tarry long at Ferebee, but paddled smoothly past Delabar's Rock. Below Quarry Rapid, John hit a roll. Eddying out at Whirlpool, I flipped, waited for the eddy to sweep me closer to the bank, and pushed off the bottom, thankful to be upright again. Whirlpool is a squirrely rapid that is easy

The scenic views from Forest Service Road 711 are endless.
Tusquitee Bald and Signal Bald rise to the left and loom over Nantahala Lake.

to misread. It wasn't the first time I'd been upside down in its eddy, and I'm sure it won't be the last.

John was anxious to lead the way through Nantahala Falls and show me his new moves. I waited in an eddy for him to exit before making my move. We hit river right, then executed ferries to river left before ending up back river right immediately above the suck hole located in the middle right of the channel. Since this eddy was big enough for both of us, I pulled in and threw my paddle across his bow to stabilize my kayak, which almost caused both of us to flip. The shuttle team—still following our progress down the river—hooted and hollered.

"What next?" I queried.

"Micro eddy. Follow me," John replied.

He paddled out of the eddy, the nose of his boat pointed upstream across the current at a 45-degree angle. He made two strokes, shifted his weight downstream, and went spinning across the river. With an effortless pivot, he eddy-turned into Micro and sat motionless for an instant before he stroked back into the turbulence and scooted down the tongue, landing in the eddy at the base of the rapid. He made it look easy.

I mimicked his ferry in the general direction of Micro. As I shot across the river, I realized I was a day late and a dollar short. The nose of my kayak slammed into the rocks lining the bank river left. The current pushed my tail downstream, and I dropped backwards over the ledge into the hydraulic below. I braced hard right and was immediately rewarded by the sight of blue sky, which told me I was upright. Instantly, the hydraulic sucked my entire boat down nose-first. I disappeared into the hole, disoriented, my mouth open. All noise ceased. Time had no meaning. I was one with the river and totally in its grasp. Without warning, the river spit me and my kayak into the air, free. A pop-up. I paddled hard for the eddy and the end of the ride.

Eleven and a half miles of some of the hardest hiking in the southern Appalachians separated us from our goal. There was still no sign of the McKnight brothers. We later learned that after breaking camp, they had helped some folks with car trouble and missed us at the put-in. They ended up paddling the river, but John and I were long gone.

Luke and Joy had everything ready for us. After loading our paddling gear and boats on the car, which already had three bikes hanging on the rear, Luke, John, and I said good-bye to Joy and Dylan. They would be at Stecoah Gap waiting for us later that evening. We figured we could hike the trail in five hours. We'd meet them at nine, well after dark. We checked our flashlights, feeling confident that the moon would yield enough light for hiking.

A short distance up the Appalachian

Trail, it became evident that the day's activities had taken more out of John and me than we thought. We were behind schedule by the time we reached the section known as "the Jump Up" and began its steep ascent.

The sun was starting to sink low in the sky as we stood atop the rocky ledge and enjoyed the spectacular view of Nantahala Gorge stretching out below us. It was completely dark by the time we reached Sassafras Gap and worked our way toward the summit of Cheoah Bald (5,062 feet). The moon was starting to rise south and east of us, but it was dark, almost pitch black. We pondered sitting awhile on Cheoah and waiting for the moon, but seeing a line of storm clouds far to the west, we decided to push on.

We were on the dark side of Cheoah as we descended, which almost caused us to miss a switchback in the Appalachian Trail and take a trail leading toward Bellcollar Gap. We'd actually hiked a ways down that trail before Luke spoke up and said, "Something's wrong. We should be descending to our right." We backtracked and found the Appalachian Trail. During this steep descent, Luke caught a branch in his left eye even though he was wearing glasses, and we were forced to wait 10 or 15 minutes for his vision to clear. We should have thought to bring clear goggles, which completely protect the eyes for night hiking. Next time.

Four miles remained in the hike. It was taking us much too long. All we could do was hope that Joy and Dylan would wait for us at Stecoah Gap.

It was close to 11 by the time we reached our destination and collapsed into the car. Joy and Dylan had gotten worried about us and were within minutes of driving the nine miles down to Robbinsville to alert the local authorities and mobilize a search-and-rescue mission for three missing hikers. So much for knowing your capabilities.

As we rode home, we skirted Nantahala Gorge to the west, stopping briefly at the scenic overlook on U.S. 129 near Topton. A full moon one day past prime illuminated the depths of the gorge and shone on ribbons of water cascading downstream. Wayah Bald and F.R. 711 lay over the horizon to the southeast, hidden by Wesser Bald, but nearly the entire section of the Appalachian Trail over Cheoah Bald was silhouetted against the night sky.

A Mad Lunar Eclipse Expedition comes only once in a blue moon. Our next one isn't scheduled until 1996, just in time for the Atlanta Olympics. The plan is, we'll all meet on Wayah, then we'll . . .

A Close Encounter in Nantahala Gorge

By Rick Ardolino, as told to g. forest

After much prompting, I have finally been persuaded to relate a ghostly encounter that happened to me in December 1978 in Nantahala Gorge. My credibility will be ruined, I'm sure, but it was such an experience that it cannot remain untold.

Darkness had already engulfed Nantahala Gorge, and my belly was full from the home-cooked meal my friends, the Prices, had prepared that evening. Finally, it was time for me and my constant companion, Sadie, a mixed-breed dog, to make our way down into the heart of the gorge from the high ridge where the Price family resided. Sadie and I opted to take the short trek down the abandoned section of the Appalachian Trail, hit the railroad tracks that run along the edge of the river, cross the swinging bridge, and then hike the road back to our basement apartment.

The night was crisp and clear. Moonlight filtered through the naked tree branches and helped us see the rugged trail. Sadie, my faithful friend, led the way. It was a good night for hiking. I glimpsed stars occasionally as clouds wafted high overhead.

Deep in thought, I descended the trail on automatic pilot, as I had a hundred times before. A canopy of rhododendron loomed over the trail. As Sadie disappeared into the darkness, I followed, confident of my way. After a few moments, I hollered for Sadie. There was no response. Listening, I heard her cutting trail down the mountainside. After a rabbit, I thought to myself.

A strong-flowing creek runs parallel to this section of trail. It was not long before I could not distinguish Sadie's barking from the noise of the creek. I pushed on.

A few more steps and my heart stopped. Without warning, I had the feeling of another presence near me, sort of like when someone is staring at your back. I called vainly for Sadie. The hair on the back of my neck bristled, and suddenly the creek noise was obliterated by a high-pitched scream that intensified to excruciating pain. I tried to cover my ears, but my arms were frozen to my sides. I wanted to drop to my knees, but my legs were locked tight. My eyesight blurred, and my head began to swim. I thought I was going to pass out. Frozen to the spot, I couldn't run. Time seemed to end, and I have no idea how long I stood suspended in fright.

As abruptly as the encounter started, it stopped with a deathly silence. My knees buckled, and I fell to the ground. I could feel the coolness of the earth as I lay on the rocky trail. My shirt was soaked with perspiration, and a warm glow filled my body. A tingling sensation ran wild in my fingertips and toes.

I was exhausted. I felt like I had just

run five miles as hard as I could. I contemplated retracing my steps to the Price residence, but fearing my friends' laughter, I finally decided to push on down the trail. I cautiously surveyed every noise at every step. I peered hard at every darkened shape materializing out of night's gloom. It was the longest half-mile I have ever hiked.

I finally made the railroad tracks and thought briefly of running all the way to the swinging bridge and up the road to the safety of my shelter. It was just my imagination, I told myself. The scream that tore through my soul must have been a panther. It was the only explanation that I could come up with. Nonetheless, I set off down the tracks at a brisk pace.

About a quarter-mile down the tracks, I came to a cut through solid rock, and as I entered this man-made canyon, I realized that the sound of the river had disappeared. A hauntingly familiar quietness engulfed me. As I picked up my pace even more, I began to get chilled, the hair on the back of my neck bristling. I stopped. I stopped walking. I stopped shaking. I stopped thinking. I glanced to my side and my eyes became mesmerized by a reddish glow on the cut stone. Warily, I squatted down to investigate closer. I told myself that it must be foxfire, or a similar animal residue that glows in the dark.

I was in that vulnerable position when the fear hit me full-force again. Ice water on the back. Eyes burning a hole in me. Cotton mouth. I turned to my right and there stood an apparition. *The Chief.* An Indian warrior stood tall in the middle of the tracks. I was stunned and caught off-balance. I fell backwards into a sitting position in the ditch with my mouth agape. There was no use running, so I just sat there staring. No words were spoken, but a mental conversation ensued.

"I am Black Fox. This is the land of my fathers and their fathers before them. You will walk here unhindered. Go safely."

As the apparition faded into the darkness, the chill left my body. The murmuring of the river filled my ears. My senses reeling, I turned and staggered down the tracks. A million thoughts ran through my head. What the hell did it mean? Dazed, I stumbled to my door, only to recoil once more when Sadie flew out of her doghouse to greet me. It took me half an hour to find my keys, which I dropped in the dark when she jumped.

Over the years, I have told only a few close friends of my encounter with Black Fox. None has ever laughed in my face, but I notice that shortly after I relate this story to them, they will leave the room for one excuse or another. Sometimes, they have just wandered off without saying good-bye.

I have walked the trail and the railroad tracks countless times since, always hoping for another chance to talk with Black Fox and learn more about him. But each hike has been uneventful. Even the foxfire is gone.

Biking in the Nantahala Gorge Area, Whitewater Rafting on the Nantahala River, Hiking the Appalachian Trail

WHO

Commercial rafting guests on the Nantahala are required to weigh a minimum of 60 pounds. According to Brian Mays of the Nantahala Outdoor Center, the reasoning is that children weighing at least 60 pounds will fit securely in life jackets and will most likely have enough body fat to avoid hypothermia. The 50-degree water of the Nantahala leaves children more susceptible than adults to rapid chilling. I can personally vouch for the fact that if you stick your hand in the river for five minutes, it will turn blue.

Folks of all ages bike in the Nantahala Gorge area and hike the Appalachian Trail.

WHEN

Although people paddle the Nantahala year-round, most commercial rafting operations begin their season in early March and continue to offer trips into November. I particularly like paddling the Nantahala on weekdays in July and August when the sun is approaching high noon and the air temperature is in the 90s. The contrast between the hot day and the cool briskness of the water is refreshing, to say the least.

The warm months are the peak times for biking in the Nantahala Gorge area and hiking the Appalachian Trail, though you may find folks enjoying both activities any time of year.

WHERE

Biking opportunities in the Nantahala Gorge area are virtually endless. If a trail or Forest Service road is not designated for foot travel only, or for other special uses, it is fair game for bikes. Please observe the rules of the road and ride safely.

U.S. 19 runs alongside the Nantahala River on its east-west course between Bryson City and Andrews, North Carolina. The lower part of the river through the gorge flows northeast before emptying into Fontana Lake a short distance past the Nantahala Outdoor Center. Both the lower and upper portions of the Nantahala River lie within Nantahala National Forest, which is administered by the United States Forest Service, Wayah Ranger Station, 8

Sloan Road, Franklin, N.C. 28734 (704-524-6441). Topographic maps and literature about the area are available at the ranger station.

On the Appalachian Trail portion of The Mad Lunar Eclipse Expedition, we traveled north of Nantahala Gorge in the Cheoah Ranger District, administered by the United States Forest Service, Route 1, Box 16A, Robbinsville, N.C. 28771 (704-479-6431). The Appalachian Trail follows a 2,200-mile course from Georgia to Maine. Wesser, North Carolina, where the Nantahala Outdoor Center is located, is commonly referred to as "where the AT crosses the Nantahala."

HOW

The Nantahala River is one of the premier whitewater instructional rivers in the world, due largely to the excellent and varied programs offered by the Nantahala Outdoor Center over the years. Ken Kastorff, a former NOC instructor, has helped advance the sport of whitewater paddling by developing innovative teaching techniques. His company, Endless River Adventures, offers private and group instruction.

Should you desire to paddle with a commercial outfitter, the following are licensed by the Forest Service on the Nantahala River: Appalachian River Raft Company (704-321-6065 or 803-244-0168); Brookside Campground (704-321-5209); Carolina Outfitters (800-468-7238); Endless River Adventures (704-488-6199); Fast River Rafts (704-488-2386); Great Smoky Mountains Rafting (704-488-6302 or 800-238-6302); Nantahala Outdoor Center (800-232-7238); Nantahala Rafts (704-488-3854); Paddle Inn (704-488-9651); Pigeon River Outdoors (800-PRO-RAFT); River Runners Retreat (704-321-2211); Rolling Thunder (704-488-2030 or 800-344-5838); Whitewater Express (800-676-7238); Wildwater, Ltd. (704-488-2384); USA Raft (704-488-3316).

If you're seeking guided service for hiking the Appalachian Trail, contact Trail Blazers Hiking and Backpacking, 41 Connahetta Avenue, Andrews, N.C. 28901 (704-321-2346).

Commercial campgrounds in the area include Lost Mine Campground (704-488-6445), Turkey Creek Campground (704-488-8966), and Brookside Campground (704-321-5209). United States Forest Service campgrounds include Tsali Campground and Appletree Campground, which are managed by the Cheoah Ranger District (704-479-6431).

Lodging and dining facilities in the area include Nantahala Village (outside of N.C. 800-438-1507 or 704-488-2826), known for its excellent dinners, rustic atmosphere, and scenic views of the Smokies, and the Nantahala Outdoor Center (800-232-7238), which offers a variety of facilities, including the renowned restaurant Relia's Garden.

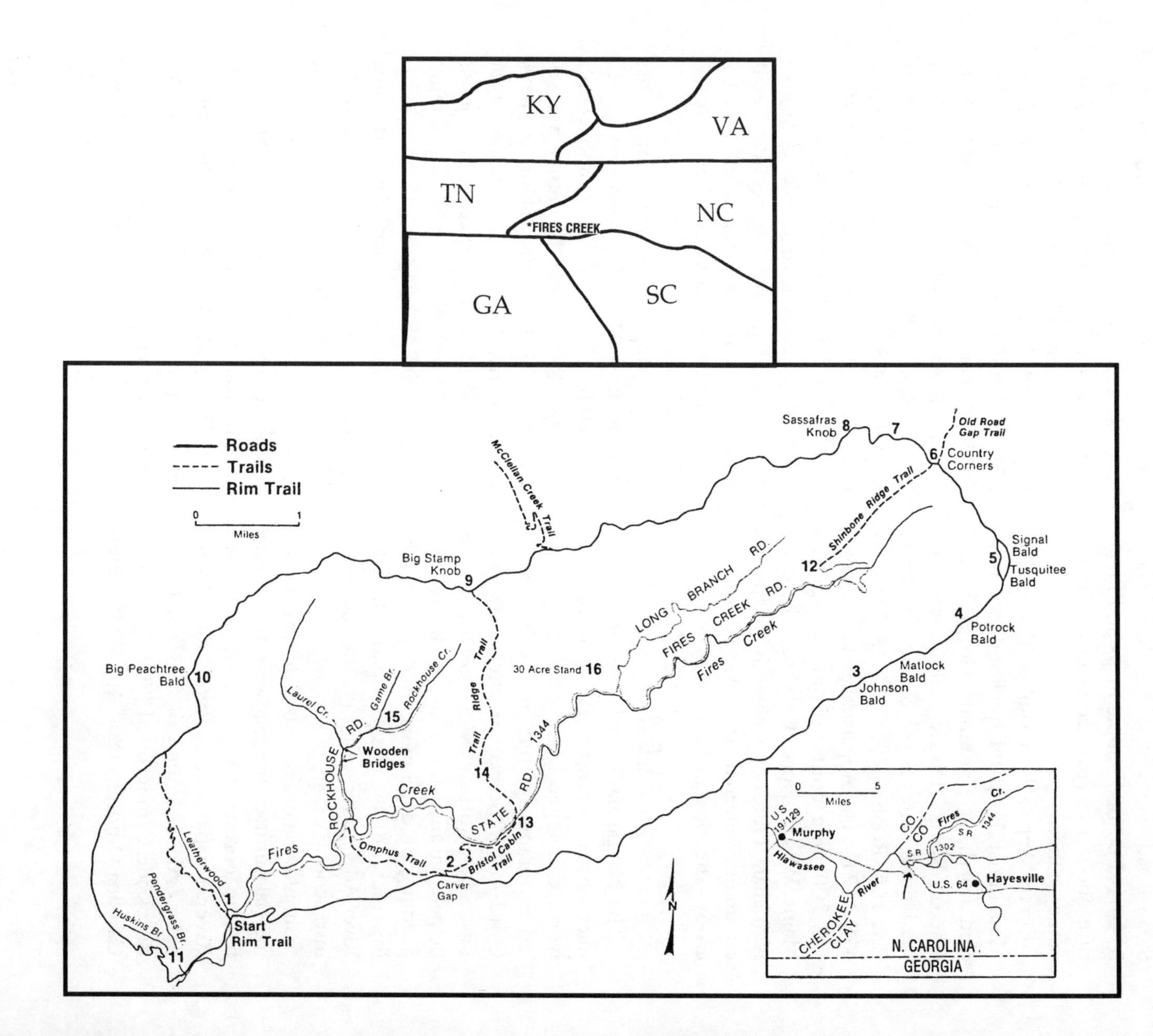
KY
VA
TN
NC
*FIRES CREEK
GA
SC
Roads
Trails
Rim Trail
0
1
Miles
McClellan Creek Trail
Sassafras Knob
8
7
Old Road Gap Trail
6
Country Corners
Shinbone Ridge Trail
Signal Bald
5
Tusquitee Bald
4
Potrock Bald
3
Matlock Bald
Johnson Bald
Big Stamp Knob
9
12
LONG BRANCH RD.
FIRES CREEK RD.
Fires Creek
30 Acre Stand
16
Big Peachtree Bald
10
Laurel Cr.
Game Br.
Rockhouse Cr.
15
RD.
ROCKHOUSE
Wooden Bridges
Trail Ridge Trail
14
1344
STATE RD.
13
Creek
Fires
Omphus Trail
2
Bristol Cabin Trail
Carver Gap
Leatherwood
1
Pendergrass Br.
Huskins Br.
11
Start Rim Trail
N
0
5
Miles
US 19/129
Murphy
Hiawassee
River
CHEROKEE
CLAY
CO.
CO.
Fires
Cr.
S.R.
1344
S.R.
1302
U.S. 64
Hayesville
N. CAROLINA
GEORGIA

SOLO TREKKING IN FIRES CREEK

Hidden away in the northeastern corner of Clay County, North Carolina, a few miles north of the Georgia border and not far from the sleepy little town of Hayesville, Fires Creek Bear Sanctuary remains virtually unknown to travelers in the southern Appalachians. I hesitate writing about it because I know that as more is printed about this chunk of public forest, more people will come.

Fires Creek lies in my backyard. Well, not exactly, but from my cabin, which sits on the ridge above Carter Cove, I can look northeast and see the Tusquitee and Valley River mountain ranges rising over 5,000 feet, culminating at Tusquitee and Signal balds. These mountains rule this segment of the Hiwassee River Valley like the ancient volcanoes they're rumored to be, forming a natural bowl—an entire watershed—called Fires Creek. Sitting up there at my old cabin, built of hand-hewn logs by Sam Fox in 1877, I can watch the mountains come alive, the ridge lines and thousands of hidden valleys changing in the sunlight, the shadows cast by clouds racing across the sky. It is my refuge.

Since Fires Creek Bear Sanctuary is so close, I go there often and drag friends and family with me. Occasionally, I venture into its terrain solo and hike its trails seeking to restore a sense of calmness in my life. Such was the case when a friend dropped me and my backpack off at Leatherwood Falls in the winter of 1993–94. I needed the space and the chance to think where I was headed in life.

I've always liked hiking the Southern forests alone. You set your own schedule. Your pace is not influenced by speeding up or slowing down for someone else.

The first major solo hike I ever did followed the completion of Sam Nunn's successful Senate campaign in November 1972. Serving as the soon-to-be senator's personal aide during five hectic months of nonstop travel, fried-chicken dinners, and endless pressing of the flesh left me, a recent graduate of the Henry W. Grady School of Journalism at the University of Georgia, overwhelmed. The senator-elect and I both realized that, as exciting as our travels across the state of Georgia had been, Washington was not for me. I had done my job. A few days after the victory party, we parted. The senator flew to Washington or to some island in the sun to escape, and I set off hiking north from the southern end of the Appalachian Trail, toward Newfound Gap and the Great Smoky Mountains. Thirteen days later, after a couple hundred miles and innumerable elevation changes, I made Sugarlands Visitor Center, just outside Gatlinburg, Tennessee.

Throughout that hike, I battled inclement weather. For 10 consecutive days, it rained, snowed, or hailed. Most of my gear was soaked after the first night on the trail. My tent and sleeping bag were blue-light specials, but the thick, 100-percent-wool blanket I carried saved me. I cooked over a Sterno can and drank water straight from the springs I found along the way. Between Stecoah Gap and Fontana Dam, I was surrounded by a herd of Russian boar and scared half to death. A female skunk with a slew of younguns sprayed my pack during a lunch break on Shuckstack. And on the night of December 4, 1972, I almost froze to death at Derrick Knob Lean-to, 4,910 feet above sea level. Despite all the hardships, I was hooked on hiking. Never before had I felt such independence and vulnerability at the same time. I was determined to upgrade my gear and improve my wilderness skills.

Since that first solo hike on the Appalachian Trail, I have hiked many of the trails in western North Carolina, but I've always come back to Fires Creek Bear Sanctuary to hike its ridges, fish its streams, splash in its mountain-fresh waters, and photograph its beauty and wildlife.

As my friend drove away and I was alone in the forest, I turned and, hiking in a southeasterly direction, quickly left Leatherwood Falls and the rushing waters of Fires Creek behind. A half-mile into the walk, as I steadily gained altitude, I was startled by the sound of a ruffed grouse drumming the air with its wings. I finally spotted the bird, raised my camera, focused, and exposed the frame. The motor drive advanced the film, but the bird was gone, startled by the noise.

I considered the grouse a good sign. I hoped to see more wildlife and few, if any, hunters using the Rim Trail during my three-day outing. I also hoped to encounter a bear. Bears leave obvious signs but are difficult for humans to track. Paw prints, unmistakable scats, and trees marked by sharp, powerful claws are good indications of a healthy bear population in the sanctuary. Finding the bears is another matter. They are shy critters and almost always hear you first. They easily slip into the deep cover of rhododendron thickets, out of sight.

Potentially a prime haven for backpackers as well as bears, Fires Creek Bear Sanctuary is a 16,000-acre tract in the middle of Nantahala National Forest. It is crisscrossed by a maze of hiking trails totaling over 40 miles. These trails enable visitors who can find the area to get a good look at several interesting archaeological sites and enjoy far-reaching mountain vistas. The longest of the paths, the 25-mile Rim Trail, portions of which are open to horse travel, is so named because it makes a complete loop around the edge of the elongated bowl formed by the meeting of the

Valley River and Tusquitee mountain ranges.

Tusquitee Bald and Signal Bald, located on the Rim Trail at the eastern edge of the bowl and separated by a slight saddle, stand 5,240 feet above sea level, providing panoramic views of the surrounding countryside.

Prior to the white man's conquest of this territory, Cherokee Indians used smoke plumes from atop Signal Bald to communicate with their neighbors in what are now Georgia, Tennessee, and western North Carolina, thus giving the mountain its name.

In his classic *Myths of the Cherokee*, recorded in the last years of the 19th century, James Moody tells of a lone hunter crossing Tusquitee Bald during a dry spell and hearing voices. Silently following these voices, the hunter finds two water dogs—large, amphibious lizards—in conversation, walking hand in hand down the trail. One water dog turns to the other and asks, "Where has all the water gone?" Both creatures just laugh, then continue out of the eavesdropping hunter's sight. Since that legendary encounter, the peak and the range of which it is a part have been known as Tusquitee, which in Cherokee means "Where the Water Dogs Laughed."

Several points of interest to archaeology enthusiasts and students of American Indian history are located in Fires Creek Bear Sanctuary. Atop Potrock Bald, a bowl carved into stone is circled by several smaller bowls, signifying a possible Indian ritual site. L. C. Loudermilk, retired from the Forest Service, is well familiar with Fires Creek's rugged terrain and history. He interprets the bowl formation as a representation of the solar system, with the large central bowl symbolizing the sun and the smaller bowls the planets orbiting it. A similar formation of bowls is located a short (but steep) distance up Trail Ridge Trail, starting out of Bristol Camp.

Prior to the federal government's purchase of the Fires Creek watershed shortly after the Great Depression, the land was owned by F. P. Colver & Sons, a tannery headquartered in nearby Andrews, North Carolina. Bark from chestnut and chestnut oak trees logged from Fires Creek's coves and ridges was used by the Colvers in drying and curing hides.

As late as 1951, much of the Fires Creek tract was still covered with virgin timber, and isolated stands remain hidden in the sanctuary today. The once-grand American chestnut forests are gone, though, a victim of the blight that swept across the land. One tabletop protected by steep ridges is overgrown with 30 acres of oak trees more than two centuries old. L. C. Loudermilk recalled that in 1956, he and a companion, John Stanley, counted 430 rings on a giant white oak felled near Big Stamp Knob.

In the high elevations, Fires Creek is a mixed hardwood forest, with maple, oak, beech, hickory, and birch trees predominating. In the lower sections along the creek, evergreens and dogwoods provide excellent cover for many forms of wildlife. Although bear hunting is not allowed in the sanctuary, in-season hunting of white-tailed deer, grouse, boar, and wild turkey is permitted with proper licenses. Fishing for brook, rainbow, and brown trout in Fires Creek and its many tributaries is a challenge for even the experienced fly-fisherman.

My outings in Fires Creek Bear Sanctuary have taught me that the weather can change at any moment, and often does. The high altitudes yield cooler temperatures than you might anticipate, and the winds blow with incredible power, sweeping the unprotected balds. Because of the rugged terrain, covering even short distances can prove a considerable challenge.

I camped that first night in the saddle between Potrock and Tusquitee balds, not trusting the weather that appeared to be building to the west. The local forecast called for fair to partly cloudy conditions, lows in the high 20s, and daytime highs reaching the mid-40s. Typical weather for this region during winter months.

They missed the call. Badly. Later, I wondered whose dartboard they were using. The skies dropped six inches of wet, heavy snow, burdening trees, rhododendron, and mountain laurel branches with insupportable weight.

The second day, hiking was a nightmare. The trail was blocked by fallen trees and an impossible tangle of rhododendron and laurel. It was a struggle to make any progress with my fully loaded internal-frame pack. I needed to cover a minimum of eight miles to stay on schedule to reach Leatherwood Falls for my rendezvous with my wife, Joy, and a ride out of the wilderness. Repeatedly, I had to shuck off my pack, toss it through a small opening, and work my way twisting and turning to it. By the time I ascended Tusquitee Bald and traversed the ridge to County Corners, I'd found the answers to all the questions I had in my mind when I started this quest. I was exhausted. Footing was treacherous and the trail a mess.

I pitched camp a scant two miles or so from my camp of the night before and pondered my options. They didn't look good. Joy was supposed to pick me up at Leatherwood Falls the next evening, and to do that, she'd have to borrow a four-wheel drive and hope the Forest Service hadn't locked the gate leading into the sanctuary. I knew I could never cover the remaining miles of the Rim Trail to Leatherwood Falls in time. Even if I hiked down Shinbone Ridge Trail to the road, it was 12 miles to a place I doubted Joy could get to.

I awoke to two additional inches of snow. Once I had zipped the tent for the night and snuggled deep into the warmth of my minus-20 down bag, I had been lost to the world, never hearing the silent assault of the frozen crystals. In the early-morning light, I got out the map. My best bet was to hike down Old Road Gap Trail, leave the sanctuary entirely, and catch a ride into Andrews.

Immediately upon breaking camp, I discovered a new challenge. Footing was impossible. The six inches of previous snowfall were frozen solid, and the new powder on top of the solid base made walking a slick proposition. I slid, fell, tumbled, and yelled the entire trek down Old Road Gap Trail, reaching Junaluska Road thankful for no broken bones, although the seat of my pride was bruised, battered, and soaked. Old Road Gap Trail is one steep descent. Many times, I found myself flat on my back, riding my pack with my feet in front, zooming down the trail. I'd invented a new Olympic sport, wilderness luge X-C, by the time I got to the road.

The lack of traffic on Junaluska Road discouraged me as I gamely hiked toward Andrews. Even trying to walk on the snow-encrusted road was wild. I flagged down the first four-wheel drive that came by and talked the driver into letting me jump in the back of the pickup and ride into town. It was cold with the added wind chill, but it sure beat walking and falling my way to town.

Joy was relieved to hear from me. She'd checked with the Forest Service and learned that getting to Leatherwood Falls was impossible. She'd come to the conclusion that she was going to have to call the rescue squad to find me. I can still visualize the headlines in the area papers: "Local Hiking Expert Evacuated from Fires Creek." How embarrassing that would have been. It was bad enough to endure the hooting from my family when they finally pulled into the shopping center where I was waiting.

Thirty minutes later, I was home soaking in a hot bath, healing my spirits and feeling my lumps. All the gear from my Fires Creek outing had been unceremoniously dumped on the snow-covered porch and forgotten. Tomorrow. I'd straighten all that out tomorrow.

Exploring Fires Creek Bear Sanctuary

WHO

Backpackers, day-hikers, mountain bikers, horse riders, photographers, handicapped adventurers, fly-fishermen, and hunters. No bear hunters, though. Bear hunting is strictly forbidden in the sanctuary. All other hunting and fishing must be done in accordance with North Carolina regulations. These activities are monitored with a keen eye by rangers and wildlife officers.

For up-to-date hunting and fishing regulations in the sanctuary, contact the North Carolina Wildlife Resources Commission, 512 N. Salisbury Street, Raleigh, N.C. 27604 (919-662-4370) and request copies of *Inland Fishing, Hunting and Trapping Regulations Digest* and *Games Land Map*.

Please keep in mind that solo trekking is not for everybody. If you don't have back-country experience and wilderness skills, don't do it. If you're determined to try, start with day-hikes and test your equipment and skills gradually. Learn how to read a map and use a compass. Carry them with you. I take notes as I hike and have lately tried using a small tape recorder. Hiking and back-country camping with companions are much safer than solo trekking. The risk of injury causes me to exercise great caution when hiking alone.

WHAT
The Trails and Sites of Fires Creek

Rim Trail

This 25-mile trail, marked by blue blazes, follows the contour of the two major ridges shaping this 16,000-acre bowl. Called "the RT" by local hiking enthusiasts, this trail has numerous elevation changes and is difficult at best. Three days and two nights are sometimes not enough to hike this trail if weather conditions are not favorable. The area averages 50 inches of rainfall a year. During winter, snow is a frequent inhabitant of the balds.

A mile inside the sanctuary boundary, just above Leatherwood Falls (1), you will begin the ascent of the Tusquitee Mountains, which contain four balds over 5,000 feet (Signal, Tusquitee, Potrock, and Matlock balds). After 2.2 miles, Omphus Trail joins Rim Trail half a mile from Carver Gap (2), where Bristol Cabin Trail also joins the RT. Follow the ridge line 4.5 miles to Johnson Bald (3). Note the wreckage of a light plane among the rhododendron on the right and scattered along the trail.

When this single-engine Cherokee Six crashed in May 1974, Dr. George Size of Pasadena, Texas, and George Westmoreland of nearby Murphy, North Carolina, suffered severe injuries and died. Westmoreland's 14-year-old twin sons, Gary and Larry, miraculously survived. After pulling his injured brother from the wreckage, Gary set off in search of help, but was unsuccessful. He returned to spend the night with his brother. Rescue workers, following the Mexican pesos Gary had left on the trail, found them the next morning while Gary was carrying his injured brother out of the wilderness.

Matlock and Johnson balds rise between Johnson and Tusquitee balds. At Potrock Bald (4), 0.9 mile from Johnson Bald, are the bowls carved in stone by Cherokee Indians.

Dylan pops up out of the cold waters of Fires Creek after jumping off the bridge.

During the final ascent to Tusquitee Bald, the Rim Trail splits. The lower, left-hand fork circles west of Signal Bald. The right-hand fork ascends Tusquitee and runs across the saddle to Signal Bald. Chunky Gal Trail drops off the ridge eastward between Signal and Tusquitee balds and offers 20 miles of strenuous hiking to its terminus at the Appalachian Trail three miles north of Deep Gap.

From Signal Bald, the Rim Trail swings north by northwest toward County Corners (6). There are excellent views from Signal Bald and the section of trail leading to County Corners. Numerous rock outcroppings afford hikers a chance to rise above the laurel and rhododendron and see the rest of the world. Note Nantahala Lake spread out below, with Wayah Bald rising beyond it to the east. Past Nantahala Gorge and Cheoah Bald, Clingmans Dome (6,640 feet) is clearly visible in Great Smoky Mountains National Park.

County Corners (6), so named because Macon, Clay, and Cherokee counties meet in its vicinity, is roughly halfway around Rim Trail, 10.3 miles from the start. Another 13.7 miles of trail lie westward toward Big Stamp Knob and beyond. Shinbone Ridge Trail and Old Road Gap Trail intersect the Rim Trail at County Corners, the former connecting with the end of Fires Creek Road, the latter leading down for about a mile to a gravel road northeast of the sanctuary's boundary.

A half-mile northwest of County Corners, you will ascend Weatherman Bald (7), which rises 4,960 feet, and skirt its summit to the south. At Sassafras Knob (8), the trail cuts sharply to the right and affords a good view of Andrews, North Carolina, and the long Konnehete Valley.

During the 7.25 miles between County Corners and Big Stamp Knob, you will note the extreme drops off the north face of the ridge, some exceeding 70 degrees. About 1.4 miles before reaching Big Stamp, you'll see a marker for McClellan Creek Trail, which leads downhill toward Andrews, a three-hour walk.

Following a logging road, the Rim Trail skirts south of Big Stamp Knob (9), where a fire tower once stood. At the point where the trail crosses an unmaintained road leading up to Big Stamp, a couple of options are available. You can either cross the road and continue on the Rim Trail or follow the road uphill 0.25 mile to the knob. Big Stamp overlooks Andrews, to the north, with the Snowbird Mountains rising on the other side of the Konnehete Valley. Beyond the Snowbirds rises Stratton Bald, the highest peak in the Joyce Kilmer-Slickrock Wilderness. On the northeastern horizon, you can view the Smokies, 40 miles distant. South of Big Stamp lie Hayesville and Lake Chatuge. Brasstown Bald, Georgia's highest mountain, and several other major ridges rise farther to the south. From Big Stamp, you can easily hike westward along the ridge and descend amid the decaying trunks of chestnuts to the Rim Trail.

The 6.5 miles between Big Stamp and Huskins Branch Hunters' Camp is characterized by steep drops to the north, yet is relatively easy hiking. Big Peachtree Bald (10), frequently visited by Cherokees who lived in the Peachtree Valley below, is the last ascent worth mentioning on this trail. You will descend to Leatherwood Falls (1) to complete the Rim Trail.

Shinbone Ridge Trail (12)

To reach this trail from Huskins Branch Hunters' Camp, follow Fires Creek Road nine miles up the creek. At 8.5 miles, the road makes a sharp cutback to the left; note the iron bar blocking the road straight ahead. Continue to the left and crest Shinbone Ridge a short distance farther. A small parking area and a sign for Shinbone Ridge Trial are at the trailhead.

The trail climbs steadily northeast for 1.5 miles to County Corners (6). From County Corners, you can hike a short distance toward Signal Bald for an excellent view of Wayah Bald, the Chunky Gal Mountains, Standing Indian, and the Smokies.

Shinbone Ridge Trail provides backpackers an opportunity to split their hike of Rim Trail into two outings. It is also a good departure point for day-hikes.

In 1991, Doyle Smith and I decided that our sons needed to go backpacking with their fathers and camp a night on Tusquitee Bald. As we began ascending Shinbone Ridge Trail, his son, Jeremiah, and my son, Dylan, started moaning and groaning. Every time they complained, we tried to encourage them, to no avail. As the hike wore on, Doyle and I figured out ways to slip rocks unnoticed into their packs. We'd help them adjust their straps or get their water bottle and load them up while doing so. By the time we made Tusquitee, they were each carrying an additional seven to 10 pounds. You can imagine their indignation when they got their sleeping bags out for the night.

We pitched camp on top of the bald. Doyle had just finished pan-frying the Mexican course when a storm blew out of the northwest with a fury. Hail struck hard as we scrambled to get in the tent. I could hear thunder rolling across the sky as our camp became engulfed by a solid wall of rain. Within minutes, lightning played across the summit of the bald, and during flashes, we could see each other's hair standing straight up. We looked like Einstein clones. We debated fleeing camp for a mad dash to a more-protected spot until the storm passed, but we were transfixed by nature's awesome display, frozen in its grip.

As quickly as the storm struck, it was gone, marching eastward toward the neighboring range. We watched as it unleashed bolts of lightning and spread along the ridges of Wayah and Wine Spring balds. The night was alive and, luckily, so were we. The moral of the story is this: Do not camp on high balds during electrical storms.

Trail Ridge Trail (14)

At Bristol Camp (13), five miles inside the sanctuary, Trail Ridge Trail takes off northward from a log-staging area at the upper end of the camp. Logging operations often make this trailhead difficult to find. Trail Ridge Trail is no longer listed in the trail system.

The trail starts with a climb of nearly 50 degrees and is not recommended as an ascent to Big Stamp and the Rim Trail unless you are training for a Denali ascent and need a real challenge.

It is, however, a convenient descent from the Big Stamp area. An unmaintained Jeep road crosses the Rim Trail just below Big Stamp. Follow the road down for less than 0.25 mile. Trail Ridge Trail is marked by blue blazes, the same as the Rim Trail. It takes off from the right-hand side of the road. Remember, though, that this trail has been dropped from the system and is no longer maintained.

If you want to see the Indian bowls on Trail Ridge Trail, hike up the steep grade from Bristol Camp to the first major shelf in the ridge line. A short distance farther up the hill, note the surveyor's bench mark embedded in concrete in the center bowl. Smaller bowls are cut into the surrounding stone.

Bristol Cabin Trail (13)

This trail crosses the open fields of Bristol Camp to a footbridge spanning Fires Creek. You can then hike 1.25 miles to Carver Gap (2), where Bristol Cabin Trail joins the Rim Trail. Bristol Camp is the former site of Arthur Bristol's cabin. Bristol, the caretaker for F. P. Colver & Sons, watched over the entire Fires Creek area. Bristol Cabin Trail is all uphill to Rim Trail, but it is marked and maintained.

Omphus Trail

Three miles from Huskins Branch and 1.7 miles past Leatherwood Falls (1), Omphus Trail ascends 0.75 mile to the Rim Trail at a point half a mile west of Carver Gap. Hiking Omphus Trail, then the Rim Trail to Carver Gap, then Bristol Cabin Trail makes a good day-hike.

Rockhouse (15)

Rockhouse is a natural rock shelter roomy enough for a dozen people. To reach it, follow Fires Creek Road for 2.8 miles past Huskins Branch (11) and turn left on Rockhouse Road, marked 442-A. Follow this road north across the concrete bridge spanning Fires Creek and continue across two wooden bridges within 200 feet of each other. After the second bridge, take a sharp right up Rockhouse Creek. Proceed 0.25 mile to Game Branch. Leave the road and scramble 50 feet to Rockhouse. A recently fallen segment of rock weighing several tons makes a comfortable sitting ledge.

Thirty-Acre Stand (16)

No trails lead to this unnamed and unmarked 30-acre stand of virgin oaks, and if you try to follow my directions, you'll surely get lost. Over 200 years old, these trees measure 10 feet around and were left unmolested because of the steep slopes surrounding them. Evidence indicates that much of Fires Creek was burned in the mid- to late 1700s, either by Indians or natural causes. This is the oldest and largest stand of timber remaining in Fires Creek, and efforts have been made to encourage the Forest Service to preserve it from future logging.

To reach this portion of virgin forest, follow Fires Creek Road approximately 7.1 miles from Huskins Branch Hunters' Camp (11) to a small branch that runs through a culvert beneath the road. A short distance farther is a sign for Bald Springs Horse Trail (the old Mule Flat Road). Leave the road on the left (north) and follow this branch uphill over steep, rocky, unmarked terrain. Travel beyond where the streambed goes dry and disappears into the rocky mountain slope, then continue over and around the large rock outcroppings. After these rocks, the terrain levels off to a more gentle incline overgrown with thickets of rhododendron and other wild shrubs. After making your way through this vegetation for about 100 yards, you'll emerge from it and enter the virgin forest, situated on a 30-acre tabletop. Hopefully, it's the right one.

When considering this walk, keep in mind that this terrain is much more difficult than the aforementioned trails in Fires Creek Bear Sanctuary. It is a steep ascent with numerous obstacles, and the absence of trails and signs increases the possibility of error.

In September 1993, Doug Oliver, planning forester for the Tusquitee Ranger District, and I searched in vain for the 30-acre stand. It was eight years since I'd last visited the stand, but I was sure I knew where it was. So much for my wilderness skills. Stay posted. I'm going back. We did measure one white oak that hit 11 feet in circumference 4.5 feet above ground level. At least we determined that this compartment of the forest has not been logged, and that the 30-acre stand is still there somewhere. As veteran forester L. C. Loudermilk said when giving me directions to the stand, "It's only 500 yards or so, but it seems like it's five miles."

Horse Trails

Portions of the Rim Trail are open to horses. Little Fires Creek Horse Trail cuts south just beyond Bristol Camp and intersects the Rim Trail west of Johnson Bald. From there, the Rim Trail is open to horses to the junction of Bald Springs Horse Trail, which lies south of Tusquitee Bald. This loop is a great day-ride that covers a lot of miles in the high country.

The Rim Trail is also available for horse trekking from Big Stamp north to Sassafras Ridge.

The route from Huskins Branch Trail (an old portion of Rim Trail) to Will King Gap and the intersection with Phillips Ridge Trail makes a good horse trip.

Rockhouse Creek Trail is open to horse travel. It leads to Rim Trail near Big Stamp.

WHEN

I hike in Fires Creek every season of the year. Prior to hiking here or elsewhere, I check to see if any hunting season is open in the area. If so, I wear bright outerwear and an orange ball cap.

Note that logging activities occur inside the sanctuary at times. You should drive the narrow tracks within its boundaries defensively and slowly.

WHERE

To reach Fires Creek Bear Sanctuary, take U.S. 64 west from Hayesville, North Carolina, toward Murphy. Travel 4.7 miles to the Citgo gas station at Fires Creek, where S.R. 1302 cuts right (northeast). Note the sign for Fires Creek Recreation Area at this turn. Follow S.R. 1302 across the Hiwassee River at Shallowford Bridge. After 3.7 miles, you will reach S.R. 1344, which cuts left (north). It is easily identified by another sign for Fires Creek; a field is on the right and a bridge over Fires Creek immediately ahead. Turn left on S.R. 1344 and follow it for one mile, entering the southwest corner of Fires Creek Bear Sanctuary at Huskins Branch Hunters' Camp (11).

RESOURCES

U.S. Geological Survey maps of Topton, Hayesville, and Andrews, North Carolina,

Jumping off the footbridge at Leatherwood Falls is a favorite summer activity.

each contain parts of Fires Creek Bear Sanctuary. These maps are available from the Tennessee Valley Authority, Mapping and Services Branch, 200 Haney Building, 311 Broad Street, Chattanooga, Tenn. 37401. They are also available at the Tusquitee Ranger Station.

EMERGENCY INFORMATION

Clay and Cherokee counties dispatch ambulances, rescue squads, fire departments, and law officers through a 911 system. Both counties predict that enhanced 911 systems will be in operation before the end of 1994. An enhanced system automatically tells the dispatcher the origin of the call, which is plotted on a map. This helps cut response time. Call 911 first in any true emergency. If you ever have to make an emergency call, be calm and give accurate information as to location and the number of people needing assistance.

Clay County Sheriff's Department, Hayesville, N.C.
704-389-6354
Cherokee County Sheriff's Department, Murphy, N.C.
704-837-2589
Murphy Medical Center, Murphy, N.C.
704-837-8161
Tusquitee Ranger Station, Murphy, N.C.
704-837-5152

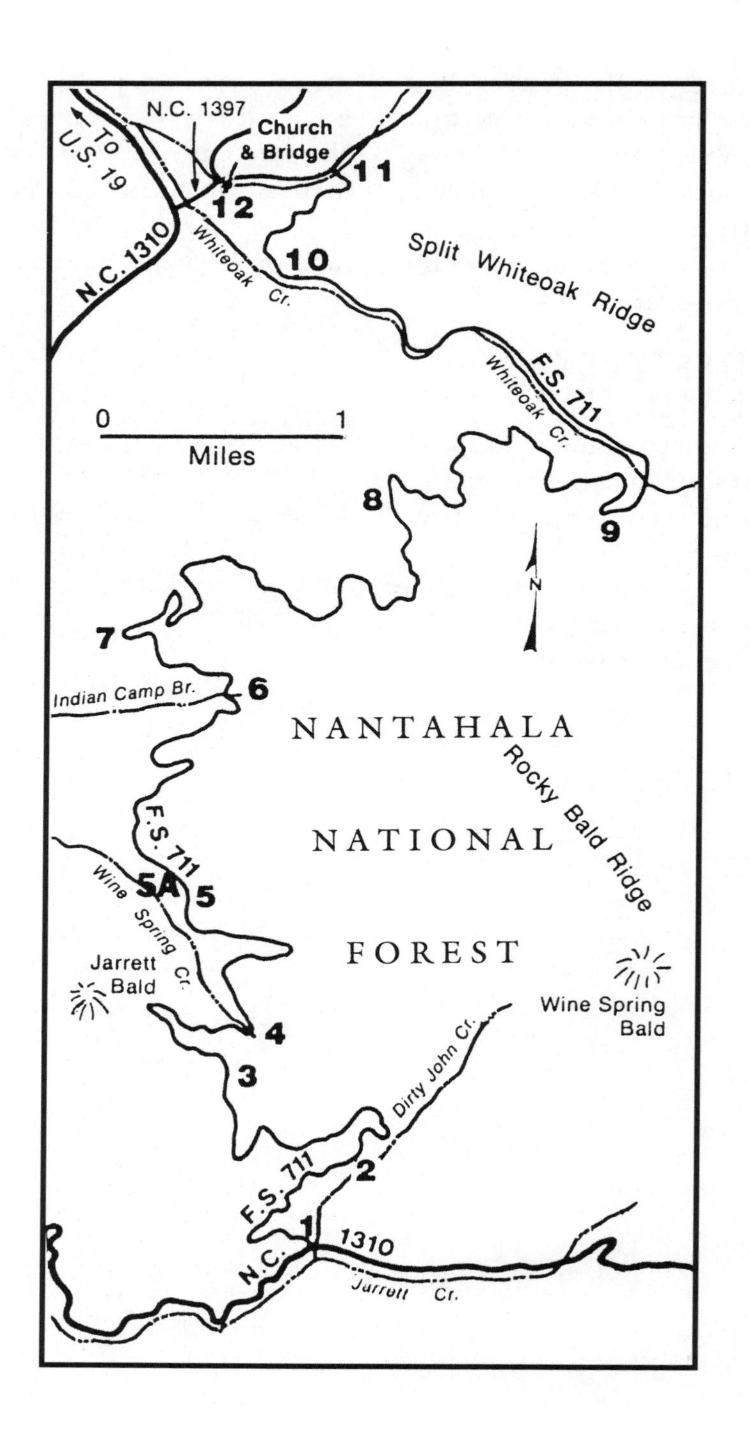
To U.S. 19
N.C. 1397
Church & Bridge
11
12
N.C. 1310
Whiteoak Cr.
10
Split Whiteoak Ridge
F.S. 711
Whiteoak Cr.
0
1
Miles
8
9
N
7
6
Indian Camp Br.
NANTAHALA
NATIONAL
FOREST
Rocky Bald Ridge
F.S. 711
5A
5
Wine Spring Cr.
Jarrett Bald
4
3
Wine Spring Bald
Dirty John Cr.
2
F.S. 711
1
1310
N.C.
Jarrett Cr.

CROSS-COUNTRY SKIING

A Frozen Odyssey

One ski lay smashed across the jumble of rocks that plunged sickeningly out of sight, its spruce cores exposed to the wintry elements. I was apparently stranded four miles from Newfound Gap. Collecting myself and my gear out of the two-foot snowfall that blanketed the Appalachian Trail in Great Smoky Mountains National Park, I peered over the precipice called Charlie's Bunion and thanked the good Lord for not letting me disappear into oblivion.

I was lucky that day. I was able to render the ski "skiable" with tape and two small fir branches stripped of their bark.

When John Gibney and I finally made our way back to the gap and skied down the final bit of trail into the mammoth parking lot, a park ranger stopped us, and for a moment I figured we'd just committed some obscure park violation.

"Did you boys just ski down the trail?" he queried. "Wasn't that a mite dangerous?"

In all truth, skiing the Appalachian Trail, or any other trail, has numerous dangers. Like going over the edge at Charlie's Bunion.

"Yes, it was dangerous," John replied.

"Grabbers," rocks hidden from view by the white powder, are a skier's deadly foe. Low-flying tree limbs are a threat to the eyes, although ski goggles offer some protection. Switchbacks in the trail test your agility and turning quickness, not to mention your ability to stop abruptly. Several times, I've had to abandon my snowplow and sling my body along the trail to avoid a head-on collision with one of mother nature's stands of timber.

Obviously, trail skiing is not for everybody. More than once, I've skied a short distance down what appeared to be a promising trail, only to have to abandon my skis and hike back up. Although trail skiing requires a certain devil-may-care attitude, common sense and safety must always be foremost.

On the other hand, road skiing—like that done on the gated and closed sections of the Blue Ridge Parkway, F.R. 711, and Clingmans Dome Road—is relatively tame and provides a great opportunity to strap on the long skis for the first time. Since the Blue Ridge Parkway has a smooth surface, narrow, lightweight skis and boots work quite well when the snowfall ranges from five to 10 inches. Again, you have to watch for "grabbers," isolated slick spots, and wind-swept pavement. For off-track skiing on back-country trails in deep snow, wider, steel-edged skis yield better control. Steel edges also make a difference on ice.

Through the ages, much has been writ-

Gibney heads out the Appalachian Trail from Newfound Gap
towards Charlie's Bunion.

ten about skiing. The first known account is found in the *Sagas*, a piece of classical literature from the time of the Vikings. The Norwegian Vikings were excellent skiers and even had their own god and goddess of skiing: Ull and Skade. The Ourebo Ski, on display in the Ski Museum at Oslo, Norway, is over 2,500 years old and has a turned-up, pointed tip, just like today's skis. Other skis found in Finland and Sweden date back 5,000 years.

Jon Thoresen Rue immigrated to America from Telemark, Norway, at age 10. In a new land, and with a new, American-sounding name, he became a legend among skiers: John "Snowshoe" Thompson. In 1856, Thompson responded to the Sacramento, California, postmaster's plea for someone to carry mail from Placerville, on the west side of the Sierra Nevadas, to Genoe, Nevada, on the east. Two snowshoers, Daddy Dritt and Cock-Eye Johnson, had failed in their efforts three years earlier, but Snowshoe Thompson managed to reach Genoe in three days despite the blizzard raging in the high passes. Using "gliding shoes" that he built from his memory of his early days in Norway, Snowshoe cross-country skied the 90 miles back to Placerville in a short two days. For 13 winters, from 1856 to 1869, he carried the mail across the Sierra Nevadas on his cross-country skis. When the Central Pacific Railroad was completed across the mountains, Snowshoe was relegated to the ranks of early American folk heroes.

Cross-country skiing was originally called "snowshoeing." Early skis such as the ones Snowshoe Thompson used measured as long as 12 feet. But that was only one ski. The other ski was comparatively short, six to seven feet, and was used as the kick ski. A single, thick pole helped the skier balance himself, slow down, and alter course. One technique for slowing down called for a skier to drag the large pole between his legs with his skis in the snowplow position—tips together, heels turned outward. That technique is still useful with today's equipment, though holding two poles firmly requires a bit more dexterity than holding just one.

Just about anybody can cross-country ski. One friend of mine can't hit a snowflake on the downhill slopes using Alpine equipment, but put him on a set of long, skinny Nordic skis and he glides right alongside the rest of us.

Unlike the footwear used in Alpine skiing, where the entire boot is clamped to the ski, cross-country boots are held to the ski only at the toe, which allows the heel freedom to move. Although cross-country skiing is basically similar to walking, there are subtle differences I'm still learning. When skiing on fairly level terrain, I find myself stretching my step as far as possible before putting all my weight on my forward ski as I prepare to kick off with it and bring my rear ski forward. Kick and glide. Stretching exercises are good warmups for cross-country skiing. Once you master keeping your skis pointed in the same direction, the kick-and-glide becomes a natural movement and the miles pass quickly.

Steep climbs can be accomplished by utilizing a herringbone step, a technique that is as effective as it is awkward to learn. Imagine walking with your toes pointed 45 degrees outward. Add skis that measure 180 to 220 centimeters in length and you have to squat and waddle to get up the hill. The result is a herringbone pattern left in the snow for you to admire from the vantage point you've just attained.

In 1976, Bill Koch, America's Olympic silver-medal winner in the men's 30-kilometer race, helped popularize cross-country skiing in the States. He also introduced the "skating" technique to the general public. Today's cross-country racers use it on level terrain and even going uphill. When "skating," a racer uses his skis like skates, pushing off to one side with a powerful kick that yields great acceleration and extended gliding.

Skiing with someone better than you is the quickest way I know to improve your techniques and learn new ones. I was fortunate that people like Dennis Counts tolerated my early attempts at cross-country skiing. With a few tips from Dennis, my telemarks—turns in which one ski is placed forward of the other and its tip angled inward—were sharper. Watching him execute "helicopters"—360-degree turns on cross-country skis—does get me jealous, though. I can see how he does it, but I just can't master the move. My attempts have culminated in some classic head plants and sore body parts.

Sir Arnold Lunn, a British philosopher and one of the true pioneers of skiing, stated that the main reason to go skiing is "to absorb mountain culture." That statement remains true today. Cross-country skiing provides the means to experience different terrains on their own terms. Intimate contact with remote wilderness areas and wildlife is no longer limited to summer outings. With a kick of the ski, a whole new season becomes the adventurer's personal playground.

Cross-country skiing tests balance and endurance. The unpredictability of the weather and the possibility of accidents demand good sense and good preparation. A sprained ankle, a broken ski, hypothermia, rock slides, and avalanches can spell big trouble for skiers.

In January 1982, Gordon Black and I decided to do some night skiing on the section of the Blue Ridge Parkway leading to Waterrock Knob. Getting to Soco Gap was an adventure. Ice and snow rendered sections of the highway virtually impassable. We snuck up to the gap behind a snowplow. It was a winter wasteland. No kids were sledding. There were no signs of recent skiers. Oak trees frozen solid by a mixture of sleet, frost, and snow stood silhouetted and lonely, their branches white against the stark blue sky.

Immediately upon leaving the thin shelter of Gordon's VW, we both realized the intensity of the situation. The night was clear—clear and cold. Wind gusts of 20 to 30 miles per hour chilled us to the bone. The cold made us hustle, cramming last-minute items into our packs and grabbing more clothing to put on. On one of the coldest nights on record in western North Carolina, we put our packs on, adjusted our skis, and set off on the snow-closed parkway toward Waterrock Knob, all 6,292 feet of it.

The moon was past high and dawn's arrival not far off by the time we made the large parking area just below the crest of Waterrock. The wind was howling. Sudden gusts kept jerking items out of our hands. For every minute that the moon rose higher on the horizon, the temperature seemed to drop two or three degrees. The wind whipped so hard that we could not converse without shouting.

My bag of gorp was frozen shut and a heavy frost lined my beard and face by the time we reached the pinnacle on Waterrock. Undaunted after the night's chilling ordeal, we worshipped the sun's arrival in its early-morning splendor.

The sun rose high in the sky before we departed the summit and skied down the quarter-mile trail to the parking area and began our trek back to Gordon's VW.

Since that odyssey on Waterrock, I have suffered through other cold nights in the wilderness and endured long uphill pulls on skis that made me question why I hadn't stayed home. But upon reaching a mountain's peak and catching the majestic tapestry smothered in fresh snow as far as the eye can see, I always know why I'm there. Telemarking down the smooth contours of a natural bowl or across a mountain meadow lifts my spirit to heights previously unattainable.

Cross-Country Skiing

WHO

I hope to be cross-country skiing when I'm in my 80s, like some of the active senior skiers I've seen. Cross-country skiing knows no age. My kids started before they were old enough to go to school. As youngsters, they loved hiking through the snow to the golf course nearby, where the wide-open slopes provided them a great practice field.

WHEN

In the far western region of North Caro-

Downhill: Skiing Alpine-Style

You push off and point your ski tips down the mountain. Amazement flashes across your face as the slope races past. Wind whips across your exposed flesh. Your goggles fog and leave you momentarily blind.

"What were you thinking?"

"How did it feel?"

"Did you take lessons?"

"Did the ski patrol have to carry you off the slope?"

Your friends are full of questions once they learn you've "downhilled." You are idolized, however briefly. You took the risk, accepted the challenge, and lived to tell about it.

To the vast majority of us Southerners, snow is alien terrain. We hardly ever see it, much less go out and play in it. It seems an impossible task to strap two long boards, slicker than bear grease, onto your feet, encased in moon boots, and jump onto the slope. Add the fact that downhill skiers travel at high speeds and it's no wonder people question your sanity. But you cast all those risks aside. It is the lure of powder, that perfect snow that billows as your skis carve the mountain.

Remember the first time you snowplowed to a complete stop without falling down? Not long afterwards, you mastered the art of turning and gliding across the face of the slope in absolute control. You rapidly learned to keep your shoulders pointed downhill with the fall line as you shifted your weight to the downhill ski and executed a perfect parallel turn.

Soon, you were linking turns on the intermediate slope. Secretly, you came to the realization that you were God's gift to downhill. Nothing could stop you. When they started calling you Jean-Claude, you knew you were ready for the big test: the black-diamond run, for advanced and expert skiers only.

Getting on the chairlift gives you your first hint of trouble ahead. After struggling into position and crossing your ski tips twice, you grab both ski poles with your inside hand and twist your body to the outside, looking behind you for the approaching chair. As the chair clips you right below the buttocks, you fall backwards into it. The Mr. Perfect chairlift operator bellows over the loudspeaker for you to lower the safety bar. You do so pronto.

When the chairlift passes the getting-off point midway up the mountain, you know you are committed to skiing the black diamond. Just before you reach the summit, the chairlift comes to a halt, leaving you dangling 50 feet above the slope, facing a stiff wind and boredom. However, this interruption in your immediate plans affords you the opportunity to study the upper section of the run. It looks horrible. Nothing but moguls swiped clean of all powder by countless skiers. Finally, the lift moves and brings you to the end of the line. You raise the safety bar and prepare to exit. As you push away from the lift, your right ski hits a patch of ice and you head-plant into the snowbank. Fortunately, you are out of other skiers' way as they disembark. Their laughter fades into nothing as they disappear over the edge of the mountain.

After collecting yourself and getting upright again—no easy task—you peer over the edge, a rigid snowplow holding you steady. There's no turning back. One last sigh and you're skiing the Big One. Immediately, you hit the mogul field, humps and bumps, and lose control. You pick yourself up numerous times, dust yourself off, clear the snow out of your goggles, and start again, picking your way through the moguls that stand between you and the lodge at the base of the mountain. You ski to spot A, stop, and scan the slope for your next destination, already savoring that hot toddy.

You work your way down the black-diamond trail. Relief overwhelms you when you finally reach the midway point. Your confidence soars. You can ski now. The lower part of the mountain is easy. Nothing to it. You swoop down to the lodge thinking, "A few more trips from the midway point and I'll tackle the Big One again. Hey, I've got this licked. I love it."

The first time I took my daughter Callie downhill skiing, we spent 30 minutes on the bunny slope showing her how to sidestep up the slope, how to snowplow to a complete stop, and how to turn and work the slope. From then on, she went for the chairlift and tackled the big slopes with abandon. Some are naturals, while others, like myself, have to work constantly on technique and accept the bruises that accompany the learning process.

Alpine skiing is a sport for all ages, from the very young to senior citizens. Two organizations, Outdoor Vacations for Women over 40 and Over the Hill Gang International, attest to the fact that skiing doesn't end at midlife. It only gets better.

Downhill slopes in the southern Appalachians generally operate from mid-November through March, but heat waves sometimes postpone opening day. All the following slopes have advanced snowmaking capabilities that complement the natural snowfall: Ski Beech at Banner Elk, North Carolina (800-438-2093 or 704-387-2011); Sugar Mountain Ski Resort at Banner Elk (800-784-2768); Ober Gatlinburg at Gatlinburg, Tennessee (800-251-9202 or 615-436-5423); Appalachian Ski Mountain at Boone, North Carolina (704-295-7828); Hawksnest at Banner Elk (704-963-6561); Ski Cataloochee at Maggie Valley, North Carolina (800-768-0285); Ski Scaly at Scaly Mountain, North Carolina (704-526-3737); Sky Valley Resort at Dillard, Georgia (800-437-2416); Ski Wolf Laurel at Mars Hill, North Carolina (800-817-4111 or 704-689-4111); and Snowshoe at Snowshoe, West Virginia (304-572-1000).

It's good advice to go to ski school and benefit from lessons from a pro. One hour with these folks and most people get the hang of the sport and are off on their own, challenging the mountain.

Please note that anyone who violates the Skier Responsibility Code can have his or her lift ticket removed and skiing privileges revoked. The code, endorsed by the American Ski Federation, includes such things as skiing under control and in such a manner that you can avoid other skiers and objects; avoiding skiers below you when you are overtaking them; not stopping where you might obstruct a trail; not stopping in a blind spot; yielding to other skiers when entering a trail; wearing retention straps or other devices to prevent runaway skis; keeping off closed trails; and observing all posted signs.

Ski safely. Have fun. Carve the mountain to shreds.

lina where I live, the best snowfalls generally occur in January, February, and early March.

The blizzard of 1993 dumped over two feet of snow on our home and left my wife and kids sequestered around the house for eight days without power and water. All they could do was read, sit around the wood stove melting snow for water, and go cross-country skiing out the back door. I got caught by the blizzard in West Virginia without my skis and missed one of the century's greatest snowfalls.

Since we live in a temperate region, we have to be ready to go when snow is in the area. We prefer a minimum base of three to four inches, but during warm winters, we have been known to ski when only a thick frost blankets the ground. You've got to watch out for those thin spots, though. They'll send you crashing headfirst.

WHERE

The Blue Ridge Parkway offers excellent opportunities for both beginners and experts. Access is generally easy, since the main roads crossing the parkway are kept open year-round, but note, cross-country skiing is only permitted on gated and closed sections of the parkway. Soco Gap rises 4,400 feet above sea level between Cherokee and Maggie Valley. If there is snow in western North Carolina, it's usually there. Balsam Gap, between Sylva and Waynesville, North Carolina, on U.S. 23/19A, is a good starting point, though not quite as high as Wagon Road Gap on U.S. 276 between Waynesville and Brevard. Excellent views of the monolithic Looking Glass Rock are afforded skiers who climb west of Wagon Road Gap a short distance.

Moses H. Cone Memorial Park, just north of Blowing Rock, North Carolina, on U.S. 321, offers 25 miles of carriage paths that lead through beautiful white-pine forests. Access to the Appalachian Trail is nearby.

F.R. 711 runs below Wine Spring Bald off S.R. 1310 in western North Carolina. This 15-mile road winds through a rugged section of Nantahala National Forest before ending at S.R. 1397 near the community of Nantahala. Skiing the route up to Wayah Bald is one of my favorites.

The backroads in Pisgah and Nantahala national forests are laid out in fine detail in the maps available from the Forest Service. They offer skiers a multitude of choices, provided there's snow.

Given the right conditions, the parking lot at Newfound Gap, in the heart of the Great Smoky Mountains, overflows with cross-country skiers attacking the road to Clingmans Dome. I have skied down the ramp from the top of the observation tower at Clingmans Dome several times. This is very similar to bobsledding in that it's a bit scary and not recommended.

Roan Mountain lies along the Tennessee–North Carolina border, rising 6,285

Ice Water Springs Shelter on the Appalachian Trail

feet above sea level. In late June, it boasts the largest natural display of blooming rhododendron in the world. With its high elevation and the trails crisscrossing its grassy balds, which stretch 10 miles from Carver's Gap north to Big Hump Mountain, Roan Mountain is a cross-country skier's dream. Roan Mountain State Park, near Hampton, Tennessee, offers lodging, hiking, and a host of festivals and programs. The park maintains three trails totaling 8.5 miles for cross-country skiing. For information, contact Roan Mountain State Park, Route 1, Box 50, Roan Mountain, Tenn. 37687 (615-772-3303) or the Tennessee Department of Conservation, Division of State Parks, 401 Church Street, L & C Tower, Nashville, Tenn. 37243 (615-532-0001 or 800-421-6683).

Some cross-country skiers take their skinny skis to downhill slopes to work on their telemarks. Metal edges aid in executing linked telemarks, particularly if there's any ice or hard-crusted snow. Runaway straps, designed to prevent your skis from disappearing down the mountain, are required on all downhill slopes.

HOW

Up north in New England, cross-country ski shops are abundant, but in the South, they are few and far between. Most folks purchase cross-country skis from catalogs like L. L. Bean. Several shops in the Boone–Blowing Rock area in North Carolina handle cross-country equipment, as does Diamond Brand, located near Hendersonville, North Carolina. Expect to pay $150 to $200 for a basic cross-country set that includes skis, bindings, boots, and poles. Naturally, there is high-tech gear on the market that can drain your pocketbook but make you look sharp on the trail. My advice is that if you're just getting into cross-country skiing, start with basic gear before investing the kids' college fund in fancy equipment and Lycra suits.

Advances in cross-country equipment have come rapidly in the last few years. A wide assortment of toe-to-ski bindings designed for race, recreational, and telemark skiing are now on the market.

Most skiers prefer no-wax skis with numerous ridges in the kick zone, which provide traction while powering a glide or going uphill. For skiing in groomed tracks, lightweight, extremely narrow skis suffice. Back-country skiing and telemarking are usually tackled using wider skis with metal edges. My back-country skis require waxing the kick zone to get any push. Selecting the proper wax for variable snow conditions is an art that requires experimentation and practice. The temperature of the snow, its moisture content, what type of base lies underneath, and the air temperature are all factors that influence the selection of wax. Waxing can test your patience when conditions are constantly changing.

Anytime I go skiing, I dress in layers and stop often to shed or add clothing in order to maintain my body temperature. Warm gloves, hats, and socks are keys to keeping your body functioning properly in cold weather. My outer shell consists of a waterproof jacket with a hood and Gore-Tex pants. Goggles keep the eyeballs protected, especially in high winds and extreme temperatures. Ample water and snacks such as fruit and trail mix help me avoid dehydration and hypothermia. Skiing with friends provides an added safety factor.

RESOURCES

John Caldwell's *Cross Country Skiing Today* was originally published in 1977 and has been updated numerous times. This book contains a wealth of information for the casual skier and the serious racer. It is published by Stephen Greene Press, Brattleboro, Vt. 05301.

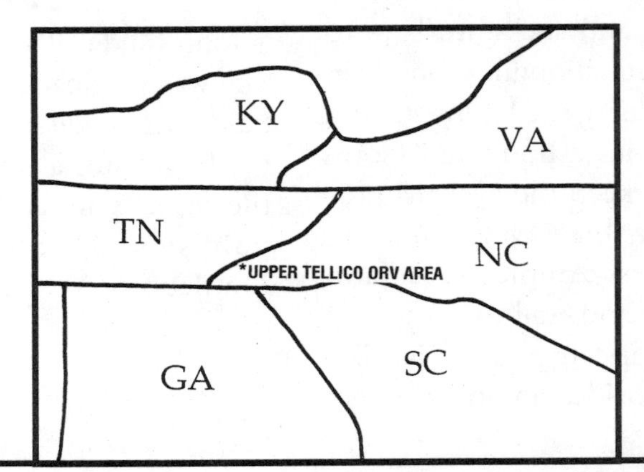
KY
VA
TN
NC
*UPPER TELLICO ORV AREA
GA
SC

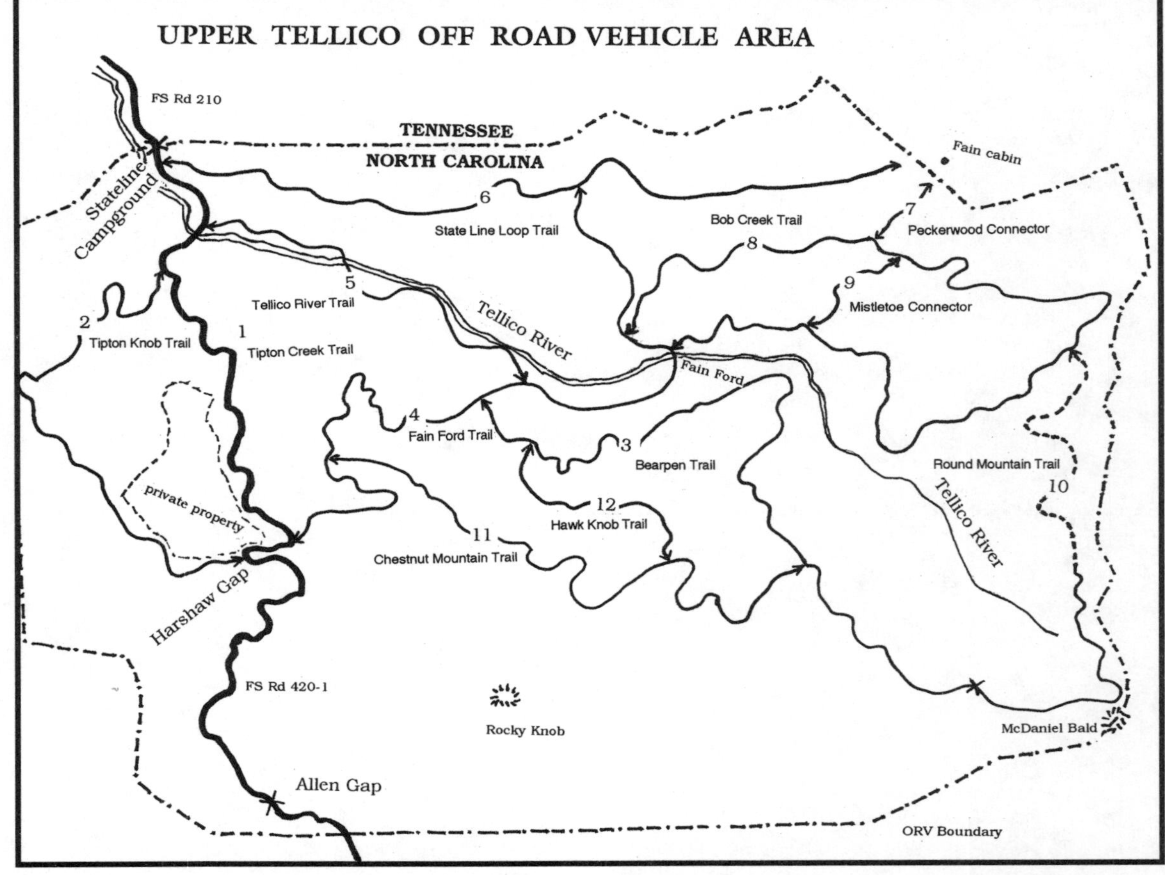
UPPER TELLICO OFF ROAD VEHICLE AREA
FS Rd 210
TENNESSEE
NORTH CAROLINA
Fain cabin
Stateline Campground
6
State Line Loop Trail
Bob Creek Trail
7
Peckerwood Connector
8
5
Tellico River Trail
9
Mistletoe Connector
2
Tipton Knob Trail
1
Tipton Creek Trail
Tellico River
Fain Ford
4
Fain Ford Trail
3
Bearpen Trail
Round Mountain Trail
10
private property
12
Hawk Knob Trail
11
Chestnut Mountain Trail
Tellico River
Harshaw Gap
FS Rd 420-1
Rocky Knob
McDaniel Bald
Allen Gap
ORV Boundary

THE TELLICO

Off-Road-Vehicle Heaven

Cub said, "No problem. I've got bikes that'll do the job. How about a four-wheeler? I've got two of them. Hell, I know that neck of the woods like I do my own backyard. Been up every creek over there. It'll be a hoot. I'll tell you what. I'll give you half a day to get a feel for the bike. We'll hit some of the easy trails. After that, we'll bust some forks. And don't you worry. We'll stick to the trails. They're rough on you if they catch you where you're not supposed to be."

"What if the weather's like it is today, Cub?" I queried.

Gator said, "This whole thing is about mud in your face, dirt in your eyes."

"Gil, you be here ready to go at high noon on Saturday," Cub said. "The rain won't bother me one bit. We'll just plan on camping on the trail somewhere. I know some good spots. Bring a couple of pounds of bacon, some cornmeal, and a can or two of beans. That'll be good eating. I'll tell you something else I bet you don't know. I'm a master of the bullwhip now. I'll give you boys a demonstration. Why, you could stand there holding a cigar and I could cut it down inch by inch at 12 feet. Want to see me do it now?"

I told Cub that his bullwhip show sounded good but that my participation would be limited to taking pictures. Gator could hold the cigar. As Gator and I piled into the Ford Ranger, I could hear Cub laughing, talking to himself: "We'll give this writer something to talk about. I don't believe he can make it. Ought to be fun."

There are times when the weather just refuses to cooperate. High noon on Saturday found us standing around Cub's place forlorn. Rain pelted the shop roof and ran down the drive. You could have kayaked the main road from Cub's all the way to Murphy, North Carolina. The forecast called for more heavy rain, and a flood watch had been issued for the tri-state area. We abandoned all pretense of reaching the Tellico and made arrangements for the next weekend.

It was still raining the following Saturday, just as hard as the week before. I left Cub's severely depressed.

Since Cub could only get away on weekends, and I already had plans for the next four weekends, I made arrangements with Doyle Smith to borrow his dirt bike. Gator volunteered his four-wheel-drive truck to haul the bike over Davis Creek to the Upper Tellico Off-Road Vehicle (ORV) Area. While I rode, he'd fly-fish for trout and have dinner cooking over the fire when I got back. Did I want my trout fried or baked? First, though, we had to wait a few days for it to stop raining and the trails to dry a bit.

The Tellico River has its headwaters in Cherokee County, North Carolina, and flows northwest into Monroe County, Tennessee. My first exposure to the river came in September 1980. Bugs Kelly and a bunch of hard-core four-wheel-drive Jeep owners talked me into going with them on a run across State Line Ridge, which now serves as the northern boundary of the ORV area. The local paper agreed to carry the story, provided it had a little action and some decent photos.

It was a diverse group that assembled at Bugs's service station on the square in Murphy that Sunday morning. At precisely seven o'clock, we departed downtown, a line of 15 Jeep Eagles and Renegades, one Hurricane 4, and Henry Wilson in his Volkswagen Beetle, heavily modified for off-road travel. There was no waiting around for stragglers. "They know where we're going," Bugs said. "They can catch up." Some of the vehicles looked a little worse for wear, due to previous outings in the Tellico. Bugs, however, was driving a brand-new baby-blue CJ5 that didn't have a scratch on it. That changed almost immediately after we departed the paved road and hit the dirt track called Davis Creek.

Today, Davis Creek is a decent gravel road as it winds through Nantahala National Forest on its ascent to Allen Gap and the southern edge of the ORV area. You could drive a Winnebago most of its length, the key word being *most*. Prior to the mid-1980s, Davis Creek was nothing more than a steep, rutted logging road overgrown with mountain laurel and rhododendron, with numerous switchbacks and creek crossings.

By the time we got to Allen Gap, Bugs had already determined he'd need a new paint job. As we bounced over boulders, he confided to me that I hadn't seen anything yet. "Just wait till we get to State Line. Now, that's a four-wheeler's dream."

Below Harshaw Gap, Henry Wilson's Volkswagen dropped an oil pan. A scant quarter-mile farther, a red CJ5 jammed its right front tire into rocks, breaking a tie rod. Two more vehicles dropped out to assist the Jeep team in getting back across the mountain. What I vividly recollect about our ride up State Line that day is my overriding desire to be wearing a helmet. Even strapped in tightly, I had to work hard to avoid smashing my head against the roll bar. How Bugs managed to hold on and drive was beyond me.

At a section of road that someone reverently referred to as Cherokee County's own Chimney Top Hill Climb, everybody stopped and got out of their Jeeps to survey the route. It was wicked.

The climb claimed a couple more tie-rod ends, and two Jeeps were left without brakes. Another Jeep bashed a hole in its gas tank climbing over rocks. The tie-rod ends were fixed easily enough by hooking a line to them and winching the curves straight. Naturally, the Jeeps drove a little differently as a result. The hole in the gas tank was plugged with some type of material that looked like clay. The brakeless wonders just kept going. It didn't faze them at all. They were going uphill, and there was no turning back.

A keen sense of competition was alive and well among this group. If I heard it once, I heard it a thousand times that day: "Jeep wrote the book on four-wheel drive." One driver in particular stood out among the group. Luke had an impressive ability to handle Jeeps in tough spots. His most spectacular run that day was up a nasty, gully-washed track at the wheel of Bugs's baby-blue jewel. As Bugs stated, "He drove it like it was his." By that point, Bugs was committed to not only a paint job but some major bodywork as well. And a new windshield.

In the late 1970s, the Nature Conservancy purchased the 9,200-acre Dabo Tract, the piece of land we circumnavigated in Bugs's Jeep. By late 1980, the land was part of Nantahala National Forest, having been purchased from the Nature Conservancy by the United States Forest Service. By 1983, the Forest Service was at its wit's end in trying to resolve all the conflicts the Dabo Tract presented. One of the major problems facing the government agency was how to deal with four-wheel junkies, who had free run on the land and were destroying it with their motorcycles, four-wheelers, and Jeeps. Water quality plummeted, and the erosion caused by all this off-road use impacted the trout waters of the Lower Tellico, waters known for their trophy-sized trout.

In September 1983, the Forest Service convened a group of private citizens and government agencies to develop a long-range plan for the Upper Tellico. Called the Tellico River Task Force, the group was charged with taking inventory of what was there, finding how it was being used, and resolving how it should be used. The citizens invited to participate represented off-road-vehicle users, private property owners—there is a parcel of land within the boundaries that is privately owned—fishermen, biologists, hunters, and backpackers. Due to my involvement with the North Carolina Bartram Trail Society, I was invited to attend the sessions and have a hand in seeing that hiking opportunities were not totally sacrificed in the Upper Tellico.

During the first session, we identified 49 separate issues, including conservation of fish and wildlife, timber management, protection of private lands, public safety and access, recreation, resource damage, noise pollution, and water quality. The rancor and harsh words that were exchanged during that session made me realize that some of the groups were fighting for a way of life.

The small group of landowners was vocal in its opposition to continued ORV use of the area. What had previously been an isolated vacation retreat with unspoiled hunting and fishing for a select few was now being violated by the obnoxious sound of Hondas, Jeeps, and ATVs tearing up the terrain at all times of the day and night. Plus, camping along the Tellico was resulting in the overuse of primitive sites. The area was simply being loved to death. Unsightly trash was, and is, an ongoing problem.

On the other hand, ORV users complained that they had no other place to carry on their activities. Since the Upper Tellico was already being used for that purpose, they felt it should continue to be available to them.

During one of the day-long sessions, the task force toured the Upper Tellico River area. It was immediately evident that unrestricted ORV use was the major cause of erosion. Trails were everywhere and anywhere. The land was being torn up by knobby tires. Obviously, there had to be some compromises by all parties involved.

What evolved from the work of the Tellico River Task Force is now evident. The Dabo Tract is promoted by the Forest Service as the Upper Tellico Off-Road Vehicle Area. The main road that once meandered through private property was rerouted and a buffer zone created to limit direct contact between ORV users and private property owners. A trail system comprised of 12 distinct routes covering 40 miles was laid out for ORV use, and certain rules and regulations were established. These rules include using designated routes only. Cross-country travel is prohibited. The maximum noise limit is 99 dBa. Tires with metal studs are outlawed. Mufflers and spark arresters are required on all motorized vehicles to limit potential forest fires. Violators are subject to a maximum fine of $500 and/or six months' imprisonment per violation.

Over the next 10 years, the harsh feelings and raw emotions that erupted between ORV users and other groups during the first task-force session evolved into a better working relationship. This is due in large part to the cooperative attitude adopted by numerous ORV groups in the region. Recognizing that they now have an area sanctioned for ORV use by the Forest Service, these organizations have spent many volunteer hours working to maintain the ORV trails by constructing water breaks, erecting silt fences to limit impact on the Tellico's water quality, and hauling out tons of trash. Most important, ORV groups stress to their members the necessity of following the regulations established by the Forest Service and respecting the rights of other users. Unfortunately, there are still some outlaws out there who don't play by the rules.

Betty Matthews, a Forest Service employee in the Upper Tellico Area, summed up the current state of affairs this way: "Management of the area is an ongoing process. We are still trying to resolve all the issues that face the Tellico. Use of the Tellico has increased dramatically in the past five years, and the fact that it is remote and difficult to get to from the North Carolina side adds to the management problems we face."

In November 1993, I wasn't concerned so much with the management problems faced by the Forest Service as I was with actually riding a motorcycle in the Upper Tellico ORV Area. I had a false sense of dominance over machines. I could make them do what I wanted. My ego had me convinced I was indestructible. I conveniently overlooked the fact that my dirt-bike skills had long been mothballed and that I had no experience whatsoever with the particular equipment I would be using. Gator had deep misgivings about helping me with this adventure and was upset that I would be riding alone. I reassured him that I could handle it, telling him that sometimes a man has to do what a man has to do. That attitude came close to bringing me to an untimely demise.

After picking up Doyle Smith's Suzuki 370 trail bike early Wednesday morning, Gator and I made our way up Davis Creek to Allen Gap and the start of the ORV area. Gator observed, "This section of road leading down to State Line is ORV trail #1. It's designated as easy. Maybe you ought to grab this bike and ride it. I'll follow in the truck. That way, you get familiar with the bike." Unbeknownst to me, what Gator really wanted was to see if I could ride. But his logic sounded good, so we unloaded the bike.

It was a piece of cake. I left Gator eating dust. I covered the 5.8 miles to State Line in approximately 25 minutes. That averages out to less than 15 miles per hour, which makes me a very cautious rider. At that point, I started thinking I could ride the remaining 34 miles of trail that day. When Gator finally rumbled across the bridge over the Tellico at State Line, I welcomed him by doing a wheelie across the road in front of him. I was feeling pretty good, even though the helmet Doyle had loaned me was constantly harassing the back of my neck and the face shield fogged up if I breathed out of my mouth. Breathing through my nose directed the air downward and eliminated that problem. A little more practice and I'd have it.

We parked at State Line. While Gator broke out his cookstove and brewed some coffee, I made my final gear check: water bottle, camera and film, compass, waterproof matches and lighter, ORV area map,

Bald River Falls joins the Tellico River on the Tennessee side of the Upper Tellico ORV area.

snacks (Snickers bar, peanuts, two apples), first-aid kit. Since I couldn't bear the thought of trying to sew myself up on the trail, this last item did not include a suture kit—just a few band-aids, toilet paper, and aspirin.

Due to the fact that deer season was open, I wore a bright red-and-blue nylon waterproof jacket made by Black Bear Weather Gear, a company I personally own. Underneath, I had a layer of medium-weight polypro and a wool sweater. I wore a pair of sturdy Vasque boots laced tight and double-knotted, the excess lace tucked out of the way.

Gator made me agree on a planned route. I was to take Tellico River Trail (#5) 1.7 miles to the intersection with Fain Ford Trail (#4), which I would follow 0.7 mile to the ford itself. A short distance up Bob Creek Trail (#8), I would photograph a picturesque Appalachian waterfall, then come back via the same route and check in with Gator before taking off on some other trail. Secretly, I figured I could follow Peckerwood Connector (#7) and get to Fain Cabin for another good photo. I told Gator that if I changed my route for any reason, I would leave a trail of breadcrumbs or a stack of three rocks with a fourth laid in the direction I was going. While pulling on his neoprene waders, Gator admonished me to be back in three hours or less. "If not, I'm calling out the National Guard."

I kick-started the Suzuki after making sure the gas was turned on, the kill button deactivated, and the key switched to start. Gator and I had already topped off the gas tank and checked the oil level and the air pressure in the tires. Since the bike was still warm from the run down Tipton Creek, it didn't need choking. As it revved to life on the first kick, I realized nothing was holding me back.

"Gator, I forgot my watch. Instead of three hours, make that on the late side of dark-thirty. I might just really get into this. Okay?"

I hadn't gone far when I heard Gator laughing. I had skirted the first mudhole. So much for aggressive dirt-bike riding. I was resolved to being careful and staying clean and dry as long as possible.

After weaving my way around boulders and mudholes a scant half-mile up Tellico River Trail, I encountered a ford of the Tellico River. At State Line, I hadn't paid much attention to the river except to note that it was running clear. What I should have looked at was how high it was running. The ford was deep. The preceding week of rain had swollen the river to three times its normal flow. From my vantage point on the cycle, it looked impossible, and I dismounted to scout the immediate area for alternatives. There were none. It was cross or go back.

I shed my boots and socks, rolled up my pants, and proceeded to wade across the creek and see how deep it was. The cold water of the Tellico sent shivers up my back and turned my feet blue. One more step and I ended up waist-deep in water, my pants soaked. Scrambling out of the creek onto dry land, I realized there was no way to get the Suzuki across. It was too heavy for me to carry, and the river was running too deep for me to drive it across the ford.

Discouraged but not yet beaten, I retreated to the bike. My frustrations mounted rapidly after I got my boots back on. Not only was I freezing to death, but the bike wouldn't crank. On the umpteenth kick, the kick-start lever flew off the bike. Since the bike had no electric starter, I was forced to figure out how to get the kick-start piece back on. It jumped off a couple more times before I got the infernal piece of machinery running and headed back down the trail to State Line. Now, I was angry as well as cold. The combination of physical discomfort and stressed mental attitude was not the appropriate baggage to be carrying on a trail bike deep in the heart of the wilderness.

Gator was amazed that I was back at State Line so quickly. I started to let him believe I had ridden up to Fain Ford and back in 45 minutes, but I just couldn't. After I leveled with him, he said, "Load that bike up in the truck and we'll book it out of here. No sense in getting hurt. That bike you're riding isn't really set up right for this stuff."

"Why's that, Gator? This bike is okay."

"This baby's got a combo tire, not the knobbies that this terrain demands," Gator explained. "Look at that rear tire. It's made for street riding and light dirt trails. First bit of real mud it hits, that tire will clog up and be as slick as a baby's ass. You won't have any traction, and that's when you get hurt."

I could see his point, but I still needed more: more trail riding, more photo opportunities, a better end to my macho visions. My ego was suffering after the river-crossing fiasco. "Gator, I'm riding up trail #2 the four miles to Harshaw Gap and then back down #1 here to State Line. There's plenty of daylight left, and it shouldn't take more than an hour or an hour and a half. I'm out of here."

Gator just shrugged, shook his head, and waded back into the Tellico, working that line back and forth in the air. I watched the fly land expertly underneath the overhanging vegetation before I struck out.

With hindsight, I can readily see the series of mistakes I made leading to my accident. It is one thing to have confidence in your abilities, especially in those activities in which you consider yourself an expert. (My expertise in outdoor adventures is limited to river running, hiking, cross-country skiing, and camping.) It is another thing entirely to let your pride dictate your actions. In the past, I had always made sure that I found experts to lead me through new activities safely. Even though I attempted to secure Cub's expertise in ORVing, I exercised poor judgment and disregarded a key safety consideration by riding alone. It almost cost me my life.

The Suzuki and I screamed back up Tipton Creek to the fork that marked Tipton Knob Trail (#2), leading to Harshaw Gap. I hadn't gone 100 yards before I found myself navigating a heavily rutted ascent. Soon, the track turned muddy. I made a couple of small jumps over water before the bike spun out from under me at a switchback. Shaken, I struggled to right the bike, then surveyed the scene. I hoped that if I got past a few more curves, the track would even out, the ruts would disappear, and I could cruise on up the trail. After another frustrating interlude with the kick starter, I finally got the bike cranked, and with the throttle to the wall, I screamed up another section of trail. The bike spun out from under me again when I hit a mudhole. This whole experience was getting to me, but I resolved to try it one more time. Don't they always tell you to get back on that horse that threw you?

My final attempt to climb onward and upward ended in disaster. The rear tire, choked with mud, started spinning like crazy, then the front tire slipped off the middle of the track into a two-foot rut. I flew over the handlebars, and my left shoulder—arm extended—jammed into the earth. The last thing I recollect seeing was the bike coming down on top of me.

I must have passed out because when I next looked up, daylight was fading. From my vantage point underneath the bike, I could make out some objects circling in the sky. It took me a minute or two to realize they were vultures. There were 15 or 20 of them. I wondered what looked appetizing to them: me or the bike.

I knew instantly I was hurt and cold, but still alive. My right hip and knee were pinned under the bike, and my left shoulder was jammed in its socket. Every little move sent waves of nausea through my body. Having experienced shoulder dislocations on my right side, I folded my injured arm across my waist, slipped my right hand under my left armpit, and manipulated the bone back into the socket. I almost passed out again due to the immediate relief I felt. There was just numbness in my right leg. It was difficult for me to extract myself from under the weight of the bike. When I finally got free, I took stock of my situation. Darkness was only 30 minutes or so away. The start of Tipton Knob Trail was less than a half-mile away. I started hobbling down the trail, not even bothering to remove the helmet or look at the Suzuki. Equipment can be replaced.

Meanwhile, back at State Line, Gator had pulled his waders off after a fruitless day fly-fishing, with no keepers to brag about. He started driving up Tipton Creek to Harshaw Gap, our designated meeting spot, when he just happened to spot the contingent of circling vultures. He decided to investigate and turned his truck up Tipton Knob Trail. Encountering the deep ruts, he parked his vehicle where it could be seen by anyone coming down Tipton Creek and started walking up the trail.

Gator found me lying flat on my back in a mud puddle, struggling to get up. The embarrassment I felt at that moment was overshadowed by my gratitude for his most welcome assistance. He removed my helmet, got me down to the truck, and turned the heater on full-blast. Later, he told me I exhibited all the classic signs of hypothermia, a condition in which the body loses its ability to generate heat. Gator then hiked back up the trail and retrieved the Suzuki. Turning his vehicle around, he was able to position it against a bank so that he could simply roll the bike onto the back of the truck.

Gator took the road home as slowly as possible, easing the truck over bumps and slowing down for curves as I sat on the passenger side moaning and groaning. I knew my shoulder would take time to heal and that the bruises down my right hip and thigh would disappear in time. The four aspirin helped. But I didn't think I'd ever get over the bruised ego. I knew that if it hadn't been for my good friend Tim Meaders, the Gator, I could have ended up a first-class dinner for the vultures of the Tellico.

When Gator finally helped me out of the truck back at the house, I told him, "Gator, thank you. I owe you one. You don't have to hold that cigar for Cub and his bullwhip."

"Don't worry, Gil. I wasn't going to anyway. You still owe me."

Off-Road-Vehicle Trekking

WHO

Operators of motorcycles, ATVs, and Jeeps are not required to have a valid driver's license while riding the designated trails in the Upper Tellico Off-Road Vehicle Area. At the date of this writing, no permits are needed for individuals to use the off-road area, but that could change in the near future, as the Forest Service is reevaluating management practices for the area. For group or commercial events where a fee is charged, a permit is necessary. Minors are permitted to operate ATVs and trail bikes in the area, but only under the direct supervision of adults.

Caution is urged due to the extremely rugged conditions encountered on the trails. One motorcyclist died from head injuries in the Upper Tellico ORV Area in 1993. A helmet might have saved his life. Helmets are required when riding motorcycles or ATVs.

Trails in the Upper Tellico Off-Road Vehicle Area

Trail Number	Trail Name	Miles	Difficulty	User Type
1	Tipton Creek	5.8	Easiest	All
2	Tipton Knob	3.9	More	All
3	Bearpen	4.6	More	All
4	Fain Ford	4.2	Easiest	All
5	Tellico River	1.7	More	All
6	State Line Loop	3.9	Most	All
7	Peckerwood Connector	0.6	More	All
8	Bob Creek	6.5	More	All
9	Mistletoe Connector	0.8	Most	All
10	Round Mountain	3.7	More	ATVs only
11	Chestnut Mountain	3.0	Most	All
12	Hawk Knob	1.2	Most	All

Please note that trails designated *Easiest* have gentle grades with a 15-percent maximum pitch, sweeping turns, and a track with few or no obstacles. Trails designated *More* have grades with up to 30-percent pitch, climbing turns, and obstacles in the track. Trails designated *Most* have steep climbs with almost 50-percent pitch, tight curves, switchbacks, and numerous obstacles; these trails require a high degree of riding or driving skill.

Sometimes the unexpected happens on the rough and tumble jeep trails in the Upper Tellico ORV area.
Photo by Tim Dockery

Additional Off-Road Trails in Southern National Forests

Trails in Cherokee National Forest in Tennessee

Trail Number	Trail Name	Type	District	Location	Miles	Rating
2004	Chestnut Mountain	4WD	Hiwassee	Etowah	7.75	Easy
81	Smith Mountain	MC	Hiwassee	Etowah	3.4	Moderate
82	Unicoi Mountain	MC	Hiwassee	Etowah	4.5	Moderate
62	Blue Ridge	MC	Ocoee	Benton	2.9	Easy
75	Sylco	MC	Ocoee	Benton	8.3	Easy
29	Buffalo Mountain	ATV-MC	Unaka	Erwin	12.8	Easy
2	Bullen Hollow	MC	Nolichucky	Greeneville	2.7	Difficult
56	Kenner Spur	MC	Watauga	Elizabethton	5.5	Difficult
57	Flatwoods	ATV	Watauga	Elizabethton	3.9	Moderate
202A	Little Stoney Creek	ATV	Watauga	Elizabethton	6.0	Moderate
322	Sutherland	ATV	Watauga	Elizabethton	2.4	Moderate

Trails in Chattahoochee National Forest in Georgia

Trail Number	Trail Name	Type	District	Location	Miles or Acres	Rating
11	Beasley Knob	4WD-ATV-MC	Brasstown	Blairsville	2,800 Acres	All Levels
7	Davenport Gap	ATV	Brasstown	Blairsville	5.0 Miles	Easy
8	Nottely Lake	4WD-ATV-MC	Brasstown	Blairsville	350 Acres	Easy
32	Locust Stake	4WD-ATV-MC	Chattooga	Clarksville	17.0 Miles	Easy to Difficult
	Moates Knob	ATV	Chattooga	Clarksville	3.5 Miles	No Rate Given
42	Whissenhant	ATV-MC	Chestatee	Dahlonega	700 Acres	Moderate
50	Rocky Flats	ORV	Cohutta	Chatsworth	5.0 Miles	No Rate Given
55	Windy Gap Cycle Trail	MC	Cohutta	Chatsworth	5.0 Miles	No Rate Given
48	Milma Creek	ATV-MC	Cohutta	Chatsworth	3.5 Miles	No Rate Given
54	Tibbs	ATV-MC	Cohutta	Chatsworth	3.5 Miles	No Rate Given
	Rock Creek	ATV-MC	Cohutta	Chatsworth	5.5 Miles	No Rate Given
53	Tatum Lead	4WD	Cohutta	Chatsworth	7.0 Miles	No Rate Given
	Oakey Mountain	ATV-MC	Tallulah	Clayton	6.2 Miles	Difficult
35	Anderson Creek		Toccoa	Blue Ridge	5.0 Miles	No Rate Given
68	Brawley Mountain		Toccoa	Blue Ridge	5.5 Miles	No Rate Given

Jefferson National Forest, located in west central Virginia, contains the Feathercamp Motorcycle Trail system, which runs from near Damascus, on Iron Mountain, to Skulls Gap, on Va. 600. It is open to licensed motorcycle and trail-bike use. For information, contact Mount Rogers National Recreation Area, Route 1, Box 303, Marion, Va. 24354 (703-783-5196). Recently, an ATV trail was opened on Patterson Mountain, in the New Castle Ranger District of Jefferson National Forest. For information, contact New Castle Ranger District, Box 246, New Castle, Va. 24127 (703-864-5195). Rock Run, a 12-mile road open to ATVs, motorcycles, and four-wheel drives, is located in George Washington National Forest, approximately 13 miles west of Harrisonburg. For information, call 703-433-2491.

The Wayehutta Section of Roy A. Taylor Forest, located in the Highlands Ranger District of Nantahala National Forest, contains nearly 20 miles of ATV trails. Trucks and Jeeps are prohibited. If you're interested in riding in this area, contact Smoky Mountain ORV Club at 704-586-5679, 704-586-8039, or 704-586-8772. This club is a group of volunteers who help maintain the trails so everybody can enjoy them. Trails in the Wayehutta ATV system are rated from *Easiest* to *Most Difficult*. The ATV system is located east off S.R. 1732, east of Western Carolina University in Cullowhee, North Carolina.

In the Piedmont area of North Carolina, the Uwharrie District of Uwharrie National Forest has 16 miles of ORV trails in the Badin Lake area. Four miles of trails in the Big Branch and Falls Dam area were recently closed after an environmental assessment identified the area as a potential bald eagle habitat. For information, contact Uwharrie National Forest, Route 3, Box 470, Troy, N.C. 27371 (910-576-6391).

WHERE

To reach the Upper Tellico ORV Area from downtown Murphy, North Carolina, go north on Joe Brown Highway (S.R. 1326) for 2.8 miles to a caution light. Turn right onto Hanging Dog Road (S.R. 1331). After 5.2 miles, Boiling Springs Road cuts right; cross the bridge straight ahead and continue another 0.3 mile on Hanging Dog Road to Davis Creek Road (F.R. 420). Turn right and follow Davis Creek Road for five miles to Allen Gap and the start of the Upper Tellico ORV Area.

Maps of the ORV area are available from the Tusquitee Ranger District, 201 Woodland Drive, Murphy, N.C. 28906 (704-837-5152).

WHEN

The Upper Tellico Off-Road Vehicle Area is open year-round. Several organizations sponsor activities in the area each year and secure special-use permits. Smoky Mountain Explorers sponsors activities April 23–May 2; contact Tom Hoskin, 8700 Broomsage Lane, Charlotte, N.C.

Crossing creeks on a trail bike leaves you soaked. Some you can't ford.

28217. Southeastern Toyota Landcruiser Association sponsors activities April 22–29; contact Dennis Yocom, 2211 Dickerson Road, Nashville, Tenn. 37207. Great Smoky Mountain Trail Ride takes place June 9–14; contact Rainey Kirk, 208 Reidhurst Avenue, Nashville, Tenn. 37203. Dixie Run Southern 4-Wheel Drive Association sponsors activities October 2–3; contact Greg Griffith, 206 Queen's Circle, Maryville, Tenn. 37801. Appalachian Jeep Jamboree takes place October 8–10; contact Mark Smith Off Roading, Inc., P.O. Box 1601, Georgetown, Calif. 95634. The event known as Safari takes place October 22–24; contact Bill Gaylord, Suite 1146, 6065 Roswell Road NE, Atlanta, Ga. 30328.

HOW

On the back of the Upper Tellico Off-Road Vehicle Area map, the Forest Service recommends the following:

1. Know your vehicle and its limits; practice before you get there
2. Ride within your skill level and avoid excessive speeds, the primary cause of accidents
3. Be prepared to make repairs
4. Carry a map and a compass and know how to use them
5. Wear a helmet and protective clothing; use a face shield or goggles to protect your eyes
6. Know that you might have to walk out if your vehicle breaks down; never ride alone
7. Do not use alcohol or drugs
8. Keep youngsters under constant supervision
9. Do not carry passengers on motorcycles or four-wheelers
10. Boil any drinking water taken straight from creeks and springs
11. Know first aid and how to deal with emergencies, such as accidents and hypothermia

EMERGENCY INFORMATION

In a true emergency, dial 911 first.

The number for the Cherokee County (N.C.) sheriff is 704-837-2589. The number for the Monroe County (Tenn.) sheriff is 615-442-3911.

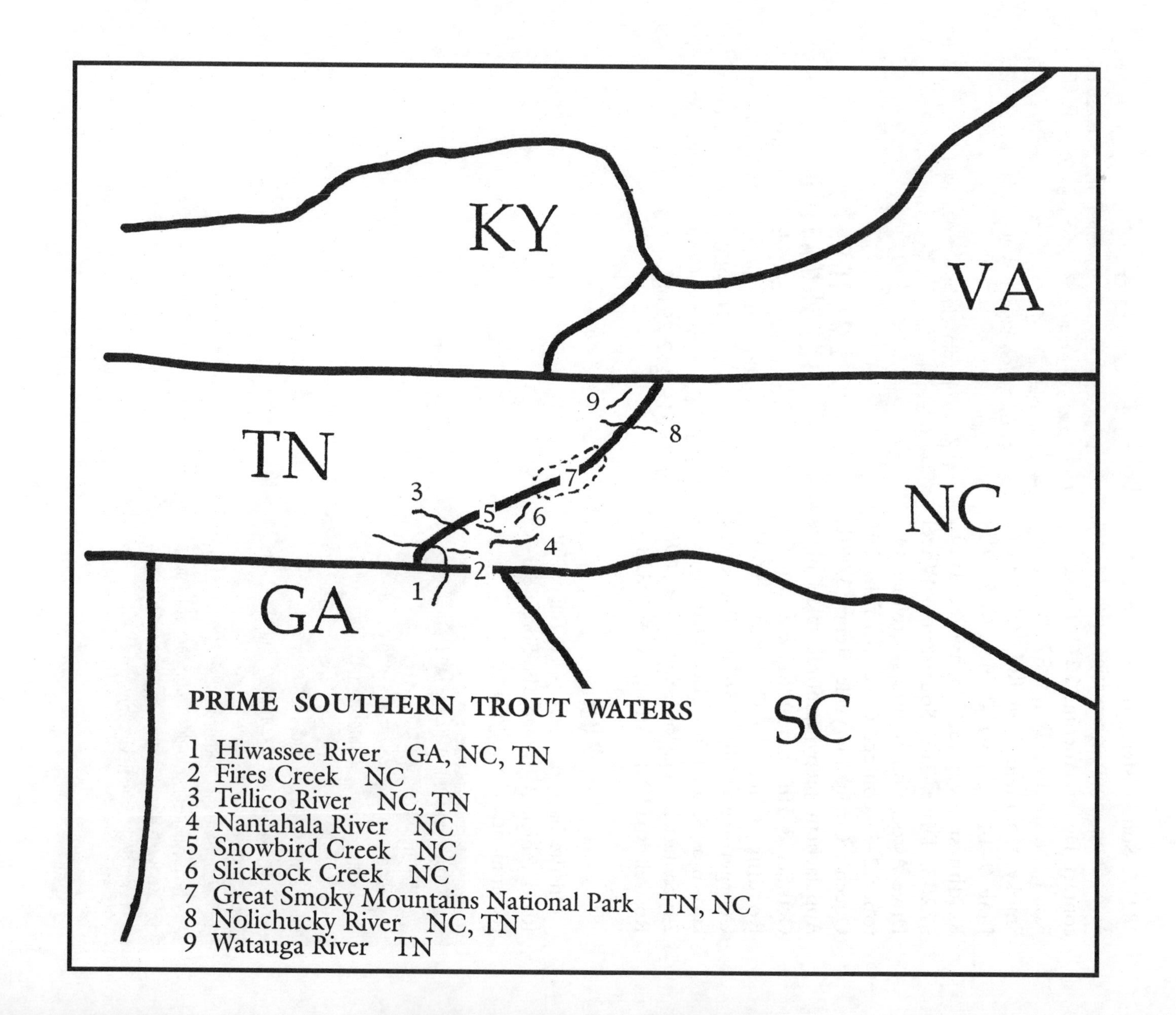
KY
VA
TN
NC
GA
SC
1
2
3
4
5
6
7
8
9
PRIME SOUTHERN TROUT WATERS
1 Hiwassee River GA, NC, TN
2 Fires Creek NC
3 Tellico River NC, TN
4 Nantahala River NC
5 Snowbird Creek NC
6 Slickrock Creek NC
7 Great Smoky Mountains National Park TN, NC
8 Nolichucky River NC, TN
9 Watauga River TN

FLY-FISHING, APPALACHIAN STYLE

Picture the silence as we drift downriver. Finally, after hundreds, maybe thousands, of casts, my fly settles gently on the water's surface, and I can see the trout as it rises out of the depths of the pool. As it strikes, I set the hook, and the battle between man and fish commences. For me, it is an epic confrontation. The fish tries all manner of tricks to shed the hook in its mouth, while I apply my elementary fishing skills to bringing it to the side of the boat and landing it in the net. Just as I am reeling it in, it rises quickly out of the water and, with a powerful flip of its tail, breaks free of the fly and disappears into the darkness of the deep. The one that got away. Another fish tale.

Fly-fishing has always held a special allure for me. I like the grace of the line as it whips against the sky, almost in slow motion. I like seeing the fly silhouetted against the sun just before it settles softly above the river's current. Suddenly, a whirl of commotion disturbs the tranquility of the water. The contest between the combatants begins. Who can outwit the other? For the fish, it is either freedom or the frying pan. Luckily for the trout, many fishermen these days play catch-and-release, better known as sportfishing.

I recollect trout fishing with friends deep in the heart of the Great Smoky Mountains back in the 1970s. We'd wander up Eagle Creek or Deep Creek, maybe hike down the Appalachian Trail from Clingmans Dome and fish the upper portion of Noland Creek, catch our limit of trout, pitch camp, and fry them up in a hot skillet with butter after rolling the fillets in cornmeal batter. Exquisite. The good life. But somehow, those days slipped away from me, and fly-fishing got boxed up and stored in the attic for two decades. I just accepted the fact that my fly-fishing days were history.

Of course, I didn't figure on the Copeland brothers, Theo and Hayden. Theo started Appalachian Angler, a guided fishing service in North Carolina. With Hayden chipping in his fishing expertise, their enterprise has become one of the hottest sportfishing outfitters in the East.

In May 1993, Tom Trawick, my son, Dylan, and I caught up with the Appalachian Angler crew outside Erwin, Tennessee. We planned to fish the Nolichucky River the next day. At base camp that night, we witnessed a typical Great Smoky Mountains thunderstorm, which dropped nearly two inches of rain in the region. The lightning show was spectacular even deep in the cove where we were camped. The thunder rocked the tents, and what had earlier been a serene, tumbling creek became a torrent of white water threatening our camp. We hunkered down, ate a superb meal, and generally yelled at each other over the din of the storm.

Morning broke calm. We left camp before 5:30, headed for the river. Overnight, the Nolichucky had silted up. It was no good for trout fishing. Theo and Hayden conferred. We opted to go look at the Watauga, a river about 40 minutes away.

Once we reached the Watauga, it didn't take us long to get the rafts outfitted with oar frames and in the water. Theo and I claimed one raft. Dylan and Tom Trawick got in with Hayden. Big Jim Cooper and Judson Conway, two Appalachian Angler guides, manned the third raft. Within minutes, we were floating downstream.

At first, Theo and I just talked fly-fishing. He walked me through the basics and shared pointers about casting a fly that I'd never thought of. Raise the rod to 12'o clock, hesitate, push. Theo then got me to study the insects floating on the water and flying about us. He discussed the importance of selecting the correct fly, one that would convince the trout lurking under the surface that what they saw was natural and edible. Theo explained the dead-drift presentation—the art of casting a fly above a pool and letting it drift downstream to the waiting trout. He taught me how to mend a line without creating telltale ripples that would alert the trout that something was not quite natural.

Throughout the course of the day, Theo kept telling me, "Strip your line. Strip it. Mend it. Quick. *Strike. Strike. Set the hook.* Let it swing. That's it. Let it swing. *Set the hook.* Gil, that's another one you let get off. You've got to *set the hook.* Okay."

Once, rounding a bend in the river, we saw a fox stalking a duck and her five ducklings. Thinking we were the danger, she took flight downstream and gave us the broken-wing act. Hopefully, the fox never saw her offspring, which she had hidden under roots alongside the river. Later, we witnessed a young river otter frolicking in a rapid, perhaps fishing. Hawks soared overhead. Near the take-out, over 100 turkey vultures eyed us from their perch on the branches of a large, dead oak.

At one point, after I had cast and cast, trying to make the line dance and the fly land in the vicinity I wanted—and failing to set the hook time and again—I laid down my rod. Theo whispered, "Gil, what are you doing? The fish are striking."

"Theo, I'm resting. I'm taking a break," I replied.

"Gil, no offense intended, but you came to fish. The fish are biting. You can rest when you're dead."

Needless to say, I got back to fishing.

Pretty soon, lunch loomed around the bend. Big Jim Cooper and Judson Conway

A youth makes a perfect cast fly-fishing the Hiwassee.
Photo by Sherry Collins

had oared down ahead of us and gotten lunch frying. Blackened trout, coleslaw, potatoes, bread, and assorted cold drinks were topped off with a great homemade array of deserts. These guys treat guests to an unparalleled experience.

After the meal, Big Jim had to try his luck in the waters flowing by the lunch area. After a few casts, he hooked a monster trout and proceeded to demonstrate his fishing skills. I thought I was watching a scene from *A River Runs Through It*. This baby looked to be in the 20-inch range. A trophy. Big Jim worked that trout for all he was worth. For all we were worth, for that matter. He got it in the net and was lifting it out of the water when, with one last convulsion, it shed the hook and soared to freedom, flipping clear of the net. From the time he hooked that fish to the time it ran back to the deep couldn't have been more than four or five minutes, but it lasted forever. Vivid.

We were devastated. Big Jim was philosophical: "I was going to release it. Even if it came close to the state records, I couldn't take it. What a fight!"

All the fishing we did that day was catch-and-release. The blackened trout we had for lunch came from a trout farm, already filleted and packed in ice for the trip downriver. The overriding philosophy at Appalachian Angler is that what's best for the fish is best for the fisherman. Theo and Hayden also have a goal of providing you with a true wilderness experience and helping you catch fish regardless of your skill level.

One of the things I came to understand from the Copeland brothers and Appalachian Angler is that there is a lot more to fishing than casting a line. It was kind of embarrassing that while everybody else was catching beauties—Tom in particular—I was getting skunked. But it didn't matter. I'd left all my headaches at home. I knew that my little girls and wife were enjoying the absence of two outspoken males around the house and were in good keeping with each other. My boy was catching fish. The river kept beckoning, waiting for me to cast. The beautiful day that surrounded us was floating by all too quickly.

Way back before our time, all a person could catch out of these Appalachian waters was brook trout, also known as speckled or native trout. The Latin name, *Salvelinus fontimalis*, means nothing to me, but if I had to guess, I'd interpret it to mean that whoever catches one salivates heavily toward the front of the mouth. Brook trout have been known to weigh as much as 17 pounds. They are pretty easy to recognize, with light, wormlike markings on a dark upper body that contrasts with white lower fins. Brook trout are found in streams with a maximum temperature of 66 degrees, though they have been known to survive temperatures up to 75 degrees. They are very sensitive to pollutants and silt. A stream that harbors trout contains good, healthy water.

About 100 years ago, rainbow and brown trout—European species—were introduced to the region. This proved unfortunate for many brook trout.

Brown trout can survive 80-degree water and will drive out brook trout from calm, warm water. Brown trout have a brown body with large, dark spots with red dots, often circled with a blue glimmer of color. The Tennessee state record for a brown trout is 28 pounds, 12 ounces. The world record, according to my 1992 *World Almanac*, was caught by Eugenio Cavaglia on December 16, 1952, near Nahuel Huapi, Argentina, and weighed a whopping 35 pounds, 15 ounces.

Gator gets a strike fly-fishing on the Tellico.

Rainbows get even bigger, with the world record exceeding 42 pounds. Rainbow trout are perhaps the best-known trout species among the general public. They are beautiful to behold, with their shimmering array of iridescent markings.

Whether baked, broiled, fried, or blackened, trout are a delight to the palate. Trout farming was once the occupation of a handful of folks trying to find a new way to survive in the hills. Now, it is a commercial industry that prides itself on providing an excellent renewable resource to an expanding market.

All trout species are highly sensitive to changes in the water. For them to grow, high water quality must be maintained. I was surprised how undeveloped the river we fished that day was, how its sparkling waters lacked eddies brimming with soapsuds and trash flushed downriver, a common state of affairs on many of America's rivers. For me, the beauty of the Watauga only added to the mystique of fly-fishing, Appalachian-style.

Super Bowl Sunday and the Tuckasegee Muskie:
A Tom Wilkes Fish Tale

By Tom Wilkes as told to g. forest

We started the day out with intentions of fly-fishing up Noland Creek, and we got there before daylight. It was so cold that the guides on the rod were freezing shut and the line couldn't pass through. I remember clear as a bell. Super Bowl Sunday 1993. I'll never forget it.

My cousin Joel Blanton and I finally give up. We were both froze solid from wading in that 33-degree water flowing out of the Smokies and were just too cold to enjoy the fishing. We headed back home and stopped in the sunlight on the road between Bryson City and Sylva to eat an early lunch.

Being it was nice and warm and the Tuckasegee River was flowing not 15 feet from where we were parked, I decided to throw my line out there. See if anything was biting. I grabbed my rod, a lightweight Ugly Stick with an Ambassador lightweight reel carrying 75 yards of eight-pound Stren premium monofilament. Had to be a trout just waiting in those waters.

I was standing on a real steep bank. The water was less than three feet away. The riverbed dropped off steeply. One step off the bank and you were chest-deep in water. Joel'll attest to that. I was casting upstream on my fourth cast with a black-backed rappella, letting it sink in a dead-drift presentation. It sunk and then swung out of the current, edging near the bank. I was just starting a slow retrieve when that lure must have floated right past him. He struck. There was no fight. I reeled him in like a log easing through the current. At first, I thought I had caught a state-record brown. My second thought as I reeled the fish closer was "My God! What a carp!" It wasn't until I saw the shape of his jaw and the color of his eyes that I had my third and final thought: "Oh Lord, I'm in trouble now!"

I hollered for Joel to get his butt over here, and directly he waddled up, still in his old rubberized canvas waders, just a-grinning at this giant fish floating calmly right next to the bank. I could see that the lure was hooked on the outside of his jaw, like after he struck at it, he tried to spit it out. And I knew I was going to lose him. There was no steel leader from the lure to the line. His teeth looked razor-sharp. It was the biggest freshwater fish I'd ever caught on eight-pound line.

Finally, this powerful muskie senses that he's caught and explodes across the river. I was letting the line go. The reel was smoking, but when he'd stop, I'd get line back on the reel fast as I could.

He ran downstream again full-bore. By the time I finally got him back toward the bank, Joel had stepped into the Tuckasegee, and I worked the fish between Joel and the bank. As Joel reached down to grab him, the fish looked him straight in the eye and proceeded to slap him upside the head with a powerful flip of his tail. It left marks across his face. The big fish then exploded back into the current. The reel whirred, and suddenly I'm down to less than a yard of line left, and he stopped. Another four feet and he'd pop the line and be gone.

That muskie proceeded to race just as hard back toward me as he'd done earlier looking for freedom. I couldn't reel the line in fast enough. Right as he got near the bank, the loop got tangled in some brush. I freed it and finally caught up with the fish. When he came between me and Joel, Joel was ready and hit him with everything he had. He ran that snout six inches into the bank's mud. I dropped the pole, and together we flipped him higher on the bank, him just a-flopping and wiggling. Pretty soon, his slimy scales were covered in sticks, branches, and leaves. We high-fived, and I considered freeing the muskie. Joel and I both thought it might be a state record for eight-pound line. We bagged it in two plastic bags and headed for the bait shop to use the scales and record the catch. We walked into the bait shop, Joel leaving a puddle of water everywhere he stepped, and proceeded to weight the fish.

Later, when I took the muskie to the taxidermist, he said, "Most folks come in with a fish and call it a trophy. You come in with a trophy and call it a fish."

I've heard it said that a man must make 50,000 casts on the average to get a muskie strike—a strike, not a catch. The Tuskasegee muskie I caught Super Bowl Sunday weighed 20 pounds and measured 42 inches in length. He was a true muskellunge, a fish that once was native to this area, and not a tiger muskie. Back in the '30s and '40s, the paper mill pumped a lot of toxins into the Tuckasegee, and the muskellunge died out. It wasn't until the '50s that muskellunges were reintroduced to the Tuckasegee. This particular fish was estimated to be 13 years old. I'm amazed to think about the number of generations of muskellunge in the Tuckasegee that this fish represents. Astounding. There's no doubt this fish is a good mount. He was a lucky catch. Now, I wish I'd let him go.

Getting back to the bait shop. We were standing there weighing and measuring the fish when the operator of the shop looked at Joel standing there, water just oozing out his canvas waders every time he sloshed about, and asked, "Did you get in the water and help land this fish?"

Joel looked him and the gathered crowd of witnesses straight in the eye and said, "Not if it's a record. No, sir. Not if it's a record."

Fly-Fishing

WHO

Everybody is a potential fly-fisherman. All you need is the equipment—a rod to cast the line and a couple of flies to catch the trout. Waders are optional. Learning the secrets of fly-fishing is truly one of life's finer pleasures. And you can always catch-and-release.

Leatherwood Falls Picnic Area, in Fires Creek Recreation Area near Hayesville, North Carolina, provides paved wheelchair access along creeks, allowing the handicapped an opportunity to try their luck and cast a line.

WHEN

Fly-fishing is great anytime, but if you're fishing designated trout waters, you'd better be aware of seasonal regulations, have the proper licenses, and know the size and number limits.

WHERE

Know the area you're planning to fish. Topographical maps and informational pamphlets are available at Forest Service offices throughout the region. I have found the people who staff the district offices to be extremely knowledgeable and helpful. Rangers and staff in the field can provide insight into fishing specific areas.

Each state in the southern Appalachian region prides itself on the quality and quantity of its "fishable" streams. Contact the respective state wildlife commissions for detailed information concerning specific areas, and remember that many rivers and streams cross state lines. Note that Tennessee and North Carolina have a reciprocal agreement for fishing licenses in Great Smoky Mountains National Park.

Areas I have fished and found to be excellent include Great Smoky Mountains National Park (N.C. and Tenn.), the Watauga River (N.C. and Tenn.), the Nolichucky River (N.C. and Tenn.), the Nantahala River (N.C.), the Hiwassee River (Ga., N.C., and Tenn.), Fires Creek (N.C.), the Tellico River (Tenn.), Slickrock Creek (N.C.), and Snowbird Creek (N.C.).

HOW

Be aware of fishing regulations. Each state requires fishing licenses. If you're 16 or older in North Carolina, or 13 or older in Tennessee, you must have a state fishing license and, in certain waters, trout stamps. Length of licenses, catch limits, and other regulations vary. Some waters are designated catch-and-release only. It's your responsibility to know the law.

For detailed information, contact

Tennessee Wildlife Resources Agency
P.O. Box 40747
Nashville, Tenn. 37204
615-781-6682 or
800-332-0900 (TWRA's Region IV office)

North Carolina Wildlife Resources Commission
512 N. Salisbury Street
Raleigh, N.C. 27604-1188
919-662-4370

Georgia Department of Natural Resources
Game and Fish Division
Fisheries Management Section
2123 U.S. 278, SE
Atlanta, Ga. 30279
404-918-6418

If you're interested in guided fly-fishing services, contact
Appalachian Angler
Route 3, Box 606
Boone, N.C. 28607
704-963-7474

This outfit is top-of-the-line, and Theo Copeland is a pioneer in Southeastern fly-fishing. Appalachian Angler utilizes both oar-rigged rafts and Western-style drift boats on the creeks and rivers of western North Carolina and the Appalachian Mountains of Tennessee.

Smoky Mountain Guides
P.O. Box 183
Brasstown, N.C. 28902
704-837-8725

Tom and Ruth Trawick, the proprietors, offer fly-fishing and bass-fishing outings in the Hiwassee River watershed.

Tom Wilkes
Route 1, Box 925C
Sylva, N.C. 28779

See "Super Bowl Sunday and the Tuckasegee Muskie: A Tom Wilkes Fish Tale," included in this chapter. Tom will gladly take you and a friend muskie or trout fishing.

RESOURCES

Over the years, there has been some classic writing on the sport of fly-fishing. The subject is also covered in numerous periodicals available at newsstands and libraries.

The Complete Fisherman's Catalog, by Harmon Henkin, published in 1977 by J. B. Lippincott Company, is an excellent source of information about fishing-related topics.

Commonsense Fly Fishing, by Ray Ovington, published by Stackpole Books, offers expert tips from an expert fisherman.

American Trout Fishing, by Theodore Gordon and a company of anglers, was published by Alfred A. Knopf in 1966. Gordon is the acknowledged father of dry-fly fishing in America.

A Primer of Fly-Fishing, by Roderick Haig-Brown, published in 1964 by William Morrow and Company, contains a wealth of information on equipment and techniques.

Techniques of Trout Fishing and Fly Tying, by George W. Harvey, was published in 1985 by Metz Hatchery.

Fly Fishing: First Cast to First Fish, by Joseph F. Petralia, was published in 1991 by Sierra Outdoor Products Company.

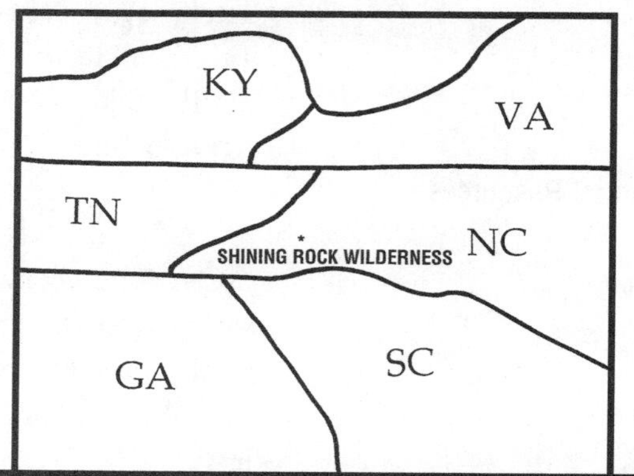
KY
VA
TN
NC
SHINING ROCK WILDERNESS
GA
SC

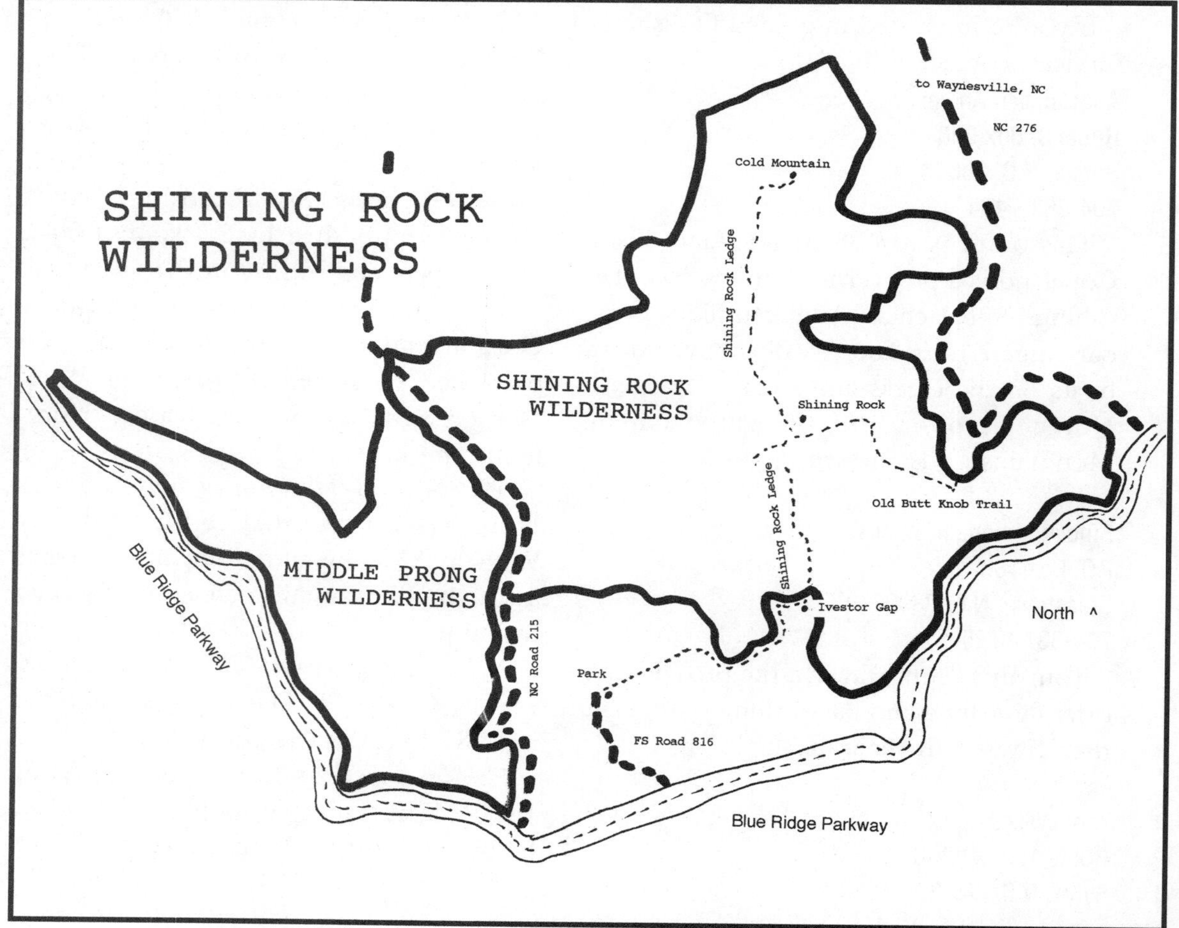
SHINING ROCK
WILDERNESS
to Waynesville, NC
NC 276
Cold Mountain
Shining Rock Ledge
SHINING ROCK
WILDERNESS
Shining Rock
Shining Rock Ledge
Old Butt Knob Trail
MIDDLE PRONG
WILDERNESS
Ivestor Gap
North
Blue Ridge Parkway
NC Road 215
Park
FS Road 816
Blue Ridge Parkway

SHINING ROCK

A Wilderness of Vistas

We prepared with serious intentions. Weeks prior to our camping trip in Shining Rock Wilderness, we inspected and washed sleeping bags. As the time drew near, we pitched tents and applied a new coating of seam sealer. We fueled and fired camp stoves. In the evenings, we gathered around the table and tried to reach an agreement on the menu. Each participant packed and repacked his or her backpack numerous times, checking flashlights, grabbing a toothbrush, discarding this or that, throwing in extra pairs of socks.

I was stunned at how serious my fellow adventurers were taking this three-day camping trip in Pisgah National Forest. Usually, I just grab what I need and hope everybody's got what they need. One aspect of backpacking I've always appreciated is people's willingness to share. It's common to omit some little item, like toothpaste or pepper. It's also common to hear around a campfire, "Here, I've got plenty. You're welcome to it." But this group was having none of that. It was every man for himself: Take what you need, you ain't getting none of mine.

We studied topographical maps for any serious elevation changes. A few members of the team thought I was trying to hoodwink them when I said it was easy hiking.

Who could blame them? These folks had been with me before on other adventures, but never on a backpacking trip high in the heart of the southern Appalachians. Let me clarify. It was the first time all five members of my family had ever attempted such a venture. Over the years, we added a child here and there, and our backpacking outings dwindled. Car camping came into vogue. Day-hikes were the ticket, followed by a sleepy ride home or a camp nestled in some national forest, where we'd tell ghost stories and roast marshmallows over the fire. Sometimes, the stories were too good, and the kids would crawl into the perceived safety of the VE-24 and the warmth of their sleeping bags wide-eyed, carefully watching the fire turn to embers and the stars crowd the night sky, waiting for Mom and Dad to enter the tent before dropping off to sleep.

These guys were pumped. Our two girls, Callie, age 11, and Cory, age eight, had promised to tell their classmates all about our trip when they got back. Once Dylan, our 16-year-old son, figured out that he'd get the honor of carrying a little extra in his backpack, he got real helpful when it came to making sure his sisters weren't carrying anything that wasn't essential. One Barbie doll per pack was the rule. No teddy

View from the Ivestor Gap Trail

bears. And one small camp pillow. No more.

Our itinerary called for a hasty exit after school on Friday. We departed Murphy, North Carolina, for Shining Rock Wilderness, which lies in the mountainous area between Waynesville and Brevard. Elevations in the wilderness range from 3,200 feet to over 6,000 feet on Cold Mountain. Shining Rock Ledge forms the backbone of these high-altitude ridges on the north slope of Pisgah Ridge.

Shining Rock Wilderness was created in 1964 with the signing of the Wilderness Act. The original 13,600-acre tract was increased to 18,500 acres by the 1984 North Carolina Wilderness Act. Middle Prong Wilderness, part of the 1984 act, added 7,900 protected acres immediately west of Shining Rock. The only thing separating Shining Rock and Middle Prong is N.C. 215, a paved secondary road that cuts off the Blue Ridge Parkway at Beech Gap, skirts Little Sam Knob, and descends along the West Fork of the Pigeon River to Sunburst and Lake Logan. It is a beautiful ride along this sparkling tributary of the Tennessee River as it drops from 5,400 feet to 3,200 feet in eight miles.

We made good time from Murphy to Balsam Gap, where we got on the Blue Ridge Parkway and headed north. A brief stop at Richland Balsam, the highest point on the parkway, tested our skill at identifying distant mountains. Immediately after we passed N.C. 215, the kids marveled at all the folks climbing Devil's Courthouse—the red, yellow, and blue of their climbing attire, the long strands of rope, the figures silhouetted on the summit.

Exiting the Blue Ridge Parkway near Milepost 420, we headed north on F.R. 816, which winds its way a little more than a mile to a low gap between Sam Knob (6,040 feet) and Black Balsam Knob (6,214 feet). After a week-long diet of education and two hours of steady driving, the gang departed the van with gusto, grabbing packs and stuffing this and that here and there.

"Which way, Dad?"

"We'll see you there."

I couldn't contain them. Dylan was first out of the gate, his backpack loaded and his gait strong. Not to be outdone, Callie closed the 100 yards that separated them on a dead run, pack bouncing and loosely secured items dropping out. A glove. Her knit hat. She didn't care. Mom would get them. Big Bro was not leaving her behind.

As I struggled into my heavily burdened, frameless North Face pack, I lost sight of Joy and Cory in a bend in the trail. I sure was starting out bringing up sweep. I double-checked the van to make sure it was locked and set off in rapid pursuit. Dylan and Callie were a good half-mile in front along Ivestor Gap Trail.

Technically, we had yet to reach the wilderness. We could have driven this section to Ivestor Gap, though there wouldn't have been much left of the van. This road is open to four-wheel-drive vehicles from August 15 to January 2. It is not open to ORV traffic.

Sharp rocks made walking this fairly level mountain roadbed a difficult task. Each step had to be calculated to avoid a twisted ankle. We skirted all water seepage and springheads to keep our boots and socks as dry as possible. I was surprised how quickly we covered the two miles from the parking area to Ivestor Gap and the signs denoting Shining Rock Wilderness.

Vegetation along these high ridges and mountaintops is scarce, even though this area is one of the southernmost reaches of the Canadian Vegetative Zone, which generally contains spruce, fir, hemlock, and hardwood forests. After the Cherokee Indians lost their land to early white settlers and the State Land Grant of 1796, three events played major roles in shaping the land. Logging operations commenced at the turn of the 19th century. Within 25 years, vast stands of red spruce, Fraser fir, hemlock, and hardwoods such as oak, hickory, and chestnut were harvested. Very little was left. Then came two fires. The first, started in 1925 by a locomotive used in logging operations, burned over 25,000 acres. The second, a massive fire in 1942, seven years after the land had become part of Pisgah National Forest, left the ridges devoid of vegetation. Only a few isolated stands of fir and spruce can be found in the wilderness today.

After a short break at Grassy Cove, we continued on Ivestor Gap Trail along the western slope of Shining Rock Ledge. Since we made our hike, the trail has be rerouted around Grassy Cove because of severe erosion. The trail to the top is no longer open, and the forest service discourages its use. In order to insure that future generations will be able to enjoy the area, avoid hiking to the top until the area has had a chance to recover.

Dylan pointed out to the girls that while the trail over the top of Grassy Cove was a little shorter, it had several elevation changes, whereas Ivestor Gap Trail stayed on the same contour line and would be easier hiking. I liked the way they were working as a team and studying the map.

It wasn't long before Callie and Dylan were out of sight. Cory was easily distracted and used all her tricks to get us to stop for a second or two. "What's that?" "My boot needs tying." "I think there's a rock in it." "I'm thirsty." "How much farther?" But she never whined or asked me to carry her pack. Once, she said she'd have a much better view if she could ride on top of my pack. Joy and I couldn't help having fun with our littlest backpacker as we hiked in the coolness of a fading day.

Shortly after entering a canopy of hemlock, we heard Dylan and Callie hastily making their way back toward us, voices filled with excitement. Or was that fear? Callie was pale. Dylan was flushed. Apparently, Callie had stepped on a snake—a copperhead, she feared. To hear her tell the story, the snake was at least eight feet long and had two heads. Dylan confirmed the snake but hadn't gotten a good look at it. It was in the shadows. He claimed it wasn't nearly as big as his sister said, and it certainly didn't have two heads. Personally, I loved it. Callie would pay better attention and appreciate the wilderness experience that much more. And neither Callie nor the snake had been harmed.

Later, Callie asked, "Why didn't that snake bite me? If somebody stepped on me, I'd sure want to bite them."

We stayed tighter after the snake encounter. Cory held my hand as we hiked the remaining mile to Shining Rock Gap. Bravely, Callie and Dylan again took the lead, careful to stay within sight. A bear scat stopped them cold.

Callie asked, "What left this, and what in the world was it eating?"

"Callie, that's Mr. Black Bear," I said. "He's been eating a lot of berries—blackberries. Although the black bear is pretty much a vegetarian, they do eat carrion and other critters. You can tell this is pretty fresh. That bear was here not long ago. If we're lucky, we'll see the bear."

That's when they started hiking right behind Joy, Cory, and me. In fact, Dylan wanted Cory to go first, thinking that after the bear ate her, it wouldn't want more of this gang. Cory kept a good grip on my hand and grabbed Joy's, too. Callie found a spot on my right, all four of us holding hands as we walked down the trail. Dylan, in the rear, was busy looking over his shoulder.

Several parties were camped at Shining Rock Gap and its abundant spring. We filled a camp bottle and headed out Old Butt Knob Trail toward Shining Rock, hoping we'd find the summit deserted. Dark was gathering and a few early-evening stars were visible as we negotiated the steep, rutted trail. Near the summit, Cory was crawling on all fours when she spotted a snake scat that contained several different types of fur. Our scatological survey of Shining Rock Wilderness was expanding.

We dropped our packs at the small campsite on the summit and, with twilight fast approaching, took off exploring Shining Rock. We moved carefully through the rock garden of exposed white stones, climbing over the tops of some, slipping between others, and crawling through tight squeezes. To the northeast, we could see the lights of Asheville.

"Cory, where are you?"

"Dylan, do you see Cory?"

"*Cory, where are you?*"

One instant, she'd been right there between me and Joy. Now, she was gone. Callie and Dylan worked their way back to us, searching. Several minutes went by, and she still didn't answer us. A bit of fear was creeping into Joy's calls for our youngest offspring. Did she fall, strike her head, and disappear into some crevice? Was she playing hide-and-seek, tucked away in some crack in the rocks? The four of us conferred. We decided to call her bluff.

"Cory, we're going back to the car to get help! We can't find you! We'll be back!" I yelled.

A voice tiny and near said, "No. You can't leave me. I'm right here."

There she was, tucked into a space within five feet of where we stood. In fact, we'd all looked in that exact spot and never seen her.

"I didn't mean to scare you," she said. "You each looked right at me. I thought you were fooling me. Let's go back to camp, okay?"

As we worked our way back toward the campsite, I couldn't help asking myself what other heart-stopping incidents could possibly happen. The day's events had certainly made us aware of our dependence on each other. The children were much more attentive, and, remarkably, we were functioning like a cooperative family. While I pitched the VE-24 and Joy got the cookstove fired to boil spring water and make hot tea, Dylan and the girls set up their dome tent and got the rain fly secured before turning their energies to inflating sleeping pads.

After supper, the west wind picked up, whistling over the bald and among the cracks and crevices of Shining Rock. With the rising moon periodically hidden by racing clouds, we alternated between deep darkness and periods of brightness, when Shining Rock was illuminated by moonbeams, much to our delight. We passed an uneventful night on the summit. I dreamed of search-and-rescue techniques, of what to do in case of snakebite, of how to tell when a 350-pound black bear is bluffing a charge.

We didn't have a campfire that night atop Shining Rock. The gang understood.

I have preached for years that backpackers should take only pictures and leave only footprints. We always police any campsite we use and scatter the remains of any firepit. Today, the emphasis for perceptive wilderness users is on no-trace use. Environmentally aware backpackers do not have campfires and avoid camping in sensitive areas, in heavily used campsites, and near water sources. Use of a "cat-hole" for the disposal of human waste is a must. My kids were learning that by doing their share to minimize impact on the wilderness, they can help ensure that others may also enjoy a pristine experience.

The sun broke clear of the eastern horizon and captured our attention from the warmth of our sleeping bags. Sometime during the night, Cory had made her way into our tent and was quite comfortable between Joy and me. I fixed coffee without getting up, and we watched the day beckon. Again, we explored Shining Rock. As we scampered around its western slopes, I looked up to see Dylan standing precariously on a slanted rock that suddenly toppled, sending him falling, disappearing from sight. I hustled up and, peering over the outcropping, saw him sitting 20 feet below, laughing, unhurt. Another day with the gang.

We hoped to hike out to Cold Mountain that day, but by the time we traveled a short distance on Art Loeb Trail to Stairs Mountain, we decided we'd hiked enough. Hiking the trail was not as appealing to the kids as hanging around camp and searching Shining Rock for hidden treasure. Besides, they knew that tomorrow would bring a forced march back to the van. Lying around camp reading started sounding good even to this old man. Backpacking with the family had taken its toll. I wasn't sure how much more I could take. After all, I had the heaviest load to carry: making sure my family survived its adventure in Shining Rock, the wilderness of vistas.

Backpacking in Shining Rock Wilderness

WHO

Hiking the rugged terrain of Shining Rock Wilderness carrying a 30- to 50-pound pack can test your mettle. Participants should be prepared for physical exertion.

WHEN

The wilderness is open year-round, but visitors should remember that access to the upper elevations via the Blue Ridge Parkway may be blocked when the parkway is closed due to snow and ice. Regardless of what time of year you hike Shining Rock's high reaches, the weather can be quite temperamental. You should go prepared with adequate shelter, sleeping bags, clothing, food, and water.

The Shining Rock area receives a tremendous amount of use. If you really want to experience solitude, the forest service encourages you to avoid holidays and weekends. Since the area is designated as a wilderness area, groups are limited to ten people—the forest service views four to six people as the ideal size for a group.

In the old days, the Forest Service used to recommend water sources, but that is no longer the case due to various contaminants. All water drawn from creeks and springs should be run through a water purifier and boiled to prevent illness.

WHERE

Shining Rock Wilderness lies west of U.S. 276, which runs north and south between Waynesville and Brevard, North Carolina, in Haywood County. The wilderness is part of Pisgah National Forest. Middle Prong Wilderness adjoins Shining Rock to the immediate west, with the Blue Ridge Parkway marking the southern border.

HOW

Preparations for an adventure in Shining Rock or any other wilderness should be made with attention to detail. I consider the following equipment essential to any backpacking expedition:

Backpack

I use an internal-frame pack made by North Face that rides comfortably on my shoulders and has a hip belt and a chest strap that help stabilize the load and distribute the weight.

Shelter

There are no trail shelters in Shining Rock. If you plan on camping overnight in the wilderness, take a tent or tarp that you know how to erect. Rain and gusting winds are frequent visitors to the upper elevations.

Hypothermia can sneak up on the most experienced of backpackers and render them helpless. Know the signs of hypothermia, which occurs when the body temperature drops below normal because of overexposure to cold and wet conditions. These signs include difficulty in keeping pace, slurred speech, chills, uncontrollable shivering, fumbling, and drowsiness. If a member of your party is suffering from hypothermia, dry and warm the victim immediately, and give him or her hot liquids to help restore normal body temperature. Sometimes, it is necessary to strip the victim, place him or her in a sleeping bag protected from the weather, and have one of the group crawl in the sleeping bag to share body heat. I have fallen victim to hypothermia more than once in the wilderness—as in the adventure in the Upper Tellico Off-Road Vehicle Area included in this book—and have been thankful for companions who knew how to recognize the symptoms and take appropriate action.

Sleeping Bag

I've found that a sleeping bag is only as good as the pad you put underneath it. A foam pad or air mattress blocks the coldness of the earth and increases the effectiveness of the bag and your comfort tenfold. The only thing better than a Therma Rest inflatable pad is two of them. Unfortunately, the weight of an extra pad is more than I can bear when backpacking.

Cookstove

Numerous lightweight cookstoves are available in backpacking stores. In winter conditions, I use an MSR stove. This model has been proven in the worst of conditions and brings water to a boil rapidly, regardless of the altitude. The most dependable model I have in my pack is a 20-year-old Svea stove that operates without pressure by using a wick to pull fuel to the burner. This simple stove rarely fails to perform, and if something is wrong with it, I can repair it with minimal tools.

Campfires are no longer permitted in Shining Rock or Middle Prong wilderness. Again, too much damage to the natural resources has caused this restriction. Violators are subject to fine.

Don't forget to carry matches in a waterproof container—or better yet, waterproof matches. I also carry a couple of lighters for insurance.

Map and Compass

Daniel Boone is reported to have said something like, "I've never been lost in the woods. Bewildered for a few days, perhaps, but not lost." A compass and topographical maps of the area you are venturing into can help you avoid taking the wrong trail and visiting a place where you hadn't thought of going.

A map of Shining Rock Wilderness and Middle Prong Wilderness is available through District Ranger Headquarters, P.O. Box 8, Pisgah Forest, N.C. 28768 (704-877-3265).

Clothing

Foul-weather gear that can be worn over multiple layers is at the top of my clothing list. Underneath, I prefer layers of polypro to keep moisture away from my skin. A wool sweater, balaclava or skull cap, gloves, extra socks, and sturdy hiking boots provide me with adequate protection during cool conditions. For winter outings, I beef up my clothing with a down jacket. Gaiters that cover the tops of my boots and prevent moisture from soaking my socks greatly increase my comfort. Remember, you can lose up to 60 percent of your body heat if your head is exposed to the elements. The old adage "If your feet are cold, put a hat on" remains true.

Food and Water

Backpacking consumes calories and energy. A trail mix consisting of dried fruit, nuts, and chocolate is great for a quick energizer as you hike. Fresh fruit is easily carried and somehow seems tastier in the wilderness than at home. Some people prefer the freeze-dried packages of food that can be purchased in backpacking stores, but not me. Cooking a full-course meal around camp can be one of the highlights of an expedition.

Maintaining a proper level of fluid in your body is important when backpacking. I probably carry more water with me than most folks, as I can't stand to be thirsty. Boil or treat all water taken from springs. The newfangled water purifiers available on the market are designed to eliminate microscopic organisms and can prevent you from becoming ill.

One rule of back-country travel that is written in stone is this: Pack it in, pack it out. Don't destroy the allure of the wilderness by leaving trash along the trail or around your camp.

Additional Gear

I consider a camera and film part of my equipment. I also carry a notepad and pen. Binoculars are fun to use for scanning distant ridges; they can also help you determine your general location. A small flashlight can be of use when you're scrounging around in the tent in the dark, or when you have to leave the security of the shelter in the middle of the night to answer nature's call. A pocketknife, eating utensils, a small cooking pot, a first-aid kit, and a personal-hygiene bag containing toothbrush and paste, soap, a washcloth, and toilet paper complete my gear.

If you are on medication, be sure to take it with you and inform your hiking companions how often you are required to take it and how to administer it should you become incapacitated.

It's important that you understand what hiking and camping in a wilderness area really means. There are no trail markers or improvements. Be prepared for the worst and know how to read a topographical map and use a compass. When you come to a creek, you won't find a bridge.

In order to keep the area in a wilderness state, try to minimize your impact on the environment. Restore your campsite to natural conditions before you leave. Avoid camping in beauty spots. These sites can quickly become overused, spoiling the site for future visitors.

EMERGENCY INFORMATION

In a true emergency, dial 911 first.

To reach the district ranger for Pisgah National Forest, call 704-877-3265. To reach the Haywood County Sheriff's Department in Waynesville, North Carolina, call 704-452-6666.

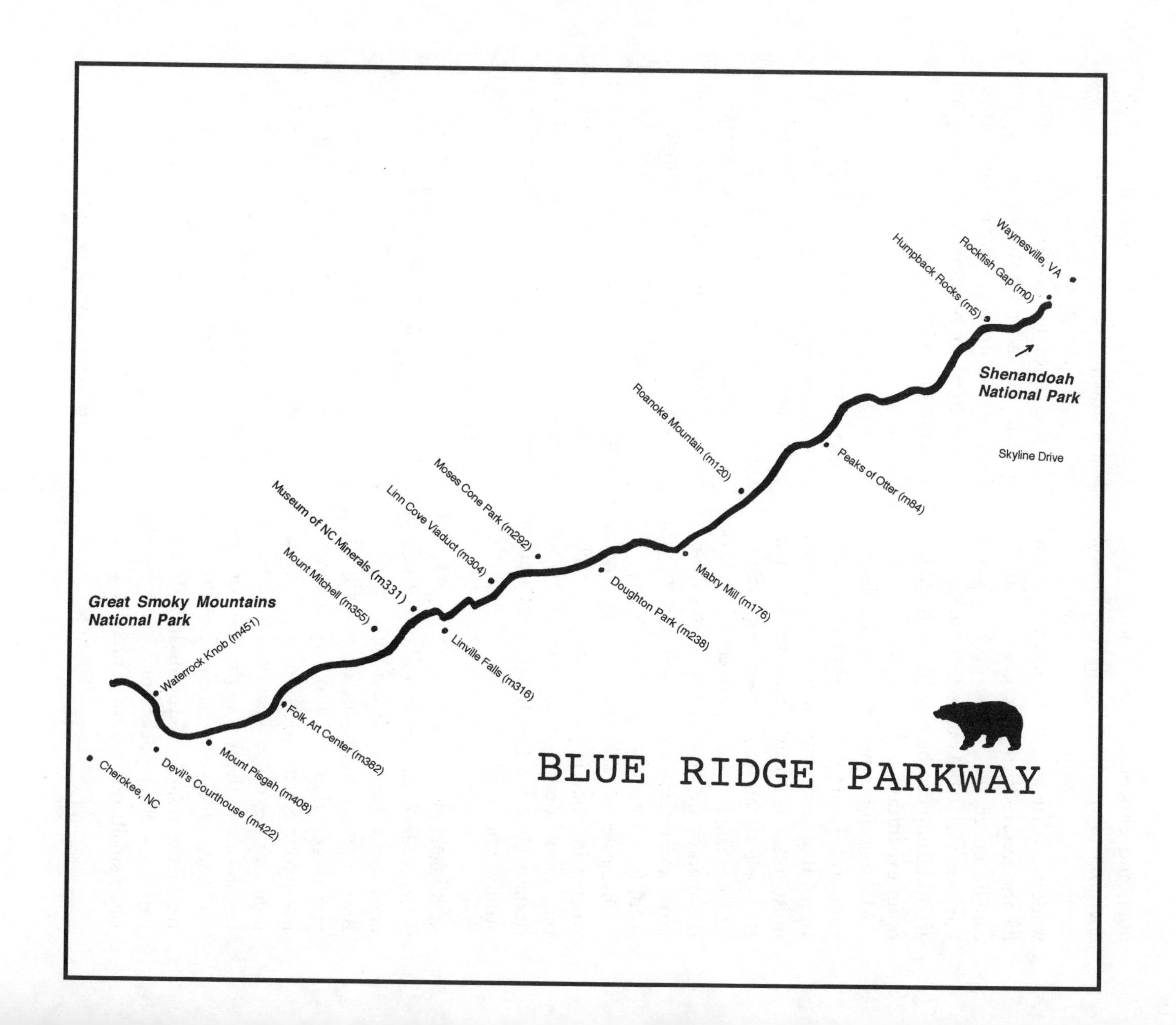
BLUE RIDGE PARKWAY
Waynesville, VA
Rockfish Gap (m0)
Humpback Rocks (m5)
Shenandoah National Park
Skyline Drive
Peaks of Otter (m84)
Roanoke Mountain (m120)
Mabry Mill (m176)
Doughton Park (m238)
Moses Cone Park (m292)
Linn Cove Viaduct (m304)
Linville Falls (m316)
Museum of NC Minerals (m331)
Mount Mitchell (m355)
Folk Art Center (m382)
Mount Pisgah (m408)
Devil's Courthouse (m422)
Waterrock Knob (m451)
Great Smoky Mountains National Park
Cherokee, NC

GOLD WINGS AND THE BLUE RIDGE MOUNTAINS

Thirty-eight degrees. Nine in the morning. The Honda Gold Wing 1100 GL was loaded. The saddlebags contained clothing, my minus-20-degree Frostline mummy bag, a Therma Rest pad, a six-by-nine space blanket to cover the motorcycle at night, a Svea cookstove, and a liter of Coleman fuel. The large lift-top compartment on the rear held food, cameras, film, extra gloves, a gallon of water, notebooks and pens, and a copy of Chilton's *Motorcycle Troubleshooting Guide*, second edition. Red Bear would start the journey there. The locked compartment over the gas tank concealed my wallet, sunglasses, a 1979 owner's guide, a small set of tools, and the gas cap. Riding directly behind my backrest, secured by bungee cords, were my North Face VE-24, complete with poles, and a sack crammed full of foul-weather gear, including my Gore-Tex action suit. I was ready. Martin was late.

I had no qualms about waiting for Martin. When he'd called at 7:45, I figured it was to say, "Have a good trip. It ought to be fun. Wish I were going along." Doyle, a Harley owner, had already backed out, after we'd juggled departure dates to ensure his participation. But Doyle marches to a different drum, if he hears one at all, and I was greatly relieved when Martin said, "I'm headed out the door." I could envision Martin Sachs cranking up his 1975 BMW R75/6 and all of Young Harris, Georgia, realizing that he was going on a ride that brisk Monday morning. Small town.

We were going to ride motorcycles the entire length—all 470 miles—of the Blue Ridge Parkway. This adventure was about places, vistas, and the people along the way. It was about friends who inspire you and the family you've left behind, if only for a few days. It was about dreaming how nice it would be to do something and then really having to do it.

After Martin arrived, we spent an hour at the Hardee's in Andrews, North Carolina, awaiting Doug Drew of Beaver Dam on his BMW R80/GS. Both Martin and Doug were experienced riders. Doug and his wife, Patricia, had done a cross-country tour several years earlier, hitting every major mountain range in the continental United States and covering over 13,000 miles. In fact, Martin's bike was the one Patricia had ridden on that trip.

My experience on motorcycles was limited. My junior year at the University of Georgia, I had owned a brand-new 1971 Honda 350 CB. By the time it had 890 miles on it, it had been wrecked three times. A bike shop gave me $75 for the pieces. I walked away alive, thankful, and owing only $900 on the bike. In 1984, I had gotten back on a motorcycle, a 125cc street-legal dirt bike, and tried riding some back-country roads. After a few spills, I gave it a rest. Until now. Needless to say, I didn't mention all this to Billy Crisp, a fellow river guide and adventurer from Murphy, North Carolina. I did a good enough job convincing him I could ride a bike that he agreed to lend me his Honda Gold Wing. All 1100 cubic centimeters of it.

My family expressed concern over my ability to ride a motorcycle the entire length of the parkway. It was suggested that we load up the van and hit some overlooks where some motorcyclists were parked. A few snapshots of me standing near a bike—any bike—and the story would be in the can. Money was mentioned. We could pay motorcyclists to let us follow them to overlooks, where I'd take a series of photos. I was reminded that I'd once written a hiking story without ever leaving an air-conditioned vehicle. I countered that that had been a rather unique situation.

My confidence was helped by the fact that Billy had no problems loaning me his bike. I had ridden 15 miles with him on the back. "Gil, anything happens to it, it's yours," he said. "Have fun."

I felt I needed the challenge of riding the parkway. It would be a personal quest. My goals were to seek adventure and survive. A good friend of mine likes the old saying, "Adventure is hours, even days, of sheer boredom and hard labor interspersed with moments of sheer terror." Another friend likes to ask, "What's adventure if you don't get dirty, get hurt, or lose something?"

Needless to say, there was tension in my family the night before I left. After I picked up the bike from Billy, I took each family member on a short ride. I was scared to death—a borrowed bike, a loved one, and a driver short on ability to control 1,000 pounds of hot, vibrating steel. A car forced Joy and me to the far right as we crested the ridge at our driveway. We shimmied down the rut and managed to stop by our mailbox. I think at that point she was glad she hadn't been able to work out child care and thus wouldn't be accompanying me. If anything happened, the kids would have one parent.

The morning of my departure, Cory, my second-grader, loaned me Red Bear, one of her favorite stuffed animals. "Daddy, I don't want you to be lonely. Red Bear will ride good, I promise. He won't take up much room, and he's real light. It will be like me being with you. Okay? Now promise!" Reluctantly, I stuffed Red Bear into the rear compartment.

Martin and I had not ridden five miles from my home outside Warne, North Carolina, before my inexperience showed. I was frozen to the bone and shaking. We stopped at Fires Creek Citgo Station, where I added clothing and motorcycle gloves to my attire. The hot coffee at the Hardee's in Andrews gave me a needed lift.

The sun grew warmer and the day prettier as we waited for Doug. When he rolled into the parking lot, I thought it was Robo Man. He was dressed in a complete set of leathers made by Hein Gericke. Designed for serious biking, these leathers had reinforced padding in the shoulders, knees, elbows, and slide pads. His bike was just as impressive. The R80/GS was a production bike designed by BMW to run in the Paris to Dakar Race, over 3,000 miles of extreme conditions. It won the first year it was entered. A wide assortment of saddlebags and tank packs complemented Doug's look. I was particularly impressed with the toe of his left motorcycle boot. It had been patched with a thick piece of leather where the gear shifter hit. He'd changed a lot of gears. You got the feeling that this guy could go anywhere on his bike. Great confidence. A man and his machine.

Martin didn't look too shabby, either, in his black leather jacket and his wool scarf thrown casually around his neck. It was only I—in a paddling jacket I'd made myself, a pair of blue jeans, and hiking boots with Vibrams—who looked out of place. Nobody would mistake me for a biker.

We blew through Nantahala Gorge, leaves billowing in our wake, and made Cherokee and the Qualla Indian Reservation before noon. A brief pit stop allowed Doug to give me some pointers about road riding: "Lean into the curves more. Always start on the outside of the curve. That way, if someone is in your lane coming at you, you're already outside. If you can see several curves ahead, you can lean in further toward the centerline. Skirt all road hazards. If you have to hit them, hit them straight. And always use your rear brake first. It's better to brake before you enter a curve than while you're in one. Power out. You're doing great."

I was feeling better. The bike was running great. We weaved our way through the congestion of Cherokee and made our way toward the entrance to Great Smoky Mountains National Park. Just inside the park, within sight of the Oconaluftee Visitor Center, the Blue Ridge Parkway turns northeast. It is the southern terminus of the parkway, Milepost 469. My goal was to reach Milepost 0 at the northern terminus, outside Waynesboro, Virginia. Doug could only ride one day out and one day back in order to make work on Wednesday. Martin's plans were vague. He wasn't feeling great. He'd have to see how it went.

We were cruising. There was no rush. The speed limit on the parkway is 45 miles per hour, and there were leaf-lookers galore. The colors were exquisite. The mountains faded from different shades of yellow, orange, and green into blue sky. The day was made for cruising. We were lucky we'd waited until Monday to ride. I could imagine what the traffic must have been like the previous weekend. As the *Asheville Citizen* reported, it was an exceptional color show that season.

The Blue Ridge Parkway was conceived in the 1930s as a means to connect two national parks—Shenandoah and Great Smoky Mountains—via a back-country road. It would follow the crest of the Blue Ridge Mountains and yield vistas to dazzle the eye. Construction began in 1935 near the North Carolina–Virginia border and was not completed until 1987, when the Linn Cove Viaduct, near Grandfather Mountain in North Carolina, opened. In 1993, more than 22 million people visited portions of the parkway, stopping at the more than 250 overlooks or camping at the 9 campgrounds along the way. Ten visitor centers are spaced along the parkway, offering everything from displays of folk art to a reconstructed log homestead to the Museum of North Carolina Minerals. And there's Mabry Mill at Milepost 176 in Virginia, a picturesque gristmill that still grinds corn, much to the delight of travelers from the world over.

We'd not traveled far on the parkway before I encountered my first test: a tunnel. When we entered, the world was transformed from brilliant sunshine and sublime colors to a cave lined with reflective flashes of yellow, red, and silver. Without warning, horns started honking, and both Martin and Doug cut loose with yells of delight. I was startled and at first thought that a park ranger was requesting us to stop. It was with relief that I saw daylight at the end.

Over the course of the parkway, there are 25 tunnels. The ceilings of some of them are coated with concrete that conforms to the rocky, irregular, blasted surface—a mogul field turned upside down. Others have been left naked, and chunks of rock occasionally drop onto the road. A few of the tunnel roofs have been lined with heavy wire mesh to prevent rocks from hitting the highway.

Later in the day, I had two close encounters of the deadly kind in tunnels. For no apparent reason, a carload of youths was stopped dead in one tunnel. It took me a moment to figure out the interruption in the reflective flashes of the tunnel. In another tunnel, I luckily deduced that the dancing reflections in front of me were not lightning bugs but bicyclists. Needless to say, I entered all tunnels cautiously and with trepidation.

As the day progressed, it was hard not to stop at every overlook and gawk. The majestic ridges of Great Smoky Mountains National Park exert a powerful call. The diversity of wildlife and flora in the Smokies makes for a biosphere unmatched in the world. At Waterrock Knob, Milepost 449, we reminisced about outings on the Appalachian Trail; about seeing panhandling bears at Newfound Gap; about skiing out to Charlie's Bunion. We then made our way north to the highest point on the Blue Ridge Parkway—Richland Balsam, 6,047 feet above sea level—and looked south and west, back toward our homes. Far to the west rose Standing Indian and Wayah Bald, local stomping grounds for this band of road warriors.

Riding toward Asheville, we saw a group scaling Devil's Courthouse, while others stood proudly atop that rocky promontory jutting out over empty air. A short distance past the haunting beauty of the Graveyard Fields, on the edge of Shining Rock Wilderness, the mammoth outcropping of granite called Looking Glass Rock compelled us to break out the cameras and burn film. I took several shots with the motorcycles in the foreground and Martin and Doug surveying the land. The day was glorious. As I climbed back on the Gold Wing, I knew I had to handle only nine more tunnels before we stopped for the night.

I was so glad to park the bike that evening that when I stepped off, I forgot to put the kickstand down. Fortunately, Doug helped me catch the bike. That wouldn't happen again.

The next morning, we had breakfast at Shoney's near Oteen. And that's where I left them. Doug had to go back. Martin decided to go with him. As I walked out

Mabry Mill in Virginia sits silent at the end of the season, but it'll grind meal again next season just like it always has.

to the bike, I was depressed and apprehensive about continuing the journey alone. Sure, riding with Martin and Doug had boosted my spirits immeasurably, but now I was solo. As I opened the rear luggage compartment, Red Bear popped out. It was like Cory telling me I wasn't alone, or like Red Bear telling me he wanted a better view. Either way, it was a sign. I snapped his legs under the bungee cords holding my tent and rain gear, and I felt better. Several people in the parking lot pointed and laughed, thinking Red Bear looked cute. Martin and Doug waved good-bye from their table on the veranda.

It was too early for the Folk Art Center at Milepost 382, so I cruised on to Craggy Gardens, hoping that the early-morning fog would be cleared by the time I got there. It wasn't. Nor had the overcast day brightened when I arrived at Mount Mitchell State Park. Mount Mitchell is the highest point east of the Mississippi, at 6,684 feet. The air was heavy. Cold found little cracks in my clothing and occasionally sent chills down my back. Once, as I came out from the lee of the mountain, a gust of wind whipped the bike violently on the exposed road. I tightened my grip and hunkered behind the windshield as I eased back on the throttle and released the cruise control. The bike, the road, the weather, and increasing traffic had my full attention. I rode with the wind in spells of fog and rain. Cold and alone.

My goal that day was to make Virginia. Over the years, my wife and I have explored the parkway in North Carolina on many occasions. We've toured the Museum of North Carolina Minerals and seen wonder in our children's eyes as they learned of the earth's riches and how man mines and uses minerals and precious stones. We've hiked Linville Gorge and camped near Wiseman's View, hoping for a glimpse of the famed and mysterious Brown Mountain Lights. We've taken the gang to the privately owned Grandfather Mountain, touring the animal habitats and the nature museum and hiking across the Mile High Swinging Bridge. We've ridden back and forth across the Linn Cove Viaduct to fully appreciate that engineering marvel. On other occasions, we've camped in Julian Price Memorial Park and cross-country skied in Moses H. Cone Memorial Park. As I cruised past all those familiar places, I drew comforting thoughts of family and friends and what the Blue Ridge Parkway has meant to me.

The miles flew by. At Doughton Park, I got gas for the bike and a hot drink. I'd already covered 150 miles. Virginia wasn't far. At Pilot Mountain View, I met Al Brunelle and his wife, Phyllis, from Bonifay, Florida. They liked Red Bear. Later, I visited with them at Mabry Mill in Virginia and traded parkway stories as we wandered around the mill site and the gift shop.

Early evening found me on the outskirts of Roanoke at Poages Mill Overlook, talking with Dan Rodriguez and Syd Dorsey as the lights blinked on in the city below. These two IBM executives were out for a cruise on Dan's BMW R100/5 and having a blast in the cool of a fading day. Two park rangers screamed by, lights flashing, and disappeared the way I had just come. Dan and I cranked our bikes and parted ways. He was going to chase the rangers, see what was up. I made for Roanoke Mountain Campground, 20 miles down the road.

I called home from the pay phone at the ranger hut and reassured the family I was okay. They couldn't believe I'd made Roanoke. I got back on the bike and went to pick a campsite for the night. Only two spaces were occupied. I picked one close to the bath facilities. I was tired as I pitched the VE-24, right after total darkness had set in and just before the moon rose. It was then I discovered that when I'd bounced over the speed bump entering the campground, the rear compartment had popped open. Things were missing. What, I couldn't tell in the dark. With flashlight in hand, I walked to the bump in search of whatever I'd lost. There, in the middle of the road, were a spare pair of gloves, a baggie containing crackers, and my wallet. Back at camp, a hot cup of tea, a peanut butter bagel, and an apple served as dinner. Utterly exhausted, I crashed for the night. It was 7:21.

I dreamed of mountains, motorcycles, tunnels, and wallets lying in the road. The city of Roanoke rumbled through the night. Occasionally, a siren injected itself into my dreams. I was always in a tunnel when it happened. I awoke at 4:30 and broke camp immediately. By 5:00, I was sitting at a service station in downtown Roanoke having my second cup of coffee and reading *USA Today*. A quick inventory of my gear told me I was missing a camera. I had to go back by the campground to get to the parkway, so I checked the area again, to no avail. Using chewing gum, I stuck a note to the side of the ranger hut giving my name and address in case the camera was found. I apologized for the gum. It was all I had.

It was a mile or so back to the parkway. In the bright beam of the headlight, I spotted a herd of deer grazing off to my left. Suddenly, a young buck was running stride for stride alongside me, less than 10 feet away. For 50 or 60 yards, we raced side by side. I was fearful that he would swerve into the Honda, and I hesitated in slowing down. When I did and the sound of the motor changed, the buck shot away and disappeared into the morning's darkness. I traveled on exhilarated, pleased with my decision to do some predawn riding.

From Pine Tree Overlook, I watched the sun break over the Peaks of Otter. A solitary bat performed its sonar flight, feeding, I suppose, in the soft morning glow. Low-lying fog engulfed the valleys and townships far below, and I sat mesmerized by the world awakening.

I ate breakfast at the Peaks of Otter Restaurant. Shortly after departing the Peaks of Otter area, I gained the highest point of the parkway in Virginia, 3,950 feet near the Apple Orchard. Within 10 miles of that point, I was at the lowest elevation on the parkway, 649 feet near the James River Visitor Center. My descent was slow. More deer lingered by the road. Several work crews were already out mowing and clearing. Patches of wet leaves covered the road in places. On a sweeping curve to my right, I lost control momentarily on leaves. It was like hitting a watery stretch where your tires hydroplane, or sliding on an isolated, nearly invisible patch of black ice. It left me with a rubbery feeling.

At House Mountain Overlook, I fed bits of bagel to a wounded pigeon. Banded on both legs, this pigeon was comfortable around humans, although it would not let me pick it up. A couple of other travelers and I agreed that the pigeon had probably been struck by a bird of prey—a large red-tailed hawk, perhaps—on its right shoulder. The right wing drooped and was virtually useless. There was nothing we could do. The pigeon had found its final

I took a short break at this overlook to rest my arms and stretch my legs as House Mountain hovered in the far distant haze. Note Red Bear, my faithful yet silent companion, bungi-corded to the Honda Gold Wing 1100 right behind the saddle.

roost. Survival. I kept that in mind as I settled onto the Gold Wing's seat and set off down the road, a bit unsettled by the experience.

At Humpback Rocks Visitor Center, I purchased Tom Anderson's *Black Bear: Seasons in the Wild.* I'd hoped to see a bear as I cruised the parkway; it was a good time of year for it. At that point, I figured Anderson's book was the next best thing to actually seeing a bear. It was something tangible I could take home and share with the family, at least.

My time on the parkway was nearing an end. Waynesboro, Virginia, at Milepost O, marks the southern end of Shenandoah National Park and the start of the 105-mile Skyline Drive. I celebrated the completion of my quest at the Exxon station at Rockfish Gap. Actually, I pondered the wisdom of my next move.

I jumped on I-64 and pushed the bike up to 70. It was different being out there with those big 18-wheelers flying by and rocking the whole bike. I flinched every time and constantly watched the rear-view mirrors. Even on a bike the Gold Wing's size, I could feel every variation in the road surface, every ridge, every pothole, every patch. I worked my way back to North Carolina and camped that night in Winston-Salem behind the office of John F. Blair, Publisher. Not only did I want to meet the people who would be working on my book, I wanted to inquire about hazardous-duty pay and life-insurance policies. An impressive lightning show brought to my attention the fact that I was camped under a nice array of electric lines. After 346 miles on the bike that day, I resigned myself to my fate and slept peacefully as the city and the storm went about their business around me.

The fourth day of the journey found me a scant 250 miles from home, but it wasn't until I got on the western side of Asheville that I really started thinking I was going to make it. I was having to stop every 50 or 60 miles to take a break. My back was sore, my arms ached, and I couldn't get comfortable on the bike. I pulled into the house just as my family arrived home from school. We quickly unloaded the Honda. Dylan jumped on the back and we rode it home to its master, stashing it in the barn at Harshaw Plantation. I left a message at work for Billy Crisp that his bike was at Milepost 0, Waynesboro, Virginia.

The adventure was over. I had ventured and gained without getting dirty or hurt. The journey had opened my eyes once again to the beauty of our country, and I was more aware of the struggles our ancestors overcame in settling that vast stretch of mountains called the Blue Ridge.

Each mile on the parkway is an adventure that awaits you. Each overlook opens new horizons. Ridges upon ridges drift into the endless sky. Hawks soar overhead. From the depths of the valleys to the peaks of the tallest mountains, their wings speak of freedom. Get on that road and ride. The experience will never leave you.

Grandfather Mountain:
International Biosphere

Daniel Boone used to hunt on Grandfather Mountain in the 1760s. He most likely knew it by its Cherokee name, Tanawha, which refers to a fabulous hawk or eagle. Rising majestically out of the Blue Ridge, Grandfather Mountain stands 5,964 feet above sea level and because of its massive rock outcroppings appears taller than any of its neighbors. Early pioneers called it Grandfather because they could make out an old man's face in one of the many cliffs. Today, guests at Grandfather Mountain can hike Profile Trail for a glimpse of that face.

Geologists believe the mountain was formed about 620 million years ago when two of earth's plates collided. Some of the rock formations on Grandfather are believed to be over a billion years old.

Over the years, Grandfather Mountain has entertained millions of visitors, including my family. As I rounded a curve in the Blue Ridge Parkway on a motorcycle in the fall of 1993 and saw Grandfather Mountain dominating the sky, I couldn't help thinking of all this mountain offers. Standing on Calloway Peak and viewing miles of mountains fading into the horizon brings soul-lifting inspiration. Hiking across the 228 feet of the Mile High Swinging Bridge is a unique thrill. Exploring the 12.5-mile trail system through a high-altitude forest, using ladders and cables to scale sheer cliffs, introduces you to a wide variety of fragile ecosystems. Witnessing black bears, eagles, and mountain lions in their natural habitat deepens your commitment to the preservation of all life on earth.

In June 1993, Grandfather Mountain was recognized by the United Nations as an International Biosphere Reserve. Of the 311 International Biosphere Reserves in 81 countries, Grandfather Mountain is the only one that is privately owned. That is significant in light of the fact that only 10 percent of the national parks in the United States are designated biospheres. Created in 1971, the United Nations Man and Biosphere Program is intended to provide a global framework for developing solutions to environmental problems. Grandfather Mountain was selected primarily because its 16 distinct habitats shelter 43 rare and endangered plant and animal species. Another important factor in its selection was the numerous scientific research programs under way on the mountain, ranging from the reintroduction of peregrine falcons to the assessment of air-pollution effects on spruce-fir ecosystems. Grandfather Mountain also offers interpretive programs for the general public and environmental education programs for schoolchildren.

In 1991, the owners of Grandfather Mountain entered into conservation agreements with the Nature Conservancy to protect the mountain and its endangered plants and wildlife. These agreements permanently protect 1,766 acres that lie above the Linn Cove Viaduct and the Blue Ridge Parkway on the south slope and another 434-acre tract on the north slope. The environmental consciousness of Grandfather Mountain's owners irked rock-climbing enthusiasts when Ship Rock, a popular climbing spot offering difficult routes, was closed to the public. But the Nature Conservancy and the land owners recognize that Grandfather Mountain is unique, with more globally rare species than any other mountain east of the Rockies. They are dedicated to preserving the area.

I remember the first time my children experienced Grandfather Mountain. We toured the Nature Museum, which includes the largest exhibit of North Carolina gold on public display, along with a replica of a tree Daniel Boone carved with the inscription, "D. Boon killd a bar on this tre 1775." We were dazzled by the displays of minerals and gems found in North Carolina, from smoky quartz to brilliant rubies.

Later, we stood 15 feet from bald eagles as we walked through the natural habitat. At first, the children hesitated to peer over the railing into the mountain lions' den, afraid of the leaping ability of cats and the sharpness of their claws. Their reservations quickly cast aside, they warmed to Mildred the Bear and her frolicking cubs. Before her death at the age of 25 on January 1, 1993, Mildred the Bear raised 10 of her own cubs and, to the amazement of wildlife professionals, other cubs she adopted when she had none of her own. As Catherine Morton stated in her booklet *Grandfather Mountain*, "She will always be remembered as the friendliest bear there ever was."

I remember how my kids' hands slid along the heavy cable—never letting go—as we swayed our way across the Mile High Swinging Bridge. They loved scrambling over the rocks and climbing the ladders up the sheer cliffs, always too near the edge for this concerned parent. We snacked on crackers, peanuts, and apples on Calloway Peak amid the spectacular backdrop of mountains upon mountains.

Grandfather Mountain is truly special.

Grandfather Mountain lies 18 miles south of Boone, North Carolina, and approximately 70 miles northeast of Asheville. The entrance is located two miles north of Linville on U.S. 221, only a mile from the Blue Ridge Parkway via the Linville exit at Milepost 305. Visitors are welcome to explore the mountain and its various attractions. An admission fee is charged.

Grandfather Mountain is open year-round, though snow and ice occasionally prohibit operation during winter. Singing on the Mountain, a nationally known gospel event held at Grandfather Mountain since 1925, takes place annually on the fourth Sunday in June. The Grandfather Mountain Highland Games and Gathering of the Scottish Clans are alive with pageantry, music, and athletic events during the second full weekend in July, luring thousands. Other special events include Nature Photography Weekend, held the weekend following Memorial Day; the Grandfather Mountain Camera Clinic, held the third weekend in August; and the Raymond Fairchild Bluegrass Music Festival, held in mid-August.

Cruising the Blue Ridge Parkway

WHO

The Blue Ridge Parkway is a national park designed for motor recreation. It is open to the public. No fees are charged to drive this scenic highway.

One outing on the Blue Ridge Parkway will lure you back again and again. Some people devote years to exploring all the nooks and crannies and photographing the Appalachian valleys, mountaintops, and people. It is truly one of America's finest roadways. A journey along this blacktop ribbon exposes you to the true character of the Southern pioneers who forged a living out of these rugged mountains and left a legacy of crafts, homespun humor, and the work ethic that helped build this country. Folks like me who live close to the parkway take advantage of its offerings frequently. I'm glad that I can say I've traveled its length on a Gold Wing and felt its breezes of endless splendor across my face.

WHEN

The majority of services, such as lodging, campgrounds, and nature programs, are available from May through October; keep in mind that camping facilities are limited during the winter months. Due to the high elevations the parkway traverses, many sections are closed in winter because of ice and snow. Cross-country skiers welcome the closing of the gates, as it provides them the freedom to ski undisturbed.

WHERE

The Blue Ridge Parkway begins south of Shenandoah National Park, near Waynesboro, Virginia, and winds its way 470 miles southwest to its terminus at the entrance to Great Smoky Mountains National Park, on the outskirts of Cherokee, North Carolina.

During your visit to the parkway, be sure to take advantage of the host of possible side excursions.

In North Carolina, Oconaluftee Visitor Center offers an introduction to Great Smoky Mountains National Park and an early 1800s Appalachian farm. Pisgah Inn is famous for its great food and views. Biltmore Estate is George Vanderbilt's famous country manor and gardens. Chimney Rock is a giant granite monolith that lords it over Hickory Nut Gorge. Linville Falls is an exquisite waterfall in North Carolina's most spectacular gorge. Grandfather Mountain offers the famous Mile High Swinging Bridge, on which visitors can sway in the mountain wind while they watch the world below. Doughton Park offers bluegrass downs and endless bluffs.

In Virginia, Mabry Mill just keeps on grinding that corn. You can see the mill grinding during regularly scheduled demonstrations. Roanoke Mountain Loop offers grand views of old Virginia. The Peaks of Otter offer three peaks—Sharp Top, Flat Top, and Harkening Hill—that will test your hiking skills and reward your efforts with endless vistas. Natural Bridge is surely one of the natural wonders of the world.

HOW

If you're planning a trip on the Blue Ridge Parkway, give yourself five days to a week for a leisurely excursion that will allow you to enjoy all the sights. Even though it's only 470 miles, it's a different pace than on the interstate. There are stretches of the parkway where you won't average 30 miles per hour, due to the curves, the spectacular scenery, and other travelers.

A comprehensive map of the parkway is provided free at the visitor centers. It not only lists by milepost the numerous highlights along the parkway, but also provides a complete list of campgrounds, visitor centers, demonstration areas, services, and activities. It is a great aid to traveling the parkway. To obtain a copy, contact Blue Ridge Parkway, National Park Service, U.S. Department of the Interior, 200 BB & T Building, Asheville, N.C. 28801.

RESOURCES

Blue Ridge Parkway: The First 50 Years, by Harley E. Jolley, with photographs by William A. Bake, is a stunning pictorial of the parkway that provides a wealth of background material. This book is currently out of print, but you might be able to find a copy at your library.

Blue Ridge Range: The Gentle Mountains, by Ron Fisher, with photographs by Richard Cooke III, depicts man's interaction with the mountains in vivid action shots. Fisher's interviews with folks who live in the shadows and on the ridges of the Blue Ridge Mountains capture the spirit of the southern Appalachians and the resourcefulness of their people.

The Blue Ridge Parkway Merchandise Catalog lists publications such as *A Naturalist's Blue Ridge Parkway, Bicycling the Blue Ridge Parkway*, and even *The Blue Ridge Parkway Video Guide*. Cassettes of Blue Ridge Mountains music are also available.

The Blue Ridge Parkway Directory is the official publication of the Blue Ridge Parkway Association, P.O. Box 453, Asheville, N.C. 28802. It supplies travelers with information about area attractions such as Grandfather Mountain, Biltmore Estate, Chimney Rock, and the Cherokee Indian drama *Unto These Hills*. Included in the directory are accurate maps of the parkway and lists of hotels, motels, resorts, and campgrounds. In 1995, the association will be publishing its 45th edition of the directory.

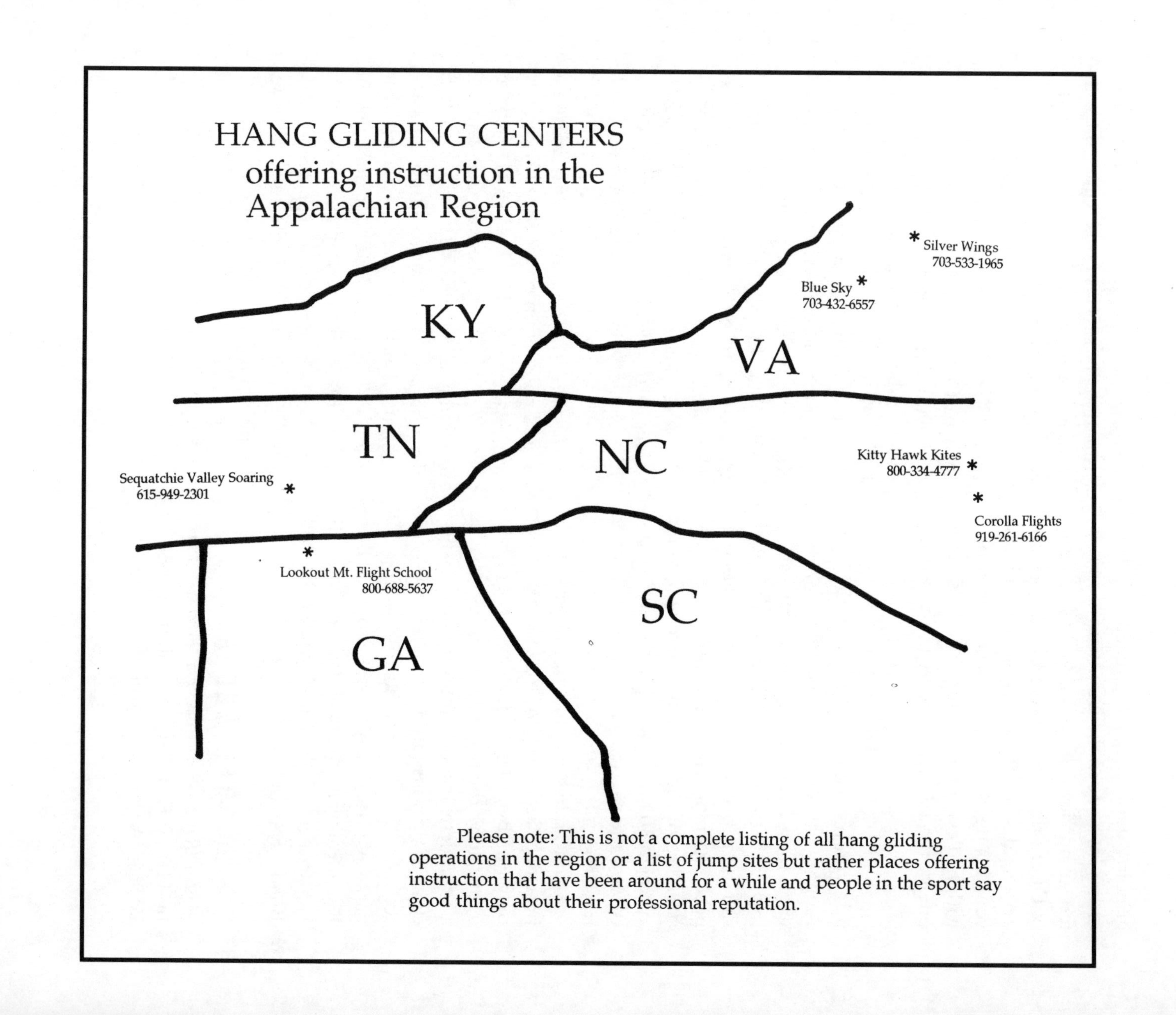
HANG GLIDING CENTERS
offering instruction in the
Appalachian Region
KY
VA
TN
NC
SC
GA
Silver Wings
703-533-1965
Blue Sky
703-432-6557
Kitty Hawk Kites
800-334-4777
Corolla Flights
919-261-6166
Sequatchie Valley Soaring
615-949-2301
Lookout Mt. Flight School
800-688-5637
Please note: This is not a complete listing of all hang gliding operations in the region or a list of jump sites but rather places offering instruction that have been around for a while and people in the sport say good things about their professional reputation.

HANG GLIDING AND THE PERILS THEREOF

Who doesn't dream of freedom from gravity? Who can stare at the sky and not see currents drifting, twirling, swirling, and spinning among the wispy clouds? Look long enough and you will feel the invitation these currents extend as they race across the atmosphere.

Imagine accepting that invitation, that challenge to extend your limits and soar with the eagles, silently performing pirouettes, swoops, and dives. There is a select group of people who literally cast their fate to the wind by launching themselves from the tops of mountains, from dunes rising out of deserts and oceans, and from cliffs buffeted by the surf of the open seas. Hang gliders are their means of escaping earth's bonds. The sky is their limit.

My quest for adventure brought me to the edge of a very tall escarpment, one that drops over 1,300 feet to the valley below. Winds gusting 30 miles an hour rushed uphill over the lip of the ridge and were instantly absorbed by the turbulent sky. Lookout Mountain Flight Park, south of Chattanooga, Tennessee, near Trenton, Georgia, was deserted. Fog rolled in and obscured the launch pad, a scant 40 feet from where we'd parked. Intermittent rain pelted the old Volvo, and wind rattled the windows.

My son, Dylan, and I were early. We'd departed our home in Warne, North Carolina, in the wee hours of the morning, while the crew of the space shuttle *Endeavor* was still rearming the Hubble Space Telescope for a better look at the outer reaches of the universe. While they worked in space, we fought heavy rains and big rigs on the four-lanes and interstates. Buzz Chalmers, director of promotions and advertising for Lookout Mountain Flight Park, had stressed the importance of being on time during our telephone conversations. Ground school started promptly at nine. All the literature I received had reiterated that central theme: Be on time on the top of the mountain. Fortunately, the directions that accompanied the brochures were excellent, and we had no difficulty finding the flight park. No way was I going to be late. Not to go hang gliding.

We got there an hour early, thus explaining the absence of activity. The nasty weather precluded any early-morning launches, and although the front was expected to pass by early afternoon, it threatened to cancel all launch activities for the day. It would not, however, affect my introduction to the sport of hang gliding. Ground school was on.

All dreams of flight start with the myth of Icarus, who flew so high that the sun melted the wax holding his wings together, causing him to fall to his death in the sea. During the Renaissance, Leonardo da Vinci prophesied that man would one day conquer the invisible currents of the air and fly. A large number of early glider pilots met their end much like Icarus, attempting to fly with the eagles. A German named Otto Lilienthal was the world's greatest glider builder and pilot before the 20th century. The Wright brothers took Lilienthal's bamboo basics a step farther in their glider experiments on the dunes at Kitty Hawk, and the rest is history.

The sport of hang gliding got its start in the late 1960s, based on the flex-wing glider designed by Francis Rogallo. In 1963, Rogallo, a NASA engineer, was experimenting with different parachute designs in an effort to devise a better recovery system for rockets when he came up with the flex-wing concept. A few years later, some brave souls decided to strap themselves under such a wing and see what happened. Dave Kilborne is generally acknowledged to have been the first person to test Rogallo's delta-wing design, off a mountain in California.

In the mid-1970s, an average of 34 deaths per year were attributed to hang gliding. The sport was in its infancy. It was unregulated. It attracted true daredevils who had little respect for mortal limitations. There were no rules. There was no national organization pushing for improved equipment, basic safety procedures, and systematic training for pilots. If you had a buddy with a hang glider and could talk him into letting you use it, all you had to do was pick a launch site and set a time. It was your funeral, so to speak.

By 1986, the sport averaged fewer than six deaths a year. The dramatic decrease was a direct result of pilots regulating themselves. What had begun in December 1971 as the three-member Peninsula Hang Glider Club, under the leadership of Dick Eipper, later became the Southern California Hang Gliding Association, which evolved into the United States Hang Gliding Association. The association even has its own monthly publication, titled *Hang Gliding*. Governed by a board of 20 regional directors, the USHGA is dedicated to promoting safe flying practices and disseminating information about the sport and advances in glider construction and flying techniques. The association has developed a training program for pilots and a rating system that denotes their skill level. In the early days of the sport, pilot skill was rated according to the "Hang System." Hang One denoted a beginner, Hang Two a novice, Hang Three a pilot of intermediate skill, Hang Four an advanced pilot, and Hang Five a master pilot. Today, the system is called the Pilot Proficiency Program and goes beyond the old "Hang System," with TOW, tandem, basic instructor, advanced instructor, and tandem instructor classifications.

Thanks to the USHGA and manufacturers, hang gliding is safer than ever. However, there is still a very real risk associated with the sport. Pilots die every year. Remember, you're throwing your fate to the wind. The vast majority of hang-gliding fatalities are due to pilot error, such as launching in unfavorable conditions or in conditions that exceed the skill level of the pilot.

Lookout Mountain Flight Park has a excellent safety record and certified instructors who take students through every phase of hang gliding. Since 1978, the flight park has provided safe, personal training for over 7,500 men and women. I was impressed with the fact that Buzz Chalmers has made over 1,100 flights and logged over 600 hours of air time since his first mountain jump in 1978. After three jumps, he was hooked and quit his full-time job as a computer programmer to be "out there with the open air," as he put it. "The natural high of flying alone, separated from the ground with nothing near you but the control bar of your glider, is unlike any other sport I ever tried. It changed my life, and I love it." From 1980 to 1985, Buzz served as editor of *Glider Rider*, overseeing the publication of 60 issues; today, that magazine, now called *Ultralight Flying*, deals with powered flight. Not only does Buzz hold his master rating, he is also certified by the USHGA as an advanced and tandem instructor, with over 230 tandem flights logged. This was the man I wanted on the control bar during my planned tandem flight.

The only other person I considered was Matt Taber, the owner of Lookout Mountain Flight Park. An avid hang-glider pilot, Matt has been a partner in the flight park since 1980 and sole owner since 1986. When he bought out the other partners, he set out to make his facility the best. Today, Lookout Mountain Flight Park is recognized as the number-one hang-gliding school in the country. Three times as many students become mountain pilots at Lookout as at any other training facility in the United States. Annually, a sixth of all mountain pilots in the country earn their wings at Lookout. Matt also has the distinction of being the publisher of the USHGA's official training manual, *Hang Gliding for Beginner Pilots.*

On the ride to the flight park, Dylan had commented, "Dad, they'll have to break out a 747 to get you airborne." I countered his observation by saying that one of the main reasons I had let him duck a day of school was that if my 210 pounds did not permit me to jump tandem with an instructor, he would take my place. I would sign the necessary waivers permitting such an event with no qualms. I now had his full attention. "Dad, I sure hope you're kidding me! I don't plan on jumping off any mountains, today or ever. You've got to do it. Besides, how can you write about it if you don't do it?"

"Surrogate hang gliding via offspring.

Haven't you heard of it? It's really hot in the publishing field right now. Older adventure writers like myself never have to subject themselves to the possibility of permanent injury. They just write up whatever happens to their kids."

Dylan didn't know whether to believe me. After a long silence, he rose from his reclining position in the back seat and started making a list. It took me awhile to realize that he was willing away his possessions in case he failed to make it home.

Shortly before nine, the flight-park crew began arriving and things started happening. Phones were already ringing as I was presented with a waiver form for my signature. I'm sure that just reading the "Acknowledgment of Danger and Release from Liability" waiver weeds out the weak of heart. But you've got to sign it if you want to jump. Buzz Chalmers freed himself from the phone to welcome us and introduce us to Daniel Jones, who would be my ground-school instructor.

The training video Dylan and I watched that morning broke down each aspect of hang gliding. We watched as a glider was slid from its protective nylon cover, almost 20 feet long. An instructor demonstrated how to rig the control bar before flipping the glider over and unfolding the wings. Performing a preflight check on all parts of the glider was deemed paramount. Establishing a systematic approach to the required preflight inspection enables students and pilots to check every aspect of the craft and its assembly thoroughly. Threads should be seen on the backside of every bolt. Every cotter and safety pin should be double-checked and all cables inspected for kinks. All parts of the control bar and other aluminum tubing should be eyed for external damage. The sail itself should be inspected for imperfections, including tears and frayed stitching. The battens that extend from the leading edge of the airfoil and give it tautness should be given the once-over to ensure they are installed properly. Finally, the pilot should perform a careful inspection of the harness that attaches him to the glider.

We continued watching as the student pilot, under the supervision of his instructor, performed a final harness check, twisting around and grabbing the steel D-ring locking carabiner to ensure that the primary and backup loops were in the D-ring and that it was locked snug. From his stretched-out position on the ground, hanging in the harness, the student checked his helmet one last time before standing up and balancing the hang glider on the outside of his shoulders. With arms extended earthward, he grasped a tube of the control-bar triangle with each hand, using a light two-finger grip. It is important not to hold the bar tightly, as that diminishes a pilot's feel for what the craft wants to do. As Daniel so accurately told me later, "You've got to let the glider fly."

One common mistake beginners have to overcome is looking down at the ground in front of them as they prepare to launch. The pilot, having already inspected the terrain immediately in front of him, must look outward with level vision and pick a spot to aim toward. This allows him to readily check his angle of attack, which is critical to launch. On takeoffs, where you run down an incline, the nose of the craft should be angled slightly above level. If it is angled downward, the nose will whack into the earth, leaving the pilot in a crumpled heap beneath the glider. If it is angled too high, the glider will stall and flip backwards on its tail. A perfect compromise must be reached in order for the wing to create lift and get the pilot airborne. Interestingly, the mixed-breed mutt that patrols the grounds of the flight park is named Whack.

In the initial stages of launch, the pilot begins walking with the glider balanced on his shoulders, maintaining level pitch, before picking up the pace into a jog, then running down the hill. As speed increases, the flow of air quickens, and the wing is lifted off the shoulders of the pilot, who leans forward slightly into the harness, still running. A few more steps and the pilot is plucked off the ground by invisible forces. He is airborne. Effortlessly, he glides across the terrain. His descent is smooth. A perfectly timed flare-out just above the surface of the field leaves him standing, smiling as the glider settles gently to earth.

The instructional film makes hang gliding appear smooth and easy. I'm sure there are people who take to the air instinctively, just as I've seen beginner kayakers know how to perform a hand roll with little or no instruction. Watching the film, I had great expectations for myself. I couldn't wait to get on the bunny hill and launch that glider into the sky.

Due to the weather, however, I got a chance to read the first four chapters of *Hang Gliding for Beginner Pilots* and expand my knowledge of the principles of flight and the things beginners must learn about hang gliding.

I learned that to progress beyond a beginner rating, a pilot must demonstrate the proper setup and preflight check of a glider and harness, make an unassisted launch with an aggressive run and a good angle of attack, and demonstrate pitch and directional control. Next comes the transition from launch to flying. A pilot must control his airspeed and be able to execute safe landings into the wind. With each successful flight, the beginner pilot moves farther up the hill, thus enabling him to make longer flights. Eventually, the beginner leaves the bunny hill for bigger ones.

Proper interpretation of wind and weather conditions is drilled into students. Brightly colored wind socks aid pilots in determining wind direction and velocity. Any obstructions that might be encountered must be taken into consideration.

When a flight is over, the beginner pilot must perform certain procedures. After

My flight instructor, Daniel Jones, demonstrates the ease of flight.

setting the glider down and unhooking, he must check both air and ground traffic to avoid any collisions. The safe removal of the glider from the landing zone and its proper breakdown and storage complete the hands-on portion of the training. Before advancing to the next level of training, the student must pass the USHGA oral exam for beginners.

Hang Gliding for Beginner Pilots is a well-thought-out publication, and the flight park is proud of the role it has played in its publication. The text is readily comprehended, and the accompanying illustrations and photos help explain the principles of hang gliding. I was interested to learn that when a glider reaches a stall angle, the nose will drop on its own in an attempt to gain speed and come out of the stall. It will literally fly itself.

After I completed my reading, Dylan and I toured the rest of the flight park. The pro shop is stocked with a wide assortment of hang-gliding paraphernalia, from helmets to altimeters to emergency parachutes. Books and magazines pertaining to the sport are everywhere. One room overlooking the escarpment serves as a classroom and video station. Snapshots of new and used gliders for sale and a wide assortment of action shots adorn the walls of the pro shop. Each photo tells the story of an individual pilot's desire to fly and speaks volumes about his or her courage and skill. A bulletin board near the coffee maker is full of letters and photos from students and pilots attesting to the flight park's elevated status in the industry. Photos of the staff at play—"And you want to fly with this guy?" one caption reads—belie the seriousness and professionalism they exhibit on the job.

Two tractor-trailer containers minus wheels sit behind the pro shop, along the edge of the ridge. They house a large number of hang gliders awaiting action. In the large, two-story workshop nearby, employees were actively performing a number of tasks. Jim Hooks, an ultralight instructor and primary tandem pilot, was helping a Kentucky man repair his damaged craft, while upstairs in the loft, Paul Mays was busy constructing a new harness system. Clark Harlow was reconstructing the leading edge of a sail spread flat on the floor, but he still took the time to explain to me that students my size train with sails measuring 220 square feet or more. I grinned at Dylan. At least it wasn't a 747. Buzz informed me later that in comparison to the sails hotshot pilots use, the craft I'd be flying was indeed a 747. Some advanced pilots use high-performance gliders that carry as little as 140 square feet of sail. That's a big difference.

The weather was still fighting us. Periods of rain mixed with heavy fog forbade any launch activity from the mountain and the training site in the valley, so Dylan and I availed ourselves of the video library there at the flight park. Watching a tape of a competition among California pilots as they performed wingovers, loops, and figure eights just above the ocean's surface left us speechless. Repeatedly, it appeared they would crash into the sea or smash into the cliffs as they executed precise aerobatics. We watched an installment of "American Sportsman" covering one man's introduction to hang gliding. His ultimate adventure was an hour-long flight off a 10,000-foot Hawaiian volcano that culminated in his missing the beach and landing short in the ocean. Unlike Icarus, he did not perish in the warm tropical waters.

After lunch, we watched the *Whack Tapes*, volumes 1 and 2, a widely assorted collection of pilots' failed attempts to land, during which they whacked the nose of their craft into the earth. Landing a glider, which had looked surprisingly easy in the training films, now gave me a nervous feeling. Although everybody appeared to survive their whacks, they took some licks that left marks on their bodies. Watching the *Whack Tapes* brought me to the realization that there was a thin line between landing a glider properly and crashing to earth. The flare-out that stalls the wing and settles the glider gently to the ground has to be executed at the precise instant at the proper height. If you push out on the control bar too soon to initiate a flare, the glider rises rapidly, only to stall and "parachute" tail-first to the earth. If you don't flare out, the glider plows a nice garden row, occasionally burying the nose in the ground and flipping the craft upside down. Fortunately, the hang gliders used for beginners usually have wheels on the control bars that help pilots avoid a nose flip. Later, my wife was greatly amused to learn that my glider had training wheels.

The weather finally broke shortly before three. As the fog and rain evaporated from the valley below, we followed Daniel Jones to the flight park's training facility, just outside Trenton. Personally, I was ready for some action, but I noticed that my "gunbearer," Dylan, was getting laconic about the situation. Knowing he needed a better-defined role, I gave him a quick review of how to operate the Nikon. It wasn't going to take me long to master hang gliding, so he'd better be quick. A few bunny-hill runs, then I was headed to the big hill, before hitting the mountain, before the tandem experience. Exuding confidence from the depths of my being, I told Dylan, "Watch. The old man is going to show you how. It'll be a piece of cake." Ignoring his uncontrollable laughter, I drove through the gate at the training site.

I liked Daniel, my instructor, even though he was awfully young. Tall, athletic, and handsome, with an easygoing disposition, he was the epitome of the young American adventurer: brave, yet possessing class, polished with a bit of humor. Twenty-four years old, Daniel had been hang gliding since a friend had gotten him started two years earlier. He had gained his instructor certification in April 1993 and had recently gotten cleared for tandem flights. His logbook recorded over 200 hours of flight.

Daniel pulled a 747—actually, a 220—out of the trailer located on the site and proceeded to instruct me in the proper assembly of the bird. After we mounted the control bar and flipped the glider over, we spread the wings and made sure everything was done to specifications. A pre-flight inspection of the craft revealed it to be ready for flight. It just needed a pilot.

First, though, Daniel demonstrated his preferred method of getting into the harness system. After I followed his lead, Daniel hooked me up to a simulator and made me go through a complete harness check before using a pulley system to lift me off the ground suspended in the harness. It felt pretty good. No problem. Just a few more steps in the learning process and I'd be airborne. I was sure of myself.

Returning to the craft, I hooked the harness system to the glider, performed a harness check, made sure my helmet was secured, and positioned myself to stand upright with the glider balanced on my shoulders. I struggled with the unfamiliar weight as I learned to walk across level ground keeping the wings on an even keel. I laughed when Daniel said it was only 70 pounds total. The wingspan was nearly 36 feet. It was rapidly becoming apparent that there was more to this sport than meets the eye in the training videos. Learning to control the pitch of the wings while jogging shook my confidence, as I came to the realization that I was not a "natural." My son's hooting and hollering at my ineptitude didn't help matters. Though I wanted to strangle him right then and there, I smiled. Show no weakness, no crack in the armor.

We walked across the quarter-mile field, Daniel now shouldering the glider, to the bunny slope. Dylan was toting two windsocks, one to place low and one for the slope's peak. I walked behind a bit awkwardly, due to the harness draped around me, and pondered what had brought me here.

Halfway up the slope, Daniel stopped and swung the glider around to face downhill. At his invitation, I stepped forward, checked the harness system, checked my helmet, and lifted the glider.

"Remember, Gil, a light grip," Daniel said. "Feel the glider. I want you to start walking down the hill. Keep your angle of attack about 15 degrees above the horizon. Then I want you jogging. Keep picking up the pace. As you feel the glider lift free of your shoulders, lean forward into the harness and pull the glider along behind you like a sled dog. Okay? You ready? Let's do it."

Together, we ran down the hill, Daniel holding onto the wing on one side. I never left the ground, but the glider did start to lift. I leaned slightly forward, as instructed. One more step completed.

Daniel carried the glider back up the hill,

and within minutes I was ready to try again. Only this time, Daniel didn't run alongside holding the glider steady. I was on my own. Everything started off okay. Soon, I was sprinting down the slope, when the wing created lift. Leaning forward, I felt my feet leave the earth. I was still trying to run. Instantly, the wing pitched left, and I spun into the ground, not even to the bottom of the hill. A solid *whack* brought the glider and me to a sudden halt. I stood up quickly, embarrassed, laughing, trying to shake it off. Daniel hauled the glider up the hill as Dylan proclaimed, "Hey! I got great shots of that, Dad. That'll look good in the book."

On my third jump, I landed on the training wheels after losing contact with the earth for at least two full seconds. I coasted to a stop, and wouldn't you know it, the nose of the glider whacked to the ground again. Two whacks. Things were not going as I'd planned.

Daniel carried the glider farther up the hill. I gamely tried to compose myself as I climbed toward him. I failed to see any humor in Dylan's comments. "You're making progress," Daniel told me, but his statement lacked conviction. I was sure he'd said that to every klutz he'd ever instructed.

I desperately wanted another run down the hill. I can do this, I told myself. Another harness check. Helmet on and buckled. I checked my angle of attack. I picked a tree across the field to aim for and started walking. A jog, then an all-out sprint down the hill. At the precise moment the wing created lift and I pulled against the harness, both of my hamstrings ripped, sending me into an ecstasy of pain. The nose of the craft rose in the air, stalled, then fell and plunged down the slope. I hung suspended and helpless as the glider landed itself and dragged me to a stop. Thank God for training wheels. My dreams of soaring in the friendly skies that day were history. The pain was intense as I hobbled along the hill. Daniel made a couple of jumps for the camera as I laboriously made my way toward the car, each step agony. It seemed so easy for him.

My gunbearer was having a field day at my expense. Dylan ended up towing the glider back to the storage facility. As he helped take the glider apart and zip it in its bag, it was evident he'd been paying attention all day.

We headed back up the mountain to the main base of operations for the flight park, Dylan now the primary driver due to my incapacitation. Glancing through the windshield, I could see some small dots in the air. On closer examination, I realized they were hang gliders flying in the vicinity of the launch site. We hustled up the mountain just as Rex Lisle was warming to the task of doing some serious mountain flying off Lookout. A former United States Army Ranger, Rex currently teaches in the Nashville area, but his thoughts were a long way from textbooks that day as he worked the gusting currents rising from the valley far below. Another pilot, Dana Dow, rode effortlessly high above Rex, meandering along the mountain and enjoying the exquisite end of the day. One instant, Rex would buzz the launch pad, missing by a few scant feet, and we'd instinctively duck as he zoomed into the void

Rex Lisle, a former Army Ranger, teaches school in the Nashville area between flights.

beyond the ridge. When he turned west after another heart-stopping swoop, Rex and his craft were silhouetted by the setting sun. Dylan and I and the other spectators watched enthralled as he circled the sinking sun one last time before turning his craft earthward and gliding swiftly to the landing site as night engulfed Lookout Valley. Just another day in the life of a hang-glider pilot.

Dylan couldn't wait to get home and share his day's experiences with the family. His reenactment of my bunny-hill flights left my wife and daughters in stitches. Joy went hysterical over the training wheels. Callie walked around giggling and whacking everything in sight. Cory unlaced my boots for me and helped me lie down. Bless that little girl, my baby.

It's taking awhile, but I'm adjusting to my new nickname. A different one follows each adventure, it seems. After my Coker Creek horse trek, the family took to calling me "Partner," until I rode a motorcycle the length of the Blue Ridge Parkway, when I became "Hog." My Tellico ORV fiasco left me with the moniker "Crash." For now, just call me "Whack." But that's okay. I'm not done yet. As soon as the black-and-blue regions below my buttocks fade and I can walk upright again, I'm going back. Buzz is waiting for me at the launch site. Look out below! I'm jumping. Forget the training program. I'm going for the tandem launch. Soon. No kidding.

Bungee Jumping: Primitive Madness

Though the male members of some South American Indian tribes have tested their manhood for centuries by jumping out of trees with only vines to stop their headlong rush toward earth, bungee jumping didn't reach the Ocoee region until the 1990s. Ocoee Outdoors was the first company on the river to set up a crane and offer bungee jumping to the public.

I was in the office at Eagle Adventure Company early one Saturday morning preparing for the day's river trips when the phone rang. Russ Miller, river guide *extraordinaire*, paramedic, cave explorer, and bungee master, was on the other end inviting me to bring all my guides down to "Double O" and experience the rush of bungee jumping free. I figured, why not? The price was right.

Imagine my surprise when I explained to my guides what an excellent opportunity had been laid at our doorstep, and not one of them jumped at the chance to accompany me. Keith and Opal preferred to go inner-tubing down the placid Toccoa River with some out-of-state friends. Darren had to mow his yard. Air T. J. was committed to baby-sitting. Shannon ducked out, explaining that his girlfriend had other plans for him. Other guides simply disappeared.

But I had an ace up my sleeve. Gator was riding with me that day. He had no choice but to pile in the car.

"As long as we're just going down to look, okay?" he said. "I'm afraid of heights."

"No problem, Gator," I assured him. "We'll just watch."

By the time we'd cruised the 20 miles to the other end of the river, where Double O operated, I was feeling young and daring. The jump site was crowded with river guides milling about awaiting their turn in the cage. Peer pressure mounted, and I finally turned to Gator and said, "I'm jumping."

His reply was unprintable.

"What's the problem, Gator?" I asked.

"If you jump, that means I've got to. I'd never live it down."

"Get in line behind me. We've got to sign the waiver forms. Standard procedure."

Silently, Gator convinced himself I wouldn't jump. He figured I'd ride the cage up, take a look, and ride it back down, thus relieving him of even having to buckle into the harness system. The Cajun boy didn't like heights—I could tell that by the sweat on his upper lip as we stood and watched others fling themselves out of the cage 120 feet above us. It was also rather discomforting to watch the ground crew move the air pillow several times in an attempt to line it up properly.

Finally, it was my turn in the cage. Gator pleaded with me not to do it. Russ started telling sick jokes. I was hooked to a bungee cord. I made sure my helmet was secured. The cage started rising from the ground. Benji, the designated jump master for the day, explained that once the cage reached its apex, he would unhook the safety line, open the door, and expect me to step out onto a small platform. At that point, I would be on my own, free to jump at my leisure.

As soon as Benji released the safety line and opened the cage door, I flung my body into the void, not even bothering to stand on the exposed platform. No way was I going to stand out there looking down and thinking about the situation in which I had placed myself. I knew that if I looked down at the tiny air pillow that had appeared so large on the ground, I would never jump.

The ground rushed toward me. Just when the cord had stretched all it was going to and the air pillow was within reach, I was snatched upward toward the cage at an unbelievable rate of ascent. A rush of adrenalin surged through my entire body, and I was filled with the meaning of life. What that meaning was, I had no idea, but I knew I was full of it. Almost before it began, the jump was over. I was lowered the final 10 feet hanging by the cord.

As I removed my helmet and reestablished contact with terra firma, I came face to face with Gator as he moved toward the cage and his date with Ms. Bungee.

"I'll get you for this, Gil, I promise. You better pay attention on the river."

With confident steps, I walked by him, headed for a beer. I had been there and done that. Gator still had to face his fears. But that was his problem. Not mine. I was a bungee master.

Hang Gliding

WHO

Although there is no established age requirement for beginner pilots, physical actions such as carrying the glider while running down a slope mandate that participants be strong and in good health. A tandem jump with a certified instructor can be done by minors, providing that parents or legal guardians sign the necessary waivers.

WHERE

The following hang-gliding centers are some of the most prominent in the southern Appalachians. For more complete listings, contact USHGA headquarters in Colorado Springs.

Lookout Mountain Flight Park
Route 2, Box 215H
Rising Fawn, Ga. 30738
(800-688-LMFP or 706-398-3541).

Lookout Mountain Flight Park offers a multitude of packages for pilots and students, ranging from the comprehensive Eagle package to programs that let first-timers get a taste for the sport.

Blue Sky
P.O. Box 212
Penn Laird, Va. 22846
(703-432-6557)

Located near Harrisonburg, Virginia, Blue Sky is owned by Steve Wendt, a veteran of 19 years of hang gliding and an instructor for 11 years. Steve has a Hang Four rating, with solo, advanced tandem instruction, and TOW certifications. Blue Sky offers sail repair and harness construction and represents three manufacturers.

Sequatchie Valley Soaring
Rural Route 2, Box 80
Dunlap, Tenn. 37327
(615-949-2301)

Soaring, catching thermals, and rising high into the sky are the ultimate goals of all glider pilots. These guys can instruct you step by step until you develop the advanced skills that can take you into the far reaches of the sky.

Though it is a long way from the Appalachians, the area around Jockey's Ridge, North Carolina, is the number-one hang-gliding spot on the entire East Coast. With its high dunes, strong winds, soft sand for landing, and historical connection to the gliding experiments of the Wright brothers, this region's importance to the sport cannot be downplayed. If you are in the area and would like a first-class introduction to hang gliding, contact Kitty Hawk Kites (800-334-4777) or Corolla Flights (919-261-6166).

WHEN

Some training centers operate year-round

and fly when the weather permits. Contact the center near you for up-to-date information and specific course schedules.

HOW

The USHGA publishes an information handbook for hang-glider pilots that offers insight into the sport and the skills required. It outlines the pilot proficiency program in detail. The USHGA also oversees the selection of United States hang-gliding teams and conducts regional and national competitions to strict standards. For information, contact United States Hang Gliding Association, P.O. Box 8300, Colorado Springs, Colo. 80933 (719-632-8300, fax 719-632-6417).

RESOURCES

Hang Gliding magazine is published monthly by the USHGA. The organization also publishes *Paragliding*, which is devoted to that aspect of nonpowered flight.

Peter Channing's *Hang Gliding for Beginner Pilots*, published by Matt Taber, is available from Lookout Mountain Flight Park.

GREAT SMOKY MOUNTAINS NATIONAL PARK
BLACK BEAR HAVEN
Gatlinburg, TN.
I-40
Foothills Parkway
Sugarlands
Davenport Gap
The Loop
MT. LeConte
6593'
Cades Cove
1800'
Elkmont
The Chimneys
AT
Newfound Gap
Charlie's Bunion
Thunderhead
5527'
Clingman's Dome
6643
AT
Chilhowee Lake
US 441
Shuckstack
3824'
Blue Ridge Parkway
Joyce Kilmer-Slickrock
wilderness
Oconaluftee
Cherokee, NC
US 129
Fontana Lake
Bryson City, NC
NC 28
AT
Nantahala National Forest

PHOTOGRAPHING THE BLACK BEAR, SYMBOL OF THE SMOKIES

The black bear, a shy giant, has come to symbolize the heritage of the Great Smoky Mountains.

I hiked countless miles with friends, family, park rangers, and bear hunters in my quest for an eye-to-eye encounter with a black bear. I saw the marks left on trees where black bears had ripped the bark clean off the trunk searching for grubs and other tasty morsels. I saw bear scat so fresh on a cold mountain morning that steam still rose from it. I ran with strike dogs as they were loosed on fresh scent, and found myself alone and out of breath as the entire pack bounded out of range. And I have had several close encounters with black bears that left me speechless, marveling at their agility and quickness.

The southern Appalachians have an abundance of plant life that supports a wide range of mammals, of which the black bear is king. Many mammals that once roamed these mountains—such as the gray wolf, the river otter, the American elk, and the mountain lion—fell prey to the pressures of hunting and trapping and disappeared. Currently, river otters are being reintroduced to Great Smoky Mountains National Park. But the black bear never left. Each year, millions of visitors vacation in the park with the hope of seeing a black bear up close in the wild. The black bear has so far managed to survive the pressures of hunting, habitat loss, drought, poaching, and four-lane highways that block access to its range. Whether the black bear avoids extinction in this region is dependent upon man.

Years ago, my good friend John Gibney and I were driving his Chevy Luv truck up Tusquitee toward Bob Allison Campground in a remote section of Clay County, North Carolina. We rounded a curve in the road and spotted a dark, massive shape nearly a quarter-mile away, at the end of a long straight. John stopped the truck and shut it off. We sat silently in the middle of the road, trying to determine just what critter lurked ahead.

At first, we thought it was a large hunting dog or a wild boar, but as it started running down the road in our direction, we knew we were seeing a black bear. We sat in stunned silence as it picked up speed down the road, unaware of our presence. A scant instant before slamming into the truck, the bear just happened to look up and note the object blocking its path. With the smoothness of a NFL tailback slanting toward an opening in the line, it angled right and missed colliding with John's truck by inches. The driver's side mirror exploded into fragments of glass and metal, with no apparent effect on the bear. It stopped and looked eye to eye at John before issuing a territorial growl and disappearing up the steep bank into a thicket of laurel and rhododendron. We sat with our mouths open, wondering what would have happened if that massive chunk of wildlife hadn't swerved. It probably would have totaled the truck.

One of the most exciting and informative hikes I've taken in recent years was in the winter of 1993 with Lawrence Robinson, a park ranger in Great Smoky Mountains National Park and a longtime friend. Raised in Bryson City, North Carolina, on the edge of the park, Robbie has worked with the National Park Service for over 20 years in a variety of positions. When he learned of my interest in black bears, he volunteered one of his days off to share his knowledge and help me learn to recognize bear sign.

We met at his house near Fontana Lake early one morning. First, we took a quick drive across Fontana Dam, where Robbie showed me a cherry tree that black bears had decimated in their efforts to eat all the fruit it had produced that season. You could see where they had climbed the trunk, ripped branches off the tree, and tossed them to the ground, where they could eat at their leisure. I mean this tree had taken a lick, a bear lick.

Next, we made our way to Twentymile Ranger Station, where we parked and started hiking up the creek.

The black bear is the largest native mammal in the Smokies. Bears generally weigh between 200 and 300 pounds, although some large males exceed 500 pounds. Great Smoky Mountains National Park contains a low elevation of 860 feet and a high elevation of 6,643 feet, and bear sightings have been recorded at all elevations. And despite their reputation for hibernating, bears have been sighted during every month of the year. Southern black bears den and enter a deep sleep but are not true hibernators. Warm spells and extreme cold can cause them to rouse and move about. Disturbed from a deep sleep, a black bear can become fully alert within minutes.

Prior to the colonization of America, the black bear had free range of the entire East Coast. In North Carolina alone, the black bear has seen its range drop from 49,000 square miles to fewer than 2,000 square miles. It now inhabits 24 western counties and 28 coastal counties. Big-game tag reports for the 1992–93 North Carolina hunting season indicate that 1,059 black bears were harvested in 41 counties.

In mountainous regions, bears prefer large hardwood forests with a thick cover

Finding comfortable sleeping quarters is no problem for this cub.
Photo by Hugh Morton

of laurel and rhododendron thickets. Recent biological studies have concluded that a typical male black bear in the southern Appalachians ranges over 15,000 acres, but that sows keep closer to home, ranging over 3,000 acres. Although black bears have been known to live 26 years, their average life expectancy in the wild is 10 to 12 years.

Recognizing bear tracks is fairly straightforward, due to the fact that they have five toes with claws and large foot pads. The track of a six-month-old cub is normally larger than that of any other large animal. The hind track of a bear resembles that of a man, in that it is long and narrow. The front track is about as long as it is wide. Expert bear trackers can often tell a bear's age and gender by the size of its tracks.

Being creatures of habit, bears often step in their old tracks on trails leading to water or to feeding areas that they use frequently. Rocks that have been rolled over indicate that a bear has been searching for insects. And logs or old stumps that have been torn apart are good signs of bears foraging for food. Interestingly, a bear will strip the outer bark from a tree to feed on the cambium layer, which leaves the tree prone to dying because it has been girdled. Robbie showed me the difference between claw marks on a tree and tooth marks made by bears. It has been speculated that bears leave tooth marks, normally five to six feet off the ground, as territorial markers.

Robbie kept throwing facts and observations about bears at me as we hiked the trail up Twentymile. This trail is typical of the park's biosphere, with its rhododendron and mountain laurel, free-flowing water, and boulders littering the creek bed and mountainside. We hiked amid this spectacular scenery, gaining altitude on Shuckstack and seeing bear sign in abundance. Confident that Mr. Bear was waiting patiently around the corner, I carried my camera poised for a photo opportunity.

Although all the books classify black bears as carnivores, Robbie informed me that they eat just about anything. Early in the century, the mast of the American chestnut was a staple in the diet of black bears, but by 1940, the chestnut blight had decimated the trees, forcing bears to depend more on acorns. Bears are also known to eat blueberries, strawberries, huckleberries, wild grapes, pokeberries, persimmons, blackberries, grasses, and fruits such as cherries.

I recollect one journey into the Smokies

Treed
Photo by Danny Heatherly

with my parents in the early 1960s. We spied a small black bear not far from Newfound Gap tearing a yellow jacket nest apart and eating it. Evidently, the stings of the yellow jackets had no effect on the bear. In fact, I was amazed to see the bear raise its paw to its mouth and eat some of the yellow jackets swarming around him. After finishing with the yellow jackets, the bear wandered up the slope and disappeared into the brush, apparently not susceptible to anaphylactic shock. No problem. Just a good treat.

Panhandling bears have been a problem in Great Smoky Mountains National Park ever since it was formed. Coming back to North Carolina one day across Newfound Gap, I was forced to stop my car in a traffic jam because three bears were on the road begging food and entertaining tourists. I finally got out of my vehicle and watched as people flocked dangerously close around the bears. One man wearing a bright-blue polyester jumpsuit ignored his wife's repeated demands that he leave the bears alone and walked right up to one of them, stuck out his hand, and offered a piece of white bread. He screamed in pain as the bear raked his forearm with its powerful claws in its attempt to get the food. Blood flowed freely down the centerline. Immediately, the spectators eased back, giving the bears a wide berth. About that time, a park ranger arrived on the scene and took control of the situation. Within a few minutes, the bears ambled into the forest and traffic resumed moving on U.S. 441.

I rode the remaining 20 miles through the park silent and angry. Not only was I mad at that particular tourist for his actions, but also at myself for not stopping him. Hopefully, he and the other sightseers learned a valuable lesson: Don't mess with the wildlife. When bears are rewarded for panhandling, it can become a way of life for them, with the result that they can end up being labeled a nuisance. Instead of foraging in the woods in their natural manner, they become dependent on man for food. They start to hang out in campgrounds, going through garbage and ill-placed food baskets and coolers. Rangers are then forced to relocate them deeper into the wilderness in an attempt to minimize contact with man. Sometimes, bears have to be destroyed, and when that happens, we have all lost something valuable. If you feel the urge to feed a bear, go to Cherokee, North Carolina, where the Tribal Council permits commercial operations to keep bears in cages. For 50 cents, they'll sell you a bag of peanuts or dog food that you can toss into the cage.

There are no known predators of the black bear other than man, his automobiles, and black bears themselves. Females breed every other year, with cubs usually being born in January or February. Newborn cubs are extremely small at birth, weighing less than a pound. Normally, they den with the sow under a rock ledge or in a hollow log until late March or April, then stay with their mother for a year and a half to two years as she wanders the forest scrounging for food. Males have been known to kill young cubs because sows with cubs will not mate. In addition to freeing sows for mating, aggressive adult males may kill cubs to eliminate potential rivals to their territory.

Of the 17 subspecies of *Ursus americanus*, the American black bear, the subspecies found in Great Smoky Mountains National Park is *Ursus americanus americanus.* Although black bears may actually vary in color from black to brown to blue to even white, bears in this region normally have black fur and a brown muzzle. A white patch around the chest or shoulders is not uncommon.

Years ago, David Allen, a biologist with the North Carolina Wildlife Commission, mistook a black bear for a Rottweiler while hiking in the Valley River Mountains on the edge of the Fires Creek Bear Sanctuary, nears Andrews, North Carolina. Thinking that the best thing for him to do was to scare the dog off, David yelled, stomped his feet, and charged, arms waving, only to discover his mistake. That was no Rottweiler on the trail. The she-bear turned, rose, and began making blowing noises. Her hackles were raised, her teeth bared.

"I thought to myself as I came to a sudden stop, 'Hold your ground,'" David remembered. "All I could hear is me and that bear expelling large amounts of oxygen. That's when I saw the two cubs in the tree just off to her left. I was in deep trouble. She charged, and I ran. When I'd stop, she'd stop. And this went on for quite a ways. It caused me some fear. For a while afterwards when I'd go into the woods, every black stump or shadow behind a tree was a black bear. Unknowingly, I had placed myself in a dangerous position. All that she-bear was wanting to do was get me away from her cubs. I had invaded her territory, and she was defending it."

By the time Robbie and I reached Shuckstack Tower after our hike up Twentymile, I was exhausted and a bit disappointed that Mr. Bear hadn't already shown up for the photo session. We ate lunch at the base of the tower as a fog settled in, limiting our vision to a few hundred feet.

As we sat there, I told Robbie that I wanted a bear encounter like David Allen's.

He replied, "Well, our best bet is to get off the trail and go cross-country. We'll work our way out Twentymile Ridge south toward Sheep Knob and eventually drop down alongside the creek. We might stumble up on one. Try to walk quieter, Gil. That'll help our chances. Oh, and keep that camera ready. If we see one, I bet it won't be for long."

We left the trail and bushwhacked through sawbriar as thick as your thumb. It grabbed at us with sharpened needles, some almost an inch long. We took our time, moving carefully over the rocky, gnarly, thicketed terrain. Numerous small-game trails crisscrossed the ridge line. Heavy bear traffic was evident.

We finally broke into old-growth forest. Robbie started wandering from dead, standing trees to hollow logs, peering into their shells. He kept looking up into the trees. "Our best bet is to catch one denning or up in a tree," he explained. "Be alert. Hey, did you ever hear the tale about two guys getting chased by a bear and one stopping to change out of his boots into running shoes? His buddy stops, amazed, and says, 'What in the world are you doing? You can't outrun a bear!' His friend looks up at him and says, 'You're right. But all I have to do is outrun you!' Look, Gil, once we find this bear, it's yours. Take all the photos you want. I'll get out of your way. Don't worry about me. And listen, if the bear charges you, whatever you do, *don't run*."

We continued southward, following the ridge line. The scenery unfolded in multiple directions. The basin forming Twentymile Creek lay to our west. To the south and east, we got glimpses of Fontana Dam, with the lake spreading out eastward.

Robbie had almost reached the crest of a knoll when we heard loud grunting noises and furious activity coming from over the edge. We were both standing there frozen when a humongous and upset black bear bounded into the foreground, snarling and expressing his—or her, I didn't have time to check for such particulars, and neither did Robbie—displeasure. We had caught him sleeping, catching a few scant winter rays in a slight saddle on the ridge. Our footsteps had alerted him. He was not a happy camper, and there were no moats, bars, or chain-link fences keeping him from tearing us apart.

Caught off-guard, I raised my camera and snapped a quick shot. Robbie stepped back as I tried to move around him for a clear view. With fluid movements, the bear halted, growled, and then suddenly bolted over the side of the ridge. Somewhere in there, the camera clicked again as I fired my second shot blind from the chest in the bear's general direction. By the time I advanced the film a second time, brought the camera to my eye, found him in the frame as he crashed downhill, tried to focus, set the f-stop, and pushed the shutter button, he was gone. From the time we heard the grunting until the encounter with Mr. Bear was over, 10 seconds may have passed.

We stood atop the ridge and stared down the mountainside, impressed. Witnessing the agility of a large black bear in the wild brought our situation into clear focus. The terror you feel in your heart and soul in the face of such raw power is unforgettable. Needless to say, our adrenaline was flowing. It took us a few minutes to resume the hike. Occasionally, we stopped, looked at each other, and shook our heads in disbelief.

We saw bear sign constantly as we headed downhill. Finally, after sliding over steep descents and picking our way through several boulder fields, we started hitting the branches feeding Twentymile Creek. We traversed hillsides under a thick canopy of forest and fought through rhododendron so thick that I lost sight of Robbie several times. But I could hear him. All of a sudden, I was not encouraged by seeing bear sign in such a close environment. This was their turf, not mine. I made a lot more noise than necessary to let those bears know I was coming. I felt better when we hit Twentymile Trail. I knew that while I might not have any good photos of Mr. Bear, I had a bear tale to tell.

Although the black bear is not an endangered species, long-range predictions about its continued presence in the southern Appalachians are hard to make, according to Gordon Warburton, leader of the North Carolina Wildlife Commission Black Bear Project.

Warburton feels there are three important keys that will determine the fate of the black bear.

First and foremost is people's attitude. Without public support, black bears may be eliminated in this region.

Loss of critical habitat is the second major key to the bears future. Many parts of the southern Appalachians are being developed with second homes, golf courses, and shopping centers, all of which consume thousands of acres that black bears once ruled. Interstate highways and road construction restrict the bears' access to prime habitat. Numerous bears are lost annually on the highways. Hunting black bears has been a way of life ever since man discovered that he could use the plentiful meat for food and the hides for clothing and shelter. Proper management of hunting seasons and increased crackdown on poaching can help protect the bear population.

And the third critical key is the ability of the black bear to adapt to man's intrusions.

Since the 1700s, the black bear has disappeared from many regions east of the Mississippi as our population has expanded. A range that was once wide and undisputed is now severely limited. A combination of poor masts for several years running and continued record bear harvests like North Carolina's 1992–93 season could throw the population of black bears into a downward spiral.

To see a black bear roaming free in the wilderness is an event that can evoke a wide range of emotions, from fear to jubilation. The chance that such encounters may occur is one of the things that calls me to venture into the mountains. It is the call of the wild. May the black bear always be more than just a symbol of the Smokies.

Riding the Rails of the Great Smoky Mountains

A Great Smoky Mountain Railway excursion train enters the 836-foot-long Cowee Tunnel.

Photo by Lavidge & Associates

We boarded the Great Smoky Mountain Railway as the conductor hollered, "*All aboard!*" A light mist was in the air in downtown Bryson City, North Carolina, lending a mystical touch to this adventure into yesteryear. Exploring the train—from its massive engine to its open-air cars to its enclosed coaches—was quite the ticket for my younguns. The engineer tooted the Great Smoky's horn and we chugged slowly out of Bryson City, heading west toward the Nantahala Gorge.

If you stop to reflect on the history of our nation, you have to consider the impact of trains in opening the West. No doubt, the early settlers rode toward the sunset on wagons and horses to stake claims all the way to California, and fought Indians every step of the way. But if wagons opened the door to the wild, wild West, railroads kicked it in. Towns grew up alongside the tracks, and if a kid didn't want to be a cowboy, he surely wanted to be the engineer who got those wheels clicking down the track.

By the time we traveled less than half a mile out of Bryson City, rain hit us hard.

Naturally, we were riding in the open car directly behind the engine. Within minutes, we were soaked. Lightning and thunder rocked the Great Smoky and added to the suspense of the ride. The chief engineer, Steve Keplinger of Murphy, North Carolina, stopped the train and, with the help of his crew, assisted passengers caught in the open cars to the shelter of the coach cars. My gang declined, hanging on in the rain as the train picked up speed and barreled into the heart of the storm.

The Great Smoky clickety-clacked along the edge of Fontana Lake, with the ridge line of Great Smoky Mountains National Park providing a natural attraction for the lightning flashing out of the darkened sky. We waved to the folks braving it out in houseboats tied along the lake's bank. Even from our distance and the relative safety of the train, we could feel their concern. Several bass boats were charging across the rough water toward the security of the boat dock. Ducks were seeking shelter.

Then suddenly, we were through it. The storm was history, and panoramic views of the Great Smoky Mountains flashed across our northern flank. Soon, we saw recreational boaters zooming up and down the lake again. Several ran alongside the train, their occupants exchanging banter with people aboard the train until the lake narrowed and blocked their passage.

Entering Nantahala Gorge from its northern end, we crossed the river and headed upstream. For many passengers, it was their introduction to the world of whitewater paddling. Kayakers, canoeists, and rafters littered the river, performing various feats of daring. We watched as one group of boaters repeatedly paddled upstream out of an eddy into Nantahala Falls, where they immediately got trashed by the water's crunching force as they attempted to execute enders, pop-ups, and pirouettes. Many of the paddlers performed Eskimo rolls, righting their kayaks after they had flipped upside down. Others showed us the infamous "wet exit" and their techniques for self-rescue.

One couple I talked to on the Great Smoky had been rafting on the Nantahala the day before and just happened to see the train with all its sightseers cruise past. At the end of their whitewater run, they had made a few inquiries and a phone call and booked themselves passage on the Great Smoky.

The tracks on which the Great Smoky Mountain Railway runs were laid in 1891. Building the railroad was an enormous task. Scores of men died in its construction. A flatboat ferrying convict workers to the Cowee Tunnel capsized in the Tuckasegee River on December 30, 1883, and 19 men locked together in chains drowned in the swift waters. Legend has it that the tunnel is haunted by the ghosts of those men, who were buried in an unmarked grave on a hillside nearby.

The Great Smoky Mountain Railway started operation in the summer of 1988 with a few excursion rides and very few passengers. Progress was rapid. In the summer of 1993, over 160,000 people rode the tracks. Today, the railway operates five locomotives—four diesel-electric engines and one steam locomotive, No. 1702—on 67 miles of track between Dillsboro and Murphy. No. 1702 gained fame for its role in World War II with the Army Corps of Engineers. It was later featured in the Paramount movie *This Property Is Condemned*, which starred Robert Redford, Natalie Wood, and Charles Bronson. More recently, the Great Smoky Mountain Railway was used in the train scenes of the 1993 movie *The Fugitive*, which starred Harrison Ford and Tommy Lee Jones. Many local residents served as extras in scenes such as the staged train crash.

Malcolm MacNeill, chief operating officer and majority stockholder of the Great Smoky Mountain Railway, is confident that the railway has a secure future. It provides visitors with an exciting adventure that combines nostalgia with panoramic views of lakes, rivers, and mountains. The railway descends through beautiful valleys, chugs over towering trestles, plunges into tunnels, and ascends a steep grade to a high-altitude gap. The company has hosted over 700,000 riders with no serious injuries. Its employees are genuinely concerned with visitors' enjoyment and well-being.

The Great Smoky Mountain Railway kicks off each season with weekend excursions starting in early April and begins offering weekday outings following Memorial Day weekend. Trips are scheduled into December.

The excursions originate in four western North Carolina towns: Dillsboro, Bryson City, Andrews, and Murphy.

The trip from Dillsboro follows the Tuckasegee River to Bryson City and travels through the 836-foot-long Cowee Tunnel, hand-dug by convict labor over 100 years ago. This is a three-hour excursion with a 45-minute layover in Bryson City.

The 4½-hour Nantahala Gorge trip starts in Bryson City and crosses Fontana Lake on a trestle 180 feet high and nearly 800 feet long. Visitors cruise in view of the Smokies and alongside one of America's most popular whitewater rivers, the Nantahala.

The Valley River excursion travels from Murphy through the Konehete Valley to the Nantahala Outdoor Center. This full-day experience lasts six hours.

The Red Marble Gap excursion is a shorter, four-hour version of the Valley River excursion. It pulls out of Andrews and follows the same piece of track alongside the headwaters of the Valley River, crossing Red Marble Gap at Topton before descending steeply into Nantahala Gorge and the Nantahala Outdoor Center.

A complete schedule detailing specific excursions, vacation packages, dates, and departure times can be obtained from the Great Smoky Mountain Railway by calling 800-872-4681. Fares vary depending upon the trip selected. With the ever-increasing popularity of the southern Appalachians as a vacation destination, the railway encourages advance reservations. Get your ticket in hand and be ready when the conductor proclaims, as only he can do, "*All aboard!*"

Go for a ride on the Great Smoky. You'll love it. We did.

Photographing Black Bears

WHO

With the cameras available on today's market, including point-and-shoot 35-mm cameras and throw-away panoramics, anyone can take photos with excellent color, contrast, and depth of field that's in focus. I started off using a 67 Nikon F that required you to manually advance the film, select shutter speed and f-stop, and adjust the focus prior to shooting. Today, my primary camera is a Nikon FE. Light and durable, with manual and automatic modes and various lenses, this camera has served me well despite being subjected to repeated bashings. For a backup camera, I carry a Nikon EM because its lenses are interchangeable with those of the other Nikon. I carry one camera loaded with color film and one with black-and-white. Regardless of what type of camera you use, getting a shot of a black bear in the wild isn't easy.

WHEN

Black bears are most active and visible during the summer months, when they forage at all elevations for soft mast. In late fall, bears are often found in mature hardwood stands loading up on acorns for the long winter ahead. The vast majority of bear sightings occur at dusk or near-dusk.

Although they are said to have poor eyesight, black bears have a keen sense of smell. They have been known to swim half a mile to raid a camp's frying pan. Mark and Lisa Skomp of Murphy, North Carolina, were vacationing at private facilities one summer. Hoping to attract a black bear, they poured a bit of grease on a rock right outside their cabin on the edge of the lake. Hours later, they wandered down to the bathhouse beneath a full moon. On their return to the cabin, they found a huge black bear engrossed in licking the rock clean. It blocked their entrance to the cabin for an hour and a half. When the bear finally quit licking the rock, now worn smooth, Mark and Lisa had no idea which way it had departed. All the shadows looked menacing as they made a dash for the cabin's door.

Like Mark said, "The thought of doing it, pouring the grease on the rock, came from my deep desire to see a black bear. I didn't really expect it to happen. The night before, some friends had startled Lisa and me by jumping out of the bushes at us, growling and pretending to be bears. For us to be standing on the edge of the lake under a bright moon with our paths blocked by a 300-pound bear was a different matter. An hour and a half is a long time to stand perfectly still. If seemed like forever."

WHERE

Many biologists feel that the key to the black bear's survival in the southern Appalachians is Great Smoky Mountains National Park. Kim DeLozier, wildlife biologist for the National Park Service, estimated that the population of black bears in the park as of January 1994 was in the 400 to 500 range.

A favorite area for bear sightings is Cades Cove, in the northwestern portion of the park. Cades Cove swarms with visitors during the summer months, like all parts of the park, but if you get up early enough and tour the cove's beautiful fields and woods before the masses awaken, you might be rewarded with your own bear encounter. Or try near dusk, when the whippoorwills sing and the owls hoot.

Bear sightings are common traffic stoppers—and headaches for park rangers—along U.S. 441 as it winds south from Gatlinburg, Tennessee, over Newfound Gap and toward Cherokee, North Carolina.

Bears are also known to frequent the shelters along the Appalachian Trail, hoping for handouts.

Note that camping permits are required in Great Smoky Mountains National Park for the use of all back-country primitive sites and shelters. Ice Water Springs Shelter and the lodge on Mount LeConte attract more than their share of black bears. Make reservations far in advance.

HOW

Rarely do black bears make themselves available for photo sessions—unless of course you're snapping shots through the chain-link fences down in Cherokee. You have to beat the bushes and be extremely lucky to get a good, clear shot of a black bear in the wild. A telephoto lens is a necessity. I normally carry a camera equipped with an auto-winder that can click through a roll of 24 exposures in a matter of seconds. Since it wasn't working properly when we went on the Twentymile hike, I left it at home.

If you want to get in some practice before you go into the woods, I recommend visiting Grandfather Mountain, North Carolina, and touring the natural habitats, which harbor black bears, eagles, white-tailed deer, and mountain lions. There, you can test your steadiness in a controlled environment behind the security of a protective barrier. (For additional information on Grandfather Mountain, see "Grandfather Mountain: International Biosphere," included in the "Gold Wings and the Blue Ridge Mountains" adventure.)

However you choose to approach your

This decaying tree trunk is a remnant of a once thriving stand of American chestnuts.

photography expedition, respect the wildlife and know that you are a two-legged intruder in the bears' natural world. No hunting or guns are permitted in Great Smoky Mountains National Park. Violators are arrested and fined, and their guns are confiscated. Penalties for poaching within the park are severe and can include prison terms.

Black bears are powerful and can inflict immense damage with one swipe of their paws. Keep a safe distance from all bears and do not attempt to pick up cubs or otherwise get between a sow and her cubs. Bears will commonly make a show of growling and charging with their hackles raised and their teeth bared, only to stop 10 to 15 feet away.

For a short distance on level ground, a bear can outrun a quarter horse. Most experts will tell you not to attempt running from a bear, as it shows fear; chances are you can't outrun it anyway. Danny Heatherly, a bear hunter from Cruso, North Carolina, told me that if you have to run, run up a hill, the steeper the better. Bears have difficulty going uphill, due to their short forelegs. Personally, I've seen bears scramble up steep banks so rapidly I wondered if I could have outrun them. I do know I would have been sufficiently motivated to try.

And don't forget that black bears, with their sharply curved claws, can climb trees with ease. I am always impressed when I see other photographers' shots of massive bears balanced high in trees on branches no bigger than my wrist. When I hike these days, I constantly scan the trees, looking up, hoping I get a chance at such a shot. I hope you get yours, too.

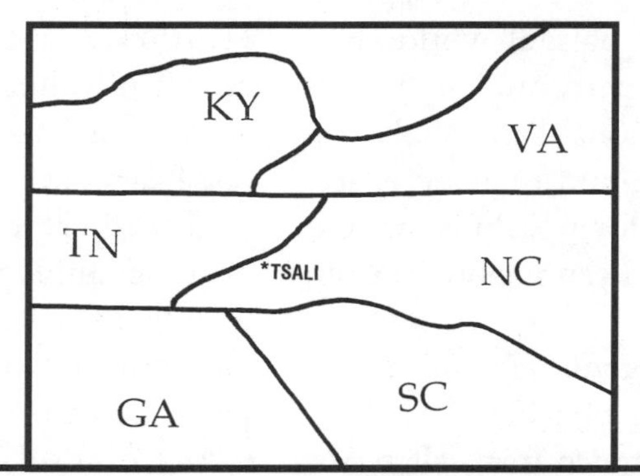
KY
VA
TN
*TSALI
NC
GA
SC

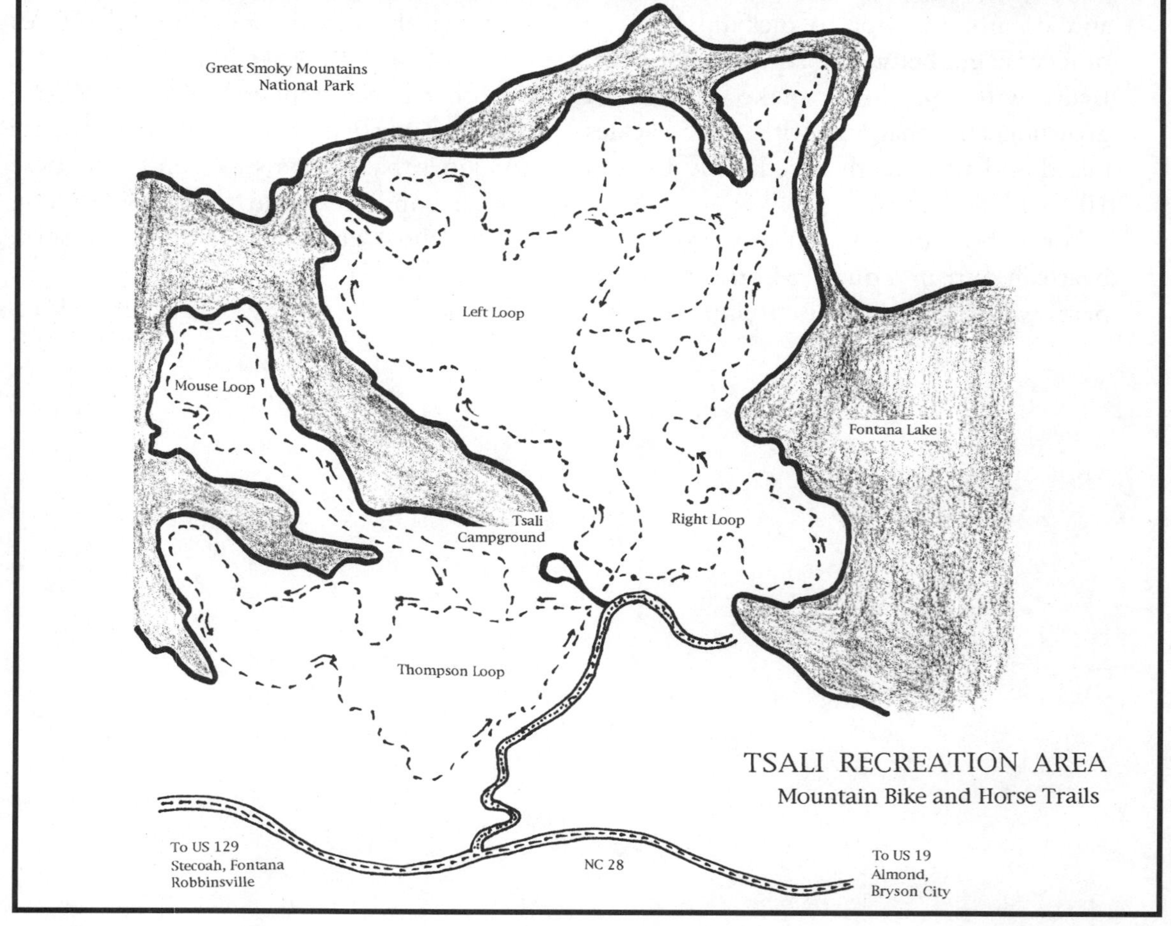
Great Smoky Mountains
National Park
Left Loop
Mouse Loop
Fontana Lake
Tsali
Campground
Right Loop
Thompson Loop
TSALI RECREATION AREA
Mountain Bike and Horse Trails
To US 129
Stecoah, Fontana
Robbinsville
NC 28
To US 19
Almond,
Bryson City

MOUNTAIN BIKING TSALI

The evolution of the modern bicycle began in 1816, when Baron Karl von Drais hit the roads around Karlsruhe, Germany, on his "Draisene," also called a "Hobby-Horse." Without pedals, brakes, or much in the way of handlebars to aid him, the adventurous baron sat on a saddle mounted between two wooden wheels and propelled himself forward by pushing with his feet. To stop, he simply dragged his feet. Even though it was expensive, awkward, and heavy, the Draisene caught on with the public. Soon, sporting events were being sponsored by numerous clubs around western Europe.

One hundred and seventy-eight years later, Callie, my 11-year-old daughter, and I hit the trails around Tsali Campground on the edge of Fontana Lake, riding the latest link in the evolutionary chain: mountain bikes. Tsali Campground is located south of the Great Smoky Mountains National Park, approximately fifteen miles west of Bryson City, North Carolina, off N.C. 28.

Since I had never had the experience of riding a mountain bike, I was fortunate to have such a good companion. Callie is an excellent athlete who has spent countless hours honing her biking skills on the roads and in the woods around our home in Clay County, North Carolina. The trail system that my kids have laid out around our 10 acres includes Quail Cove Trail, Fox Run, and Dog House Loop, none of which is rated below difficult. In fact, I refuse to try them.

Callie was tremendously excited about the prospect of riding new, unexplored terrain. The afternoon before our departure, she washed her bike, checked the air in her tires, and had me adjust her brake calipers to ensure her ability to prevent the bike from plunging downhill off the mountainous trails we'd be traversing. We fiddled with the height of her seat, raised the handlebars on her 10-speed Mountain Storm, and performed a final check on her helmet and straps. Afterwards, she packed lunches, filled water bottles, and selected her riding attire. By seven that night, she was ready to go, even though our departure was planned for first light the next day.

We pulled out of the driveway early the next morning on what promised to be a beautiful January day, even though the temperature hovered around 28 degrees. The forecast for the western mountain counties of North Carolina called for a high of 55, winds out of the northwest at five to 10 miles per hour, and mostly sunny conditions. This forecast was extremely positive considering the weather we had endured the past eight days. Sub-zero temperatures, freezing rain, hail, and snow had forced school closings throughout the entire region all week. Treacherous road conditions had kept us frozen atop our ridge, where we hiked and played when we weren't huddled around the wood stove or snuggled beneath a pile of blankets. It was still cold and brutal, but Callie and I were anxious for our adventure.

I had hoped to get a thorough introduction to mountain biking from an accomplished rider and author on the subject, but that plan fell through. I also tried to get my good friend Tim "Gator" Meador on a mountain bike, but he'd had enough of my great adventures—and his "honey-do" list had finally caught up with him, too. It was just Callie and I.

Our first stop was Robbinsville, North Carolina, where we connected with Rick Ardolino. Rick had agreed to loan me his Ross mountain bike, a 15-speed rig complete with rear rack, water bottle, flexible mirror, and air pump. I rode it around the parking lot at Graham Ford just to make sure everything was operational before loading it in the back of the pickup with Callie's bike.

A few minutes later, we cruised by Stecoah Gap and hit N.C. 28, heading east toward Almond and Tsali Campground. We were glad to see that the gravel road leading off N.C. 28 back to the campground was open. I'd figured that with all the inclement weather, the road would be closed and we'd have to begin our mountain-biking experience at N.C. 28.

Callie and I were surprised to find we were not the only bikers out that day. Numerous cars and vans equipped with bike racks were already parked around the entrance to the campground, and folks were busy making last-minute adjustments to their bikes, loading water bottles and lunches, and stretching.

One of the groups we talked with that morning at Tsali was a gang of students from Western Carolina University, led by Charles Chancellor. This hardy band of seven bikers was going to ride both Mouse and Thompson loops. Charles and his wife, Liza, pointed out different attributes of the bikes. Center-pull brakes. Built-in shock absorbers on the front forks. Twenty-one different gears, activated by Shimano derailleurs and quick-acting shifters. These bikes were mountain-ready, and so were the riders. Charles and Liza pulled a tandem mountain bike off their rack, the first one I'd ever seen. Just before they slipped past the gate and down the trail, Charles confided that "between me and the Mrs., it's the only time I have total control. I've got the brakes, the gears, and the handlebars."

"Good luck, Charles," I thought to myself.

Mountain bikes differ greatly from standard touring bikes, starting with the tires.

Clingmans Dome rises in the northern horizon behind Callie at this high point on the Thompson Loop.

Mountain bikes have knobby, two-inch-wide tires, compared with the smooth, one-inch tires on touring bikes. Twenty-one to 24 gears are standard for mountain bikes. Top-of-the-line mountain bikes have shock absorbers that are part of the frame. Mountain bikes weigh five to 10 pounds more than their cousins and have a top speed of 40 miles per hour, versus 55 for conventional touring models.

Gary Fisher is known as the father of mountain biking. In 1974, he took a beach cruiser with fat tires, high handlebars, and a single gear and converted it to a 15-speed clunker. The mountains of Marion County, California, became his test site and the trails his refuge. Soon, he was building custom bikes for friends and customers, and Fisher Bikes was born. Today, Fisher Bikes is part of the Trek company, and Gary is still out there hyping the sport and coming up with new and better products.

Callie and I rode past the gate and made our way along the old roadbed to the intersection where Thompson and Mouse loops split. Logging operations had left the roadway a mess. We hung a left and descended along the narrow trail that marks the beginning of Thompson Loop. Immediately, we saw indications of the damage inflicted on this whole region by the blizzard of 1993. Crews had been forced to clear the trail of broken rhododendron, crushed by the weight of the snow. Along portions of the trail, sharp stubs rose out of the ground. Callie and I kept our speed slow due to my concerns for safety. I could just see one of us getting thrown over the front of our bike and being impaled on a rhododendron stub. Not a pleasant thought.

Thompson Loop is named for David Thompson, a wilderness ranger with the Cheoah Ranger District. David died on March 31, 1992, in a tragic one-car accident on N.C. 28 not far from Tsali. His car plunged off the side of the mountain. He was not yet 30. A wooden sign dedicating the trail to his memory stands at one of the highest points on the loop, with panoramic views of Great Smoky Mountains National Park and Clingmans Dome, rising to the north.

Callie led us rapidly along the trail, fording numerous small branches, ducking under the trunks of fallen trees, laughing and hooting the whole time. We rode quickly along the edge of one of the many finger coves of Fontana Lake. Houseboats littered the steep banks, "dry-docked" by the low water level in the lake. They had an abandoned aura about them. Come summer and the rising waters of Fontana, these homemade floating cabins would once again serve their masters as a retreat from urban reality.

When we tackled the uphill portion of the loop, leading away from the lake, Callie suggested that I try another gear. I was still in fifth and, yes, it was easier in first, although I had to peddle faster to cover the same distance. Soon, I was walking my mountain bike up the hill and shedding layers of clothing.

We hit a short downhill run, and just as I caught up with Callie, she bounced over a log in the trail, which threw her off balance and set her on a course to go plunging down the mountainside, off the trail. I lunged to my right and managed to stick my hand through the spokes of her rear tire. With my arm jammed between the tire and frame, Callie was left pointed straight down a 45-degree slope, balanced perfectly on her bike. Gently and with great care, she dismounted, crawled up the bank, and collapsed on the trail. "Boy! That sure was close. Thanks, Dad," she said.

For the rest of the ride, I was in pain. My right hand and forearm ached from being wedged. Luckily, I hadn't broken anything, but handling the bike over rough trail, frozen ruts, and patches of ice was difficult at best. But as we passed the sign honoring David Thompson, my spirits were lifted by the vast scenery of uncluttered mountains.

After six miles of riding, my thighs were trembling from the exertion. Our final ascent on the loop was marked by rapidly thawing earth and ruts from logging trucks.

A newly completed mile-and-a-half section of Thompson Loop avoids the gravel road leading back to the parking area and contains a fast, exciting descent before making a sharp switchback onto a narrow, demanding trail. Callie hit a particularly muddy hole and flipped headfirst over the front of her bike, landing face-first and

Mountain bikes are the new kids on the block. More than 90% of all new bike sales in the United States are mountain bike designs. Note the shock absorbers located behind the center pull brake on the front fork.

spread-eagled on the trail. I was greatly relieved when she rose laughing, mud splattered across her nose, chin, and forehead. Her spirit unharmed, we continued speeding effortlessly down the trail to the end of our journey.

Upon our return home, Callie disappeared downstairs as I was relating our day's adventure to the rest of the gang, only to return a few minutes later with a written report—titled "Biking"—for my inspection:

The best part of the biking trip was that I was with my dad. My dad's a neat character. You'd just have to know him the way I do. Sometimes I don't like my dad to come to social events like dances, banquets, and other things because he's still living in the 1950's. He's just a big baby in a grownup body. But sometimes it is nice to be alone with your father.

On the trip we forded about 12 or 13 little branches. Some places we had to go under trees. Sometimes we had to get off and walk our bikes up steep, icy mountains or down steep hills. My daddy saved me once and another time I got mud on my face when I hit my front brake and the bike threw me off. The whole point of this story was to tell everyone I had a great time with my dad mountain biking.

In two paragraphs, Callie captured the essence of our mountain-biking experience and warmed her father's heart. Tsali marked a change in our relationship. No longer was Callie an offspring to be dragged along on expeditions, but a full-fledged, field-tested adventure companion. Already, she is planning new adventures for just the two of us. She has made me promise to take her parasailing. There is no doubt in my mind that mountain-biking Tsali was the dawning of a new day in my life, just as it was in Callie's.

Mountain Biking

WHO

Anybody who has a bike and a hankering for an experience of a different nature can participate in this sport.

The National Off Road Bicycle Association (NORBA) encourages mountain-biking etiquette that takes into account the rights of others. NORBA guidelines are as follows:

1.Yield the right of way to other nonmotorized recreationists
2.Go slowly when approaching or overtaking others, and let them know you're coming in advance
3.Control your speed at all times, and anticipate someone coming around the bend
4.Stay on designated trails; do not trample native vegetation; minimize erosion by not using muddy trails or short-cutting switchbacks
5.Do not disturb wildlife or livestock
6.Do not litter; pack out what you pack in; pack out even more if possible
7. Respect public and private property; leave gates as found
8. Be self-sufficient; let your destination and speed be determined by your ability, your equipment, the terrain, and present and potential weather conditions
9. Don't solo when "bikepacking" in remote areas; leave word of your destination and when you plan to return
10. Practice minimum-impact cycling, taking only pictures and memories and leaving only waffle prints
11. Always wear a helmet when riding

WHEN

It was late January when Callie and I rode in Tsali. Patches of ice and frozen creeks lent a unique air to our adventure. Experienced mountain bikers tell me that it's a hoot to ride in freshly fallen snow or hard rain because of the added element of danger due to lack of control. Those conditions do not appeal to me, a fair-weather peddler.

Once Callie and I started biking that cool, crisp morning and our bodies heated up from the exertion, we were forced to stop and shed layers. It was actually a great day for riding, with the temperature preventing us from sweating much at all. The absence of insects is another plus for winter riding. When it's hot, muggy, and buggy, I prefer paddling the river to hiking or biking mountain trails.

WHERE

The opportunities for mountain biking in the southern Appalachians are numerous. They include designated trails such as Tsali and gated and closed Forest Service roads. Mountain bikes are prohibited on trails marked "Foot travel only," such as the Appalachian Trail and the trails in Great Smoky Mountains National Park.

HOW

Beg, borrow, or buy a mountain bike, pick a spot, hop on, and enjoy the ride. Being a tightwad, I always try to use somebody else's equipment to check out a new sport. That way, I don't spend a lot of money for gear I won't ever use again.

Mountain bikes are not cheap. A decent unit that will get you into the sport can be had for around $250 or $300. But don't be fooled. A good bike costs $600 to $1,000, and super jobs are out of sight. Mountain-bike rentals are a growing industry. Check the yellow pages for listings. If you choose to go the rental route, you can try your luck on knobbies for as little as $20.

In far western North Carolina, the Nantahala Outdoor Center Outfitters Store is one of the major suppliers of bikes and accessories. The NOC sponsors the Knob Scorcher Mountain Bike Races, held over a five-mile closed loop around Nantahala Village; this annual event is sanctioned by NORBA. Open seven days a week year-round, the outfitters store rents 21-speed mountain bikes starting in late March. For information, contact NOC Outfitters Store, 13077 U.S. 19W, Bryson City, N.C. 28713-9114 (704-488-2175).

A division of the Nantahala Outdoor Center, Adventure Travel promotes fall mountain biking in the Smokies and rents 21-speed mountain bikes for its domestic tours. For information, contact NOC Adventure Travel/Cycle Tours, 13077 U.S. 19W, Bryson City, N.C. 28713-9114 (704-488-2175, ext. 333).

Euchella Mountain Bikes is located approximately 10 miles west of Bryson City on U.S. 19/74 past Nantahala Village. It offers half-day and full-day guided trips, complete rental service, and domestic and international adventure tours. Guided trips include instruction, van shuttle, high-quality mountain bikes, safety gear, and some of the best cycling in America. For information, contact Euchella Mountain Bikes, P.O. Box 177, Almond, N.C. 28702 (800-446-1603, April through August, or 704-488-8835).

In the Boone/Blowing Rock area, the following establishments offer new bike sales, touring information, rentals, repairs, and accessories: Boone Bike & Touring, 899 Blowing Rock Road, Boone, N.C. 28607 (704-262-5750); Rock & Roll Sports, 280 East King Street, Boone, N.C. 28607 (704-264-0765); and Magic Cycles, 208 Faculty Street, Suite 1, Boone, N.C. 28607 (704-265-2211).

Tsali Campground and Appletree Campground are located in the Cheoah District of Nantahala National Forest. These campgrounds are closed during the winter months, and camping spaces are hard to obtain during the summer months. Fees are charged. For information, contact Cheoah Ranger, U.S. Forest Service, Route 1, Box 16-A, Robbinsville, N.C. 28771 (704-479-6431).

The following are privately owned facilities in the area: Freeman's Cabins and Motel (704-488-2737); Lost Mine Campground (704-488-6445); Nantahala Outdoor Center (800-232-7238 or 704-488-2175); Nantahala Village (outside N.C. 800-438-1507 or 704-488-2826); and Turkey Creek Campground (704-488-8966).

RESOURCES

If you're seeking specific, detailed information about mountain-biking trails, I highly recommend Lori Finley's series,

Mountain Biking the Appalachians, published by John F. Blair, Publisher. Tsali and other trails in Nantahala National Forest are covered in her book on the Highlands-Cashiers area. The other volumes in the series cover Brevard-Asheville-Pisgah Forest trails and trails in northwestern North Carolina and southwestern Virginia. These books will tell you everything you need to know to plan your trip, and what to expect when you get there.

Off the Beaten Track: A Guide to Mountain Biking in Western North Carolina, by Jim Parham, available from WMC Publishing, covers combination rides (single-track, gravel, and pavement), gated Forest Service roads, paved roads, and the Tsali mountain-bike trails.

OLYMPIC INFORMATION

There will be a mountain-biking competition in the 1996 Olympics in Atlanta. A 70-kilometer dirt trail at the equestrian venue in Rockdale County, Georgia, will host separate fields of 40 men and 40 women. Tickets will be issued by the Atlanta Committee for Olympic Games. For ticket information, contact Games Services, 250 Williams Street, Suite 6000, P.O. Box 1996, Atlanta, Ga. 30301-1996.

EMERGENCY INFORMATION

I failed to see a telephone in Tsali Campground. To reach a phone, travel back to N.C. 28 and head east toward Almond and Bryson City, North Carolina. Several phones are available along this section of highway. Call 911 in Swain County for a true emergency.

The nearest hospital is Swain County Hospital in Bryson City, a good 15 to 20 minutes away.

Swain County Sheriff's Department
Box 1398
Bryson City, N.C. 28713
704-488-2197 or 704-488-2196

Swain County Hospital
45 Plateau St.
Bryson City, N.C. 28713
704-488-2155

Swain County Emergency Medical Services
Main St.
Bryson City, N.C. 28713
704-488-6655 or 704-488-2601

Cheoah Ranger District, USFS
Robbinsville, N.C.
704-479-6431

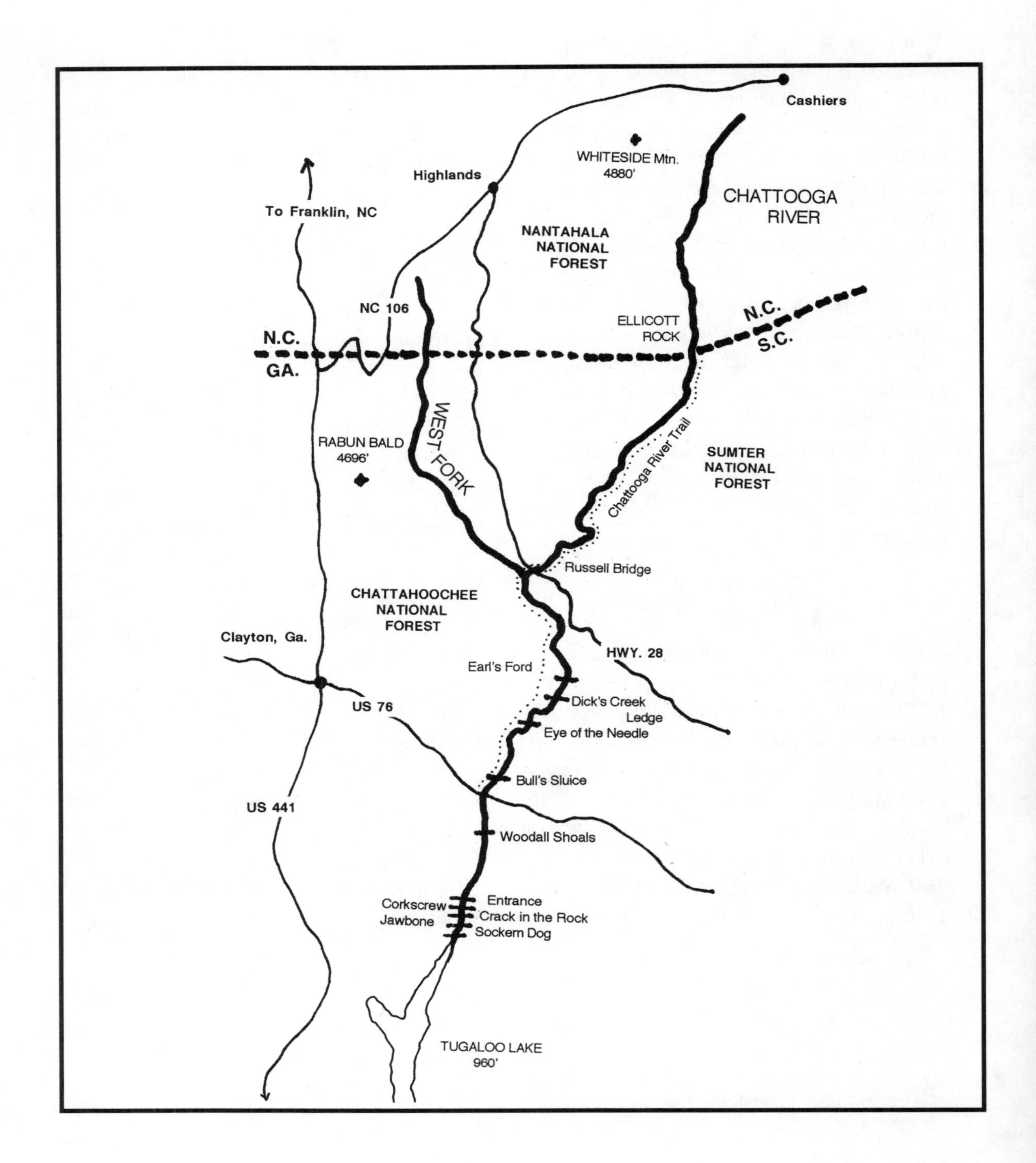
Cashiers
WHITESIDE Mtn.
4880'
Highlands
CHATTOOGA
RIVER
To Franklin, NC
NANTAHALA
NATIONAL
FOREST
NC 106
ELLICOTT
ROCK
N.C.
S.C.
N.C.
GA.
WEST FORK
RABUN BALD
4696'
Chattooga River Trail
SUMTER
NATIONAL
FOREST
Russell Bridge
CHATTAHOOCHEE
NATIONAL
FOREST
Clayton, Ga.
HWY. 28
Earl's Ford
US 76
Dick's Creek
Ledge
Eye of the Needle
Bull's Sluice
US 441
Woodall Shoals
Corkscrew
Jawbone
Entrance
Crack in the Rock
Sockem Dog
TUGALOO LAKE
960'

DELIVERANCE ON THE CHATTOOGA

It was August 1974. A heavy mist engulfed the old farmhouse at the edge of the highway just across the South Carolina border. Mummified figures lay scattered on the porch and throughout the house, belching and snoring, oblivious to passing vehicles and the light patter of intermittent rain. I stirred, uneasy, and made my way around the side of the building to the outhouse. Nobody moved. The sun had yet to announce the arrival of another day at the river. Something kept nagging at me, but I couldn't lay my finger on it.

Within 30 minutes of my awakening, the farmhouse bristled with activity. Bob Boatknight scrambled around the kitchen abusing pots and pans—just like he did first-year river guides—and proceeded to cuss breakfast into happening. Cowboy coffee and oatmeal—burned, sprinkled with sugar, and soaked in butter—stuck to our ribs and was quick and dirty. All the guides were up and hustling to finish their personal morning rituals. Sleeping bags were thrown carelessly in a corner. Packs lay in walkways. Gear was strewn about as if a plane had crashed in the middle of the room. Nobody had time for neatness.

Boatknight gave out assignments as if his hangover was our personal cross to bear. "Let's get those rafts sorted and loaded, people. This ain't no summer camp. Let's move."

The Chattooga River runs south out of the mountains of western North Carolina and serves as the border between Georgia and South Carolina. One of the last free-flowing rivers in the Southeast, it drops over half a mile from its start near Whiteside Mountain through 60 miles of rugged terrain to its terminus at Tugaloo Lake. It lay virtually undiscovered until the early 1970s. James Dickey and *Deliverance* changed all that forever. After Burt Reynolds and John Voight starred in the movie based on Dickey's novel, the river lured thousands to see its spectacular beauty and to try their luck on its currents. Between 1970 and 1975, some 17 people died in its turbulent waters, dangerous undercuts, and powerful hydraulics. As of March 1993, a total of 29 lives had been lost on the Chattooga. I was almost a Chattooga River statistic myself, but I escaped. Barely.

In 1968, Congress passed the Wild and Scenic River Act, which was designed to save America's vanishing waterways. To be protected under the act, a river had to be classified as either wild, scenic, recreational, or a combination of the three. The *wild* designation means that a river is basically unpolluted, has no dams or development along its course, and is accessible only by primitive trails. Rivers classified as *scenic* are similar to *wild* rivers but are accessible by road. *Recreational* rivers have some development and pre-existing impoundments.

When Congress designated the Chattooga a Wild and Scenic River in 1974, some 40 of the river's 57 miles were classified as *wild*, two miles as *scenic*, and 15 miles as *recreational.* A protective corridor extending roughly a quarter-mile from each bank prohibits development along the Chattooga, preserving 15,432 acres.

The Chattooga is one of America's truly wild rivers. When the river is flowing strong, paddlers from around the world come to the Chattooga to experience its beauty and test their skills against its powerful and demanding waters.

I was already headed out the door of the farmhouse when Boatknight yelled for me to help with the rafts. I'd been around long enough to know what was expected of me and the other first-year guides. We were assigned extra duty as part of our indoctrination into the world of whitewater rafting. The glamour of being a whitewater cowboy had long since faded. My life jacket no longer had its new, shiny color, and my guide knife was starting to show signs of rust. There is a lot of hard and nasty work that comes with the territory of being a raft guide. Rafts are heavy and require a remarkable amount of attention.

As I made my way to the flatbed truck used to haul the rafts, I was surprised to see Tom Bolin and Donny Dutton, two veteran guides, already out there sorting the black Zodiac rafts in the dim morning light. Payson Kennedy, the founder of the Nantahala Outdoor Center, showed up about the same time I did. Charlie Walbridge got a hand in on the task. This was a bit unusual. I couldn't understand why all the old hands were paying such close attention to each raft being selected for the day's run down Section IV. But I listened.

"The river's running high," Tom Boland explained. "Last check, it was running 2.3 and rising. If it keeps raining, it could reach three foot by the time we reach the Five Falls."

"Number nine's got a slow leak in the thwart. Leave it," somebody ventured. That raft was unceremoniously thrown off the truck.

"Hey, who used this raft yesterday?" Boatnight asked. "How'd the seam get ripped? Damn! That must have happened loading it. No way it could have made it down the river. Somebody will have to fix this raft tonight. Charlie, you and Gil fix this boat after we get back. We've got to have it ready for Sunday's trip."

"No problem," Charlie Walbridge said.

Great. Instead of going into Clayton, Georgia, with the guides that night, I'd get to spend it with Charlie. I was also concerned about the river. I couldn't recall having guided on Section IV at that high a water level.

Since there are no dams or impoundments along the Chattooga's course, the flow of the river fluctuates with changing weather conditions. During dry conditions, the flow is low. If it has been raining heavily, as was the case that month, the river exceeds its normal flow, as runoff from steep mountain slopes drains into its bed.

Located downstream of the U.S. 76 bridge, on the South Carolina side, is a measuring station that records the river's flow in tenths of a foot. Each morning of a scheduled run down Section IV, a guide is assigned to drive down to the bridge and check the gauge. Where U.S. 76 crosses the Chattooga, the river is wide and gentle in appearance. It invites the unsuspecting to throw an inner tube in its languid pools and gently flowing waters and spend the day drifting lazily downstream.

Unbeknownst to those ignorant of the river's true nature, a tenth of an inch measured on the gauge represents a potential foot of flow at Five Falls. Just a few tenths of an inch change the nature and appearance of the river dramatically. In the Five Falls area, the channel is compressed from a width of over 150 feet to a scant 10 to 12 feet in places. It gets thrashed over boulders and squeezed by steep canyon walls in its turbulent race toward the Atlantic Ocean, resulting in class V-plus rapids. That's why the Chattooga is considered the best white water in the Southeast. No other river touches its combination of scenic beauty and heavy-duty rapids.

The Chattooga had already gotten my attention.

I had seen the result of an inner-tuber getting caught in the hydraulic at Woodall Shoals. His body's release from the depths of the ledge after high water flushed him out was a constant reminder to me of the river's overpowering strength.

A kayaker's fatal mistake, refusing a safety rope and trying to swim with his equipment over the far left spillover at Crack-In-The-Rock, had left a family bereaved of a father and husband. It left this rookie guide asking why and stunned that it happened so quickly. One instant he was alive, the next a statistic.

Those deaths were on my mind as I helped load the rafts on the truck. Six of us grabbed our paddling gear, helmets, life jackets, knives, river shoes, and spray jackets and headed for the put-in on the back of the truck.

The Chattooga is divided into five sections.

The headwaters of the river, which flow out of the North Carolina mountains just

Gil and his group drop into the massive hydraulic at the bottom of Sockem Dog, the last major rapid on Section IV.
Photo by Bruce Nelson, Photocrafts

south of Cashiers, are designated as Section O. It is a wild mountain stream fed by hundreds of tiny tributaries, and by the time it reaches Ellicott Rock Wilderness Area, it is a river of great beauty. Boating is not permitted in Section O. Hiking is the only means for exploring the area. Whiteside Mountain looms over the headwaters at 4,930 feet. It is the site of the highest sheer cliffs—nearly 2,000 feet tall—in the eastern United States.

Section I of the Chattooga is the West Fork. It is marked by the merger of three major creeks: Overflow, Holcomb, and Big creeks. The upper three miles of this seven-mile run are inaccessible and are not paddled very often, although I have heard tales of "hair boaters" dragging their gear into Overflow Creek when the water is high. The lower four miles of the West Fork are easy paddling, marked by two rapids—Dam Sluice and Big Slide—with access at Overflow Road Campground.

Section II runs from Russell Bridge on S.C. 28 to Earl's Ford, a distance of seven miles. Although it contains white water and one class III rapid—Big Shoal—this section is ideal for beginners, provided the river is running at a safe level. The West Fork merges with the Chattooga a couple hundred yards below Russell Bridge and increases the river's flow dramatically.

Section III begins its 13-mile run at Earl's Ford and terminates at the U.S. 76 bridge. It is here that the river separates beginner and novice paddlers from advanced and expert paddlers. Section III offers rapids like Warwoman, Rock Garden, Dick's Creek Ledge, the Narrows, Second Ledge, Eye of the Needle, Roller Coaster, Painted Rock, and Bull's Sluice, a class V rapid. In the Rock Garden, massive granite slabs jut over the river, and paddlers must work the rapid through a maze of boulders. Dick's Creek Ledge is a class IV rapid with a double drop, requiring an S-move that should be scouted prior to paddling. Dick's Creek Falls, on the Georgia side, is just one of several scenic waterfalls along Section III. Below Sandy Ford, there is no practical way to portage the Narrows, a 150-foot class IV rapid that features numerous waves and offset holes. Downstream, Second Ledge, with its dramatic drop, slams boaters into the spray and holds their boat for just an instant. Below Eye of the Needle, the river drifts lazily for several miles and lulls paddlers into a lackadaisical state before bouncing them awake in the Roller Coaster. Bull's Sluice awaits. Normally, a roar of crashing water alerts you to its location. Scouting this class V monster is a must; river right affords excellent views of the entire rapid. This rapid has claimed eight lives. In fact, the entire Section III should be considered dangerous if the water level exceeds 2.0.

Section IV begins below the U.S. 76 bridge and stretches seven miles to Tugaloo Lake. It is one of the premier whitewater runs in the continental United States. There are numerous class V-plus rapids in the Five Falls area. Another rapid, Woodall Shoals, has been the site of seven accidental drownings. A deceptively powerful hydraulic that forms as the water pours over a dramatic ledge, Woodall Shoals absolutely refuses to release its victims. The policy of the Nantahala Outdoor Center is to skirt the shoals far river right and maneuver downstream through a host of class III jumble, or to simply portage around the hydraulic on the left (South Carolina) side of the river.

The flatbed bounced down to the put-in below the U.S. 76 bridge. We quickly dragged the limp, shapeless rafts off the truck and spread them out in the wet grass as Boatknight, the designated trip leader, headed down to the gauge station. Foot pumps were our only means of inflating the Zodiacs, and leg muscles protested after countless repetitions of pumping up and down.

Our guests arrived minutes after we had finished prepping the rafts. Payson Kennedy distributed the dry bags containing lunch. After we strapped the dry bags and the first-aid kits to the thwarts, we turned our attention to introducing ourselves to our paddlers, the people who rightly suspected that their lives were in our hands. But it works both ways. To a large degree, they control your destiny as well. It is important to establish a harmonious relationship with your crew.

Each raft was assigned four paddlers, people who had paid good money to take a calculated risk, an exciting adventure in a remote wilderness down America's *Deliverance* river, under the leadership of a river guide they didn't know and probably wouldn't have anything to do with in any other situation. But strangely, they went out of their way to make me, the guide, feel lucky to have such a strong group of paddlers. False bravado. Maybe it was nerves. I looked at my group and strove to see their positive attributes. The raft would ride light and high, that was for sure. They were no power strokers, though. They looked thin, wet, a bit shaky, as if they were wondering who had suggested this trip anyway.

I introduced them to our Zodiac, told them what a fine raft it was and how, if we worked together—them following my instructions and executing the proper strokes on my command—we could whip this stretch of white water. Finally, I got them situated in the raft so we could try a dry run. "Paddle forward. No, you've got to paddle together. Time your stroke to the person in front of you. That's it," I told them. "*Draw left! Draw left!*" I screamed without warning. We worked on draw strokes.

By the time we actually put the raft in the water, Boatknight had disappeared downstream. Silence settled over the crew. For a while, the noise of the river and the call of crows were the only sounds we heard. We hit Screaming Left Turn and worked our way from river right to river left amid the boulders. The gang was ecstatic about having run a class IV rapid.

When we reached the class III Rock Jumble, I knew that Woodall Shoals—the killer, a class III rapid with a class VI hydraulic—was around the next bend. We scouted from the South Carolina side, with no intention of running the meat of the rapid. My guests laughed at the rapid's seeming insignificance but took a second look when I informed them that it had claimed five lives in the previous four years. Nobody wanted to die that day. We ran the cheat chute that starts out hugging the right bank before turning left and dropping over numerous ledges toward the pool at the bottom.

Downstream, at Seven Foot Falls, a class IV, one of my guys popped out of the raft when we slammed into the left wall at the base. As we slid by him—a lost soul in the crashing water—I grabbed the collar of his life jacket and dragged him back into the raft.

His buddies razzed him unmercifully.

"You're supposed to stay in the boat, hero."

"We're rafting today, not swimming."

I was lucky to grab him so quickly. Obviously, I had missed the line. Outside of losing some respect from my paddlers, no harm had been done. Jeff, the swimmer, had a tale to tell. We retrieved his paddle a good ways downstream.

We stopped for lunch at Long Creek Falls, a spectacular cascade that invites you to scramble up the rocks and stand under its waters. Several guests spread-eagled themselves in the creek at the base of the falls to absorb the pounding of the dropping water.

I was distracted, thinking about the Five Falls section looming downstream. Sure enough, Boatknight walked by and chuckled, "The Five Falls gonna be kicking today. Yes, sir. I mean kicking."

Payson Kennedy stopped by to give me a word of encouragement. That's when it dawned on me that I really didn't have much experience on the river. That uneasy feeling I'd had earlier in the morning came back.

Right after we put back in the river, we ran to the left of Deliverance Rock, so named because of its several appearances in the movie. Almost immediately, we encountered the 200-foot vertical wall called Raven Rock Cliffs. We hit Raven's Chute, a class IV rapid that shoots a diagonal tongue of water from river left across the face of the drop. Sliding smoothly into the large pool, we laughed at the quickness of the rapid.

There was little activity for the next mile downstream in the section called The Calm Before the Storm. We floated, listening to the wilderness. The crew sensed my apprehension, and uneasiness engulfed the Zodiac. Everybody knew what awaited. It was the culmination of the journey.

The river started narrowing, and we entered the canyon of the Five Falls.

Boatknight, running lead, eddied out above entrance rapid, boulder-hopped

Guide trainees hit Bull's Sluice's first drop.

downstream, and set safety, ready with his throw rope in case anybody got bounced out. Payson led his crew through the rock garden above the drop and disappeared through the rapid. We ran behind Tom Bolin and his crew. The entrance flashed by us in a rush of adrenaline. Everybody stayed in the raft. I breathed a bit easier. Maybe we could pull this off. Boatknight and Payson continued leapfrogging downstream, setting safety for the rafts to follow.

Corkscrew scared me to death as we plunged into its unpredictable waters. It's a class V monster with big waves as it twists, drops, and pulsates against unmoving granite. Known for its tricky waters, this rapid trashes rafts, kayaks, C-1s, and open boats at will.

But the real danger lay downstream, at Crack-In-The-Rock, which features steep canyon walls and a riverbed littered with massive boulders. Passage downstream is through three small slots—chutes in a rock ledge—that altogether don't total 12 feet in width. I'm a happy camper when we slide over the far-right Crack, a six-foot-wide chute divided by a huge log jammed vertically into the rocks.

During lunch back at Long Creek Falls, Payson and Boatknight had let all the guides know that we wouldn't be running Sockem Dog. The river was running too high. We'd walk the Dog. That left only Jawbone. One more class V and we'd be home free.

We entered Jawbone river right, worked our way back to the center, hit a drop, and drove river left into an eddy above a violent tongue of water. We spun trying to avoid sliding under a monster rock, which almost decapitated me. I heard my right elbow crack and my collarbone snap as my right shoulder was dislocated. The impact with the rock catapulted me out the rear of the raft. My last sight before being engulfed by the river was of the raft, captainless, and my four guests headed straight for Hydroelectric, another undercut boulder that sits right in the middle of the current.

Within seconds, I found myself holding my right arm next to my body. I was pressed face-first against the bottom of the raft. Realizing my situation, I pushed and fought with my legs and feet until I was away from the Zodiac. I bobbed up, my life jacket pulling me to the surface, and saw all four paddlers hunkered flat in the bottom of the raft as it slammed Hydroelectric. The high water prevented them from being sucked down and flushed under the rock. They bounced free toward the large recovery area above Sockem Dog.

I was sucked under again, and the current held me just below the surface. I could see daylight, but I couldn't get to it. I knew I was floating dangerously close to the Dog. I popped up just in time to see Payson throw me a safety line. I couldn't get it. Boatknight shot a line, but I couldn't let go of my injured arm and stretch two feet to grab it. I floated helplessly downstream into the grip of Sockem Dog and dropped over its 10-foot ledge into the keeper hydraulic below.

The quick actions of Payson and Boatknight saved me. They tossed a raft into the hydraulic, leaped in, and pulled me free of the keeper. The next thing I knew, I was floating alongside the raft staring up at blue sky, in pain but thankful, gasping for breath. Tom Bolin threw a line out to the raft and pulled us toward shore, with help from Charlie Walbridge and some of the guests.

My arm was immobilized and the trip reorganized. We still had miles to go. The rapid called Shoulder Bone bounced me around in the raft and let me know I was still alive. Two miles of lake paddling, a strong headwind slowing our progress and keeping me chilled, took its toll. The rugged bus ride out Tugaloo Lake Road back to Long Creek let me feel every bump, every rut.

My paddling companions tried to ease my pain, but my pain was greater than physical. My guide career had come to a sudden stop. Looking back, I can realize that it was all my fault. When I hit that top eddy in Jawbone and the raft spun, I let it swing too far. Off line, I was out of luck. The river caught me but let me go.

I knew that one day I would return to Section IV and come face to face with my own deliverance on the Chattooga. I just didn't know when. At least I wouldn't be sitting around with Charlie Walbridge that night repairing a raft.

The years slipped by. It had been over a decade since my last run with Nantahala Outdoor Center down Section IV of the Chattooga. The river had my number. At least Section IV did.

After my bones healed, a surgeon in Athens, Georgia, reconstructed my shoulder. A lengthy rehabilitation period followed. Guiding rafts fell by the wayside. Occasionally, I joined up with friends like John Gibney and kayaked Section III. But I avoided Section IV at all cost.

In 1989, five years after I'd gotten back into guiding—this time on the Ocoee—I talked Southeastern Expeditions into letting me guide a few trips on Section IV of the Chattooga. It was time to confront my personal deliverance in a canyon of white water. My wife thought I was crazy. Sixteen years had passed, she kept reminding me. That was a lot of water over the dam. But I argued that my paddling skills were greatly improved. I had paddled and guided other rivers, including the Gauley in West Virginia. It was with my wife's mixed blessings that I headed over the mountains toward Southeastern's outpost on the Chattooga.

I wish I could say that I had a smooth run that day down Section IV. I didn't precisely recall every rapid, or the proper routes through them. Basically, I parked the Dibb raft I was paddling a safe distance behind Neal or Colin—two experienced Southeastern guides—and followed their lines. When they realized what I was doing, they started playing games in the smaller rapids to throw me off, trying to leave me beached on the rocks. A lot of laughter and banter passed between rafts. Twice, my crew and I had to lift the raft back over rocks to the proper channel. I couldn't remember running the river when it was so low—1.6 on the gauge. Everything looked different. The mountain scenery was spectacular, enchanting.

Two members of my group went swimming when we slammed into the canyon wall below Seven Foot Falls. Another guy got ejected in Corkscrew—at least I think it was Corkscrew—and had to grab a rope. A good throw by Neil saved him from Crack-In-The-Rock. We eddied out downstream and waited for our errant swimmer to catch up as he scrambled along the boulders lining the canyon wall. My whole group sat silently in the eddy. They had absolutely no confidence left in their guide, or their own short-term future.

Naturally, in Jawbone, we slammed Hydroelectric with enough force to send a crash-test dummy into retirement. Colin and Neal were screaming, "High side! High side!" Miraculously, we slid away and escaped upright, with no swimmers. We ran the Dog, last of the Five Falls, perfectly. Shoulder Bone, a feisty class III rapid, was like the river's farewell, a gentle reminder of the day's whitewater turbulence and spray.

We were washed clean and elated. Jubilant, we leaped from Jump Rock into the cool waters of the Chattooga. A johnboat met us at the head of Tugaloo Lake, and we motored across the two miles of flat water separating us from the take-out. I relaxed as we cruised the placid waters of Tugaloo, knowing Section IV would be easier in the future. I wasn't even upset over having to buy the guides beer—if you have swimmers, you buy. I had met a personal goal that day. I had stayed in the raft and hadn't gone swimming in Sockem Dog.

The Chattooga. My personal deliverance.

For all the hazards faced by whitewater participants on the Chattooga, not one commercial guest has become a river statistic. Since records of river users were first kept in 1973, over 650,000 commercial customers have enjoyed the Chattooga. In light of the numerous deaths that have occurred on the river, this safety record attests to the professionalism of the outfitters and Chattooga river guides, past and present.

But beware. The Chattooga has claimed innocents, daredevils, and experts without experiencing guilt. It is a river, wild and untamed.

So You Want to Be a River Guide?

The group scrambled out of the raft and pulled it up on the rocks, away from the swiftly moving current. The entire gang then followed Mark Kopeski, the guide instructor, downstream to the edge of Bull's Sluice, a renowned rapid on the Chattooga.

With an intensity that matched the roar of the river, Mark carefully pointed out to his gathered flock the correct course for running "the Bull" successfully. With vivid gestures, he identified the hidden dangers—the potholes, the pour-over, the flip routes—that lurk around and under "the Bull." Everybody listened with keen ears.

As guide trainees with Southeastern Expeditions on Sections III and IV of the Chattooga, everyone knew that "the Bull" had claimed numerous lives—eight, to be exact. It was not a time for daydreaming. Each person knew that his or her life and those of future paddling guests might depend on what they absorbed. A tremor—energy mixed with fear, anxiety, and respect—ran through the group as the river pounded and fought its way downstream.

Scooter McMillan set safety below the rapid's last drop and prepared his coiled rope for quick response. Mark led his group of four trainees back upstream and chucked the raft into the current. After maneuvering through a series of entrance rapids, the raftload of trainees and the one skilled instructor slid into the main force of the current as it sped rapidly toward the first drop and Decapitation Rock. With a pronounced river-right angle, the raft plunged over the first ledge, gently kissed the huge boulder the group had just been standing on, and back-ferried to avoid Decapitation Rock before dropping over the second ledge into the crashing waters of the hydraulic. As the raft popped free downstream, a triumphant cacophony of hoots and hollers let all observers know it was a piece of cake.

What lures people into becoming river guides? What makes them want to take the risks associated with such a powerful river as the Chattooga?

Some are attracted by the freedom and adventure. Others like the alternative lifestyle and the closeness with the wilderness. Some relish the challenge of molding individuals into a team that paddles together and conquers unknown dangers. Whatever attracts them, river guides are a special breed, whitewater cowboys carrying ropes to retrieve those who stray.

Regardless of the lure, many trainees don't make it, for a variety of reasons. The paychecks are low and the hard work wears you down. Accomplished guides must assume command and give inspired direction. Each group of inexperienced paddlers challenging the river for the first time looks to its guide to get them safely down the river, while still enjoying the scenery, the companionship, and the best white water in the Southeast. They are betting their lives on you.

Doug Allen, a former head guide for Southeastern, started his guiding career in 1973. He has seen guides and trainees come and go. "You can usually tell if a trainee is going to stick it out right after you pluck them from the river after a particularly nasty swim on one of the big rapids," he said. "There's only one type of river guide. The one who has swum and the one who's gonna swim. They are one and the same. Some day when you least expect it, the river reaches up and grabs you. The river flat doesn't care how many times you have run it.

"A few seconds caught in a hydraulic where they get recirculated three or four times really separates trainees from pretenders. That's when they realize that if they don't get it right, they could die. River action is quick, and the adrenaline rush can be intense. I've heard it said that a river guide must be an entertainer with a vast number of jokes to keep his customers happy; a physician to tend to their wounds; a psychologist to keep their spirits high; a specialist in rubber repair; a chef to prepare them the best peanut-butter-and-jelly sandwiches they ever taste; and a bus driver to shuttle them to and from the river. But above all, the guide must be good. Good at dealing with people. Good at reading water and hitting the proper lines. The Chattooga demands the best. But then everything on the edge does, doesn't it?"

Whitewater Rafting on the Chattooga River

WHO

Commercial outfitters require that Section IV participants be at least 13 years of age and Section III participants no younger than 10. Both sections require physical exertion. If you are in poor physical condition or significantly overweight, neither trip is recommended. Rafters are on the water approximately 4½ hours on Section III and five hours on Section IV. With safety orientations and shuttle rides, trips down both sections are all-day affairs.

Renee Binder, outdoor recreation planner for the Andrew Pickens District of Sumter National Forest, recently informed me that 48,212 commercial guests, 15,440 private paddlers, 3,056 clinic participants, and 315 photographers tackled Sections III and IV during the 1993 calendar year. Records indicate that nearly a million people have paddled the Chattooga in the two decades since *Deliverance* hit the silver screen.

WHEN

The three outfitters permitted to run trips on Section IV—Nantahala Outdoor Center, Wildwater, Ltd., and Southeastern Expeditions—normally schedule trips daily March through October. Call for reservations, and remember that the water level is generally higher in the spring and fall, when the rains set in. Wet suits are recommended in the cool months. Each outfitter supplies them or has rental units available. Running the river in late April or May, when the mountain laurel is blooming, adds natural beauty to the experience.

Note that during periods of heavy rainfall when water-level readings exceed 3.5, outfitters will not conduct trips down Section IV. The risk becomes exceedingly great. Remember, it is a wild river with numerous life-threatening obstacles. If you are inexperienced and not trained to guide on Section IV, then leave it to the professionals.

WHERE

The Chattooga flows out of the North Carolina mountains and forms the border between Georgia, to the west, and South Carolina, to the east, all the way to Tugaloo Lake. The closest town in the northeastern section of Georgia is Clayton, at the junction of U.S. 76 and U.S. 441.

HOW

Reservations can be made through the following outfitters: Nantahala Outdoor Center, 13077 U.S. 19 West, Bryson City, N.C. 28713-9114 (800-232-7238 or 704-488-6900); Wildwater, Ltd., P.O. Box 100, Long Creek, S.C. 29658 (800-451-9972); and Southeastern Expeditions, Route 3, Box 3178-E, Clayton, Ga. 30525 (800-868-7238 or 706-782-4331).

Three Forest Service ranger districts supervise activities in the Chattooga Wild and Scenic River area: Sumter National Forest, Andrews Pickens Ranger District, Star Route, Walhalla, S.C. 29691 (803-638-9568); Nantahala National Forest, Highlands Ranger District, Rt. 1, P.O. Box 247, Highlands, N.C. 28741 (704-526-3765); and Chattahoochee National Forest, Tallulah Ranger District, P. O. Box 438, Clayton, Ga. 30525 (706-782-3320).

Forest Service regulations for the Chattooga are as follows:

1. Each party must register its trip on the river
2. Coast Guard–approved life jackets must be worn on Section III and Section IV
3. Helmets are required for all decked boaters; rafters must wear them below Woodall Shoals
4. Inner tubes are prohibited below Earl's Ford
5. No boating or floating activities are permitted above S.C. 28
6. All commercial trips operate under special-use permits issued by the Forest Service, Andrew Pickens Ranger District, Walhalla, S.C.

According to the international classification system for rapids, class I rapids are easy, featuring slow currents, small, regular waves, and clear passage; no technical moves are required. Class II rapids are also classified as easy, with moderate currents, short drops, and minor ledges requiring turning ability; passage is still relatively clear. Class III rapids are of medium difficulty. Some scouting of rapids is required, due to numerous waves and tight channels. Boaters must have the ability to maneuver their craft around obstacles. Class IV rapids are difficult. Scouting is required, as class IV rapids are normally long, with powerful or irregular waves and numerous rocks and eddies. Class V rapids are very difficult. Undercut rocks, hydraulics, crosscurrents, and numerous obstructions demand expert boating skills; big drops demand scouting. Class VI rapids are dangerous, with all known whitewater hazards, violent turbulence, and big drops at the limit of navigability. There is a potential for loss of life. Class VI rapids should be run only by experts using all safety procedures, including scouting and the setting of safety ropes.

RESOURCES

The Chattooga Wild and Scenic River, by Brian Boyd, published by Ferncreek Press, contains a wealth of information about boating, hiking, and camping in the Chattooga corridor. Excellent maps and directions make this a must publication for those wishing to explore the Chattooga.

Whitewater Home Companion: Southeastern Rivers depicts boating opportunities on the rivers of the Southeast as only William Nealy can do, with his cartoon images and line drawings showing how to run specific rapids. Reading his text leaves little doubt that Nealy has personally experienced the rivers and been trashed by more than one hydraulic. Published by Menasha Ridge Press, *Whitewater Home Companion* is available at many outfitter stores.

The Chattooga National Wild and Scenic River Map, published by the Forest Service, is available at outfitter shops and from the ranger offices. It is regarded as the most detailed map of the area and is very helpful in planning excursions into the corridor.

EMERGENCY INFORMATION

Macon County, North Carolina, and Oconee County, South Carolina, have the 911 system. Use it first in a true emergency.

The number for the sheriff's department in Rabun County, Georgia, is 706-782-3612. The number for the sheriff's department in Macon County, North Carolina, is 704-524-2811. The number for the sheriff's department in Oconee County, South Carolina, is 803-638-4111.

Left to right:

Martin Sachs, kneeling with motorcycle helmet; Cory Hargett, on horse; Joy Sudderth, standing; Dylan Hargett, standing with caving helmet; Callie Hargett, mountain bicycle; Opal Petty, caving and climbing gear; Billy Crisp, seated on Honda Gold Wing; Buzz Chalmers, on floor with hang-gliding harness; Doyle Smith, sitting on raft holding helmet; Tim "Gator" Meaders, holding kayak paddle; G. Forest, standing; Tarp Head, in balloon basket.

Photo by Bruce Chynoweth
Southern Exposure Studios, Inc.

INDEX